On Deep History
and the Brain

ARME[...]

PERSIC[...]

MARE SIVE SI[...]

REGIO CHUS

GEHON. Fl.

On Deep History
and the Brain

Daniel Lord Smail

UNIVERSITY OF CALIFORNIA PRESS

Berkeley   Los Angeles   London

The publisher gratefully acknowledges the generous contribution to this book provided by the Ahmanson Foundation Humanities Endowment Fund of the University of California Press Foundation.

The publisher also gratefully acknowledges the support of the Harvard Historical Series.

Cover illustration and frontispiece from Athanasius Kircher, *Arca Noë, in tres libros digesta*. Reproduced courtesy of the Houghton Library, Harvard University.

A Caravan Book
For more information, visit www.caravanbooks. org.

University of California Press, one of the most distinguished university presses in the United States, enriches lives around the world by advancing scholarship in the humanities, social sciences, and natural sciences. Its activities are supported by the UC Press Foundation and by philanthropic contributions from individuals and institutions. For more information, visit www.ucpress.edu.

University of California Press
Berkeley and Los Angeles, California

University of California Press, Ltd.
London, England

Library of Congress Cataloging-in-Publication Data

Smail, Daniel Lord.
   On deep history and the brain / Daniel Lord Smail.
       p.   cm.
   Includes bibliographical references and index.
   ISBN: 978-0-520-25289-9 (cloth : alk. paper)
   1. History—Philosophy.   I. Title.
D16.9.S62   2007
901—dc22   2007011729

Manufactured in the United States of America
15   14   13   12   11   10   09   08
10   9   8   7   6   5   4   3   2

The paper used in this publication meets the minimum requirements of ANSI/NISO z39.48–1992 (R 1997) (*Permanence of Paper*).

In memory of John R. W. Smail

CONTENTS

PREFACE

In the 1970s, John R. W. Smail, a professor of Southeast Asian history at the University of Wisconsin, began teaching "The Natural History of Man," an undergraduate course that ranged freely across the millennia, paying little attention to the boundaries of modern disciplines. Looking back on it, I can see that he was influenced by evolutionary approaches to the understanding of society that were just starting to filter back into the social sciences in the 1960s. At the time, however, it seemed like a rather odd course for a professor of Southeast Asian history to be teaching. Be that as it may, I developed my own life-long fascination for natural history, evolution, and the theory of natural selection while listening to my father try out his ideas on us, a pattern that my own children will no doubt recognize. Several decades later, as my father was collapsing under the iron grip of Alzheimer's, I decided to try my own version of a deep history of humankind as a kind of intellectual memorial. The result, in the fall of 2000, was "A Natural History," a course I was to teach on two more occasions at Fordham University. This book has grown out of that course. More accurately, it first took form as a short introduction to the deep history itself, a book based on my lecture notes that I still hope to write someday. In the writing of that introduction, however, it became a chapter, then two chapters, growing ever longer, ever more complex, and even those initial forays left a great deal unsaid. Like an iceberg calving off the face of a glacier, the introduction eventually detached itself and now floats on its own as the philosophical prolegomenon to the writing of a deep history. People have reminded me how frustrating it can be to read about how and why we should contemplate a deep history without seeing the history itself, and it is hard to disagree with them. The epilogue is a small gesture toward satisfying this need. But I felt that the alternative—gluing the prolegomenon back onto the history itself—would produce one of those six-hundred-page tomes that sit, unread and reproachful, on our bookshelves. The sort of book that makes a thud when you drop it onto the table. The weight of its pages implies a claim to authority that I cannot possibly hope to make. This book is meant to be an essay, though one written with a false confidence that masks the provisional nature of the argument.

One embarks on interdisciplinary projects like this with more than the usual trepidation. The result, in my case, was a deeply felt need to test out ideas on friends, colleagues, sometimes even new acquaintances just a few minutes removed from being perfect strangers. Everyone—well, almost everyone—was kind and patient and sometimes even warmly enthusiastic. Some raised quizzical eyebrows, others noted the obvious flaws, still others zeroed in remorselessly on the less obvious, indeed the intractable flaws. All of these responses—the warm and the cold, the welcome and the painful—gave me ideas about how to choose my emphases and where to invest my energies. Members of the faculty seminar in the history department at Fordham University read or heard some of the earliest versions of these arguments, and I thank my former colleagues, among them Rick Geddes, Richard Gyug, Ann Johnson, Maryanne Kowaleski, Mike Latham, David Myers, Silvana Patriarca, Tip Ragan, Asif Siddiqi, Kirsten Swinth, Susan Wabuda, and Rosemary Wakeman, for their thoughts and comments. Doris Goldstein read an early draft of some of the arguments in the first two chapters and was generous in sharing her then-unpublished work. Lynn Hunt read an early version of the entire set of ideas; her remarks, as I found with my first book, have the extraordinary capacity to crystallize one's thinking in productive ways. Beyond that, Lynn just knew what I was talking about, and that made such a difference. Gabrielle Spiegel will probably feel chagrined to hear that she often peers invisibly over my shoulder as I write. Her comments on a draft of chapter 3 exposed some serious conceptual flaws. I would like to say I have solved them, but, even if I cannot, the final version of the chapter is certainly better for the experience. Dan Mroczek provided suggestions on chapters 4 and 5, Bruce Holsinger helped me wrestle with some difficult ideas in chapter 4, and David Roger Pilbeam gave the manuscript the much-needed vetting of a paleontologist. Morgan Sonderegger, my research assistant, contributed some crucial research to chapter 5, providing reports so lucid that my paraphrases were scarcely any improvement, and, in one crucial spot, it seemed best to let his report speak for itself. Tip Ragan has been a good and close friend for many years. He has been bound up with this project all along, for though our friendship runs to many dimensions, he was there when I first began thinking about natural history.

I presented chapters 1, 2, and 5 in various forms to audiences at Colorado College, the University of California at Los Angeles, and Princeton University, and thank Tip Ragan, Lynn Hunt, and Gyan Prakash for organizing these seminars and talks. At UCLA, Patrick Geary gave fruitful criticism and advice, and I am especially grateful for Teofilo Ruiz's hospitality, friendship, and enthusiasm. David Sloan Wilson, who read the first draft of the manuscript for the University of California Press, also gave me a chance to test out chapters 4 and 5 as a guest of the Evolutionary Studies program at Binghamton University. I thank David and his wife, Anne B. Clark, for their hospitality during my stay. After a wonderfully productive seminar, lecture, and Q&A session with dozens of students, we returned to their house to talk biology far into the night. David, as I recall, bailed out shortly after midnight, just when Anne and I got onto the subject of crows.

Kevin Padian, believing, I think, that conversations do things that reports cannot, leavened his own sharp reading of the manuscript with an invitation to dinner in Berkeley. I have done what I can to respond, though I am sure he would have liked to see more. My thanks to Kevin and Nancy Padian, Matt Wedel, Alan Shabel, and Lucia Jacobs for what proved to be a memorable evening. Readers like these are a treasure. I also want to thank Bonnie Wheeler and Jeremy Adams for an invitation to address the members of a seminar at Southern Methodist University and respond to their reading of chapters 4 and 5. I learned a lot from all who attended and delighted in their warmth and hospitality.

I ran ideas for the book past John Ackerman, David Armitage, Susan Ashley, Paul Mathews, Mike McCormick, Dennis McEnnerney, David Nirenberg, Teofilo Ruiz, Rob Schneider, and many others whose names are absent not because the author is ungrateful but because he is forgetful. David Christian read an early draft of the manuscript for the University of California Press and provided a helpful critique that set me thinking about important issues of presentation. Niels Hooper, my editor at the University of California Press, has been tirelessly interested in and enthusiastic about this project, and I am happy to acknowledge the careful production help provided by Suzanne Knott and Julia Zafferano.

Portions of the introduction and chapters 1 and 2 appeared in an article entitled "In the Grip of Sacred History," published in the *American Historical Review* 110 (2005): 1337–61, and I gratefully acknowledge permission to reuse this material. The anonymous reviewers of the manuscript gave me lots to think about. Michael Grossberg, the editor at the time, also deserves my thanks and gratitude, as does Jane Lyle, who shepherded the manuscript through production and helped with the illustration program.

For several years I collaborated with a team of teachers at Chatham High School (New York) who, under the leadership of Mike Wallace, have been engaged in a Big History project. Although they always made me feel that I was bringing something to them, in fact it was quite the other way around. It is one thing to conceive of grand schemes; it is quite another to be reminded that these schemes have to be translated into meaningful lesson plans if they are to make any difference. I have been inspired by their enthusiasm and the enthusiasm of their students. And, speaking of which, among my most important debts are to my own students, the undergraduates who took "A Natural History" at Fordham University between 2000 and 2004. These include Jordan Ballard, Ben Bowman, Laura Criscitelli, Maria

Dembrowsky, Edward Djordevic, Lori Gorcyca, Rosemary Ramsey, and many others. They objected, absorbed, and reflected with seriousness and purpose and told me, directly and indirectly, what worked and what did not work. Like others, I often teach the things that I research. With this book, I have learned how rewarding it can be to research the things that you teach.

My children, Ben, Irene, and Gregory, bring pride and pleasure in equal measure. They were probably not aware that I was doing research whenever I grilled them on the operations of gossip or status hierarchies in high schools or grade schools. Soon, I am sure, I shall be learning even more from them. My wife, Kathleen, has kept all of us together across an eventful couple of years, and she has been my source of stability, a social and moral compass, and a check on my sometimes intemperate enthusiasms. My mother, Laura L. Smail, edited the manuscript and helped correct the proofs. I hope she will see this book as the sort of thing my father might have done himself if Alzheimer's had not robbed him of the chance.

Toward Reunion in History

I have written this book for people who are interested in origins and believe that history should begin at the beginning. For centuries, in Europe, that beginning lay in the not-too-distant past, with the creation of man in the Garden of Eden. This was the story told by sacred history, and it was the platform on which history's chronology was erected. Then, with the sudden and widespread acceptance of geological time in the 1860s, western Europe's chronological certainties came crashing down. Stephen Jay Gould has called the discovery of deep time a cosmological revolution of Galilean proportions.[1] Over the course of several decades in the mid-nineteenth century, the great historical sciences—geology, biology, paleoanthropology—were made or remade as the bottom dropped out of time, exposing a nearly endless vista. Yet in those early decades, the discipline of history recoiled from that vista, fashioning instead a view of history that begins with the rise of civilization. This view dominated curricula throughout the twentieth century. There were calls for a history that dealt seriously with the time before civilization, but, with some noteworthy exceptions, they never came to much.

Only recently have historians begun to address seriously the possibility of tearing down the veil of prehistory.

Nosce te ipsum. If humanity is the proper subject of history, as Linnaeus might well have counseled, then it stands to reason that the Paleolithic era, that long stretch of the Stone Age before the turn to agriculture, is part of our history. Despite enormous strides in the field of paleoanthropology over the past several decades, however, the deep past of humanity still plays a marginal role in the grand historical narrative as measured by the history curricula offered in secondary schools and colleges in the United States and the textbooks used to teach them. Most textbooks used in Western Civilization courses include relatively little on the Neolithic era, the period between the shift to agriculture roughly 10,000 years ago and the invention of bronze tools around 5,500 years ago. The Paleolithic era, the Old Stone Age, merits even less. Some books in world history extend human history back to the outset of the agricultural revolutions, breaching the date of 4000 B.C. that used to figure prominently in many Western Civ textbooks. Yet even world history surveys currently do not deal significantly with the Paleolithic.[2] Historians, for all intents and purposes, still regard deep history as prehistory, the time before history. As Mott Greene has noted, *prehistory* is a term that modern historians have been reluctant to let drop. "To abandon prehistory," he says, "would be to postulate continuity between the biological descent of hominids and the 'ascent of civilization' of the abstract 'mankind' of humanistic historical writing. Prehistory is a buffer zone."[3]

A deep history of humankind is any history that straddles this buffer zone, bundling the Paleolithic and the Neolithic together with the Postlithic—that is, with everything that has happened since the emergence of metal technology, writing, and cities some 5,500 years ago. The result is a seamless narrative that acknowledges the full chronology of the human past. Although the themes of a deep history can coalesce around any number of narrative threads, the one I propose in this book centers on biology, brain, and behavior. In the course that I teach, I include elements of other threads—climate and ecology, disease, webs and exchanges, human morphology, sex and gender—to round out the story. Teaching this history has been a transformative experience, both for me and for a number of my students. But with each iteration of the course, their questions have made me think hard about key issues. Is all the science so necessary? Is the deep history going to make any difference to how we understand more recent history? How can you glue the Paleolithic onto the Postlithic if there are no surviving institutions around which a narrative can gel? Above all: is it really history, or is it just anthropology written in a historical key?

Struggling with all these queries, I have come to realize that the resistance to deep history does not necessarily come from my students. It comes from me. It is rooted in paradigms, in discourse, in the nameless things that one of my advisers liked to call "ghost theories," old ideas that continue to structure our thinking without our being fully aware of their controlling presence. This book is designed to explore the ideas and attitudes, common to professional historians though not necessarily shared by the general public, that quietly undermine our willingness to contemplate humanity's deep history as history, not just biology or anthropology. It is a work of frank advocacy, at once a defense of the necessity of deep history as well as an outline for the writing of it.

Of all the obstacles to a deep history, the most serious may well prove to be simple inertia. For several thousand years, historians writing in the Judeo-Christian tradition were accustomed to framing history according to the short chronology of sacred, or Mosaic, history, the chronology that frames the story recounted in Genesis. The time revolution brought an end to the short chronology as a matter of historical fact. Yet the historical narrative that emerged in U.S. history curricula and textbooks between the late nineteenth century and the 1940s did not actually abandon the six thousand years of sacred history. Instead, the sacred was deftly translated into a secular key: the Garden of Eden became the irrigated fields of Mesopotamia, and the creation of man was reconfigured as the rise of civilization. Prehistory came to be an essential part of the story of Western Civ, but the era was cantilevered outside the narrative buttresses that sustain the edifice of Western Civilization. Its purpose was to illustrate what we are no longer. In this way the short chronology persisted under the guise of a secular human history.

Yet not all resistance was due to inertia. Over the past century and more, as the ghost theories have precipitated out of the aqueous solution of historiography, several pointed arguments justifying the exclusion of humanity's deep past from the chronological framework of history have found their way into textbooks and works of general history. The authors of these works noted the absence of written documents. They proposed the idea that history concerns nations, not rootless bands. They developed the myth of Paleolithic stasis, the idea of a timeless dystopia whose unchangingness was only broken, deus ex machina, by some ill-defined catalytic event that created movement and history. That was the point of rupture, the moment in time, in or around the fourth millennium B.C., when biology finally gave way to culture.

In these and other ways, works of general history explained why there could be no narrative continuity between prehistory and history.

The intellectual obstacles that once prevented the absorption of deep time have, for the most part, dissolved. New research in the genetic and archeological archives has transformed a once-undifferentiated past of several hundred thousand years into a past punctuated by extraordinary events and adventures. Few, today, can maintain a belief in a changeless Paleolithic. The middle to late Paleolithic has now been dated with considerable precision, making available the chronological scaffolding unavailable to historians writing in the first half of the twentieth century. Archeologists have uncovered late Paleolithic towns and villages with populations numbering up to a thousand people, suggesting that complex political forms do not require agriculture's organizing power. Analyses of arrowheads and amber have shown the existence of long-distance trading networks. A new appreciation for oral composition and social memory has shown just how little the technology of writing has actually added to our ability to recall and duplicate the lessons of the past, rendering suspect the claim that writing has a catalyzing effect on culture.

Of all the arguments made by historians for neglecting the Paleolithic, the most unforgiving has been the question of evidence. The Paleolithic is an undocumented world, at least insofar as *document* has now come to mean something that is written and not, following its Latin root, "that which teaches."[4] This would seem to mark an impervious rupture between the ways in which we can know the recent past and the deep past. But the logic no longer holds up well to scrutiny. Few historians today would deny historicity to the Incans, to Great Zimbabwe, or to the illiterate slaves and peasants of societies past and present merely because they failed to generate writings through which we could touch their thoughts and psyches. A people or a nation would not cease to be historical if the ravages of time, war, colonialism, or prejudice reduced their archives to dust and ash. The ancient world is unimaginable without archeological evidence; the Middle Ages very nearly so; and the effort to reconstitute the lives of the peoples without writing has been one of the signal achievements of the twentieth century. So what does it matter that the evidence for the deep past comes not from written documents but from the other things that teach—from artifacts, fossils, vegetable remains, phonemes, and various forms of modern DNA? Like written documents, all these traces encode information about the past. Like written documents, they resist an easy reading and must be interpreted with care. The cone of available evidence, like the flower of a trumpet vine, flares out after the invention of writing. But the history itself, from the long, narrow tube to the flaring bell, is seamless. This is the logic that makes the deep past legible.

The goal of the first three chapters of this book is to lay bare some of the historiographical, epistemological, and theoretical obstacles that have hitherto obscured the legibility of deep history. Bringing these arguments into the open, we can appreciate how we no longer need to be bound by their logic. Yet not all problems are so easily overcome. As I have discovered through trial and error, one of the major hurdles to writing a deep history is the lack of demonstrable continuities between the Paleolithic past and the Postlithic present. Presenting the stream of history in introductory historical narratives, lectures, and textbooks, historians like to deal with origins and legacies, what Ernst Breisach calls "the marks of the past."[5] These take the form of institutions that endure or atavisms that are swept away in the course of revolutions. They lie at the heart of the stories we like to tell. But what possible legacies were transmitted to us from the Paleolithic? Where is our connection to that world? Deploring the very same chronological break that I deplore, and aware of the need to structure historical narratives around legacies, William McNeill once proposed making a usable past intelligible through a study of disease. It was a workable solution, used to great effect both by McNeill himself and, two decades later, by Jared Diamond.[6] McNeill has also used dance and other devices for binding the long historical narrative into a seamless whole. More spiritually based solutions have also been tried, and still other options present themselves to the enterprising historian. Yet none of these addresses what I take to be the most obvious device for making the deep past intelligible, and that is the brain.

The possibility of using the brain as a device for building a continuous narrative had already been perceived in 1912 by James Harvey Robinson when he proposed a history that pays attention to human psychology and simian mental modes. As he put it, "we are now tolerably well assured that could the human mind be followed back, it would be found to merge into the animal mind, and that consequently the recently developing study of animal or comparative psychology is likely to cast a great deal of light upon certain modes of thought."[7] As we learned during the 1990s, the decade of the brain, many features of the brain and brain-body chemistry are deeply rooted in our evolutionary history and were put there by natural selection. Among historians, this conviction has been reflected in the form of the biological or cognitive turn.[8] As the fourth and fifth chapters of this book will show, a grand historical narrative that links the Paleolithic to the Postlithic can coalesce, in part, around the continuous interplay between human culture, on the one hand, and the human brain, behavior, and biology, on the other. I take this to be what Clifford Geertz once described as the "reciprocally creative relationship" between biology and culture.[9] This is not the whole story. A narrative is built of many threads. But to pursue the biological legacies of the deep past into the present is one of the most vivid ways I know of to make that past relevant. The goal of chapter 4 is to show how features of culture can be wired in human physiology, a key to appreciating human sameness as well as cultural difference. Chapter 5 explores some of the historical hypotheses that can be generated from the knowledge that the neurochemicals associated with feelings, moods, and emotions are highly susceptible to cultural input.

It should never be necessary to explain what a book is not. All the same, any book that deals with history and the brain is capable of being misunderstood, so it is better to leave no ambiguity about the point being made in the following sentence. This book is not a proposal to bring evolutionary psychology into the realm of history. For reasons discussed at length in chapter 4, evolutionary psychology, at least as the field is currently defined, is not especially helpful to the historical enterprise. I am a firm believer that historians need to work with psychology and neurobiology. Historians have always made psychological assumptions about their subjects, and our assumptions are now decades out of date. But evolutionary psychology, with its inexorable presentism, is not, I think, the way to go. This book charts an alternative path.

What do we gain from a deep history centered on the neurophysiological legacy of our deep past? Well, one benefit is a new kind of interdisciplinarity that joins the humanities and social sciences with the physical and life sciences. This is, I hope, something we would all like to aim for. This kind of interdisciplinarity, in turn, provides an opportunity for escaping the sterile presentism that grips the historical community. In many departments of history in North America, the ancient world has already fallen off the crumbling cliff face that represents the edge of historical time. Medieval European history teeters precariously on the brink, and early modernists tread anxiously as the cracks appear beneath their feet. Time, in the hands of historians, has been a marvelously elastic concept. Made nervous by the chronological stretching that took place in the nineteenth century, historians relaxed their tension on the elastic band that marked out the time of history—and the working chronology of history contracted alarmingly, to the point where historians now contemplate far *less* time than they were accustomed to doing when the discipline was held in the grip of sacred history. To embrace the Paleolithic is to stretch the band far beyond the 6,000 years that used to represent the limits of the elastic. The refurbished chronology will make space not only for our deep history but also for our middle history, the era that came to be called "premodern" as the elastic contracted over the twentieth century.

Finally, a particular goal of this book is to advocate a history that begins where it should begin, in Africa. This is our Eden. The ancestors of non-African peoples did not leave the continent until relatively recently—about 50,000 years ago, according to the archeological evidence; 60,000 to 85,000 years ago, according to some recent estimates proposed by population geneticists. This, the most recent of several "Out of Africa" diasporas, was humanity's enduring colonial enterprise. If one of the hidden legacies of Europe's Judeo-Christian tradition is the short chronology that still frames our understanding of time, a second legacy of sacred history is the fact that history curricula still begin in the Near East. We do not intentionally mean to validate the story of the Garden of Eden in this way. Sacred history has long since been translated into secular terms. But even if the exclusion of Africa from the story of human history is the result of inertia rather than deliberate racism, I believe we are morally compelled to examine the hidden legacies that continue to prevent us from teaching a history that begins in Africa.[10] As we move from the sacred to the human, from a historical time framed by the Mosaic chronology to a time that is defined by brain and biology, we learn to think of Africa as our homeland.

Contemplating the subject of prehistory, archeologist Glyn Daniel once wrote: "Why do historians in a general way pay so little attention to this fourth division of the study of the human past; while recognizing ancient history do they not give more recognition to prehistory? . . . Historians are taking a long time to integrate prehistory into their general view of man."[11] That was in 1962. There is a real danger in this lingering myopia. The reading public is fully aware of, and largely sympathetic to, the neuroscientific and genetic revolutions of the 1990s. Historians risk alienating this audience if they continue to ignore that part of our history which consists of the deep past. In a different vein, the terrain of the historian is being contested by physiologists, ethologists, ecologists, anthropologists, and authors from a variety of other disciplines. One is free to object to the idea of applying biology too freely to history and to raise the specter of a time, not too long ago, when some historians considered it vital to explore the emergence and spread of the "master race." But this particular objection does not justify a reflexive anti-scientism. In an age when biblical literalism is on the rise, when presidents doubt the truth of evolution, when the teaching of evolutionary biology in the United States is being dumbed down and school boards talk seriously about creation science and intelligent design, it is all the more important for historians to support their colleagues in the biological sciences. We can do so by building a human history that shakes free from the grip of the sacred. We can acknowledge that humanity's natural history persisted after the rise of civilization. The archeologists, anthropologists, molecular biologists, and neuroscientists who study the deep past are also historians, regardless of the archives they consult. This book is designed to show how we might bring about reunion within all these realms of history.

ONE

The Grip
of Sacred History

Like any author engaged in the task of building a plot, the historian must grapple with the question of where to begin the story. For historians of the particular, the problem of origins is not especially acute. We choose some reasonably datable event and have that mark the beginning of our particular histories. General historians face a slightly different problem. General history, as defined by Herbert Butterfield, is a rational account of man on earth that explains "how mankind had come from primitive conditions to its existing state."[1] I use the term to embrace the universal histories of the ancient world and medieval Europe, the general world histories of the nineteenth and twentieth centuries, and the histories found in modern history textbooks, syllabuses, and lectures. Whatever their differences, all purport to begin at the beginning. But if one's object is humanity, all humanity, where, exactly, is the beginning?

For several thousand years, historians writing in the Judeo-Christian tradition were untroubled by this question of origins. Sacred history located the origins of man in the Garden of Eden, and that is where the general histories of late antiquity and medieval Europe began the story. In the eighteenth century, proposals for shortening the chronology proper to general history began to circulate, as the new fad for catastrophism brought historical attention to bear on the Universal Deluge. Since human societies were rebuilt from scratch after the Deluge—so the thinking went—it was the Deluge that marked mankind's true beginning. And in the philosophy of the Neapolitan historian Giambattista Vico (1668–1744), the Deluge made all prior history unknowable anyway, since it destroyed all the documents from which we could write such a history. As an event that set the civilizational clock back to zero, the Deluge marked an epistemological break between humanity's origin, which we cannot know, and the present stream of history, which we can.

Although the flood itself has long since receded in historical consciousness, the sense of rupture, a legacy of sacred history, remains. On the heels of the time revolution of the 1860s, historians gradually came to accept the long chronology as a geological fact. But we have not yet found a persuasive way to plot history along the long chronology, preferring instead to locate the origins of history at some point in the past few thousand years. In Western Civ textbooks, which offer a convenient distillation of widely held ideas, that point of origin has been similar to what it had been under sacred history, though the creation of man was duly transformed into a secular event, the birth of civilization. Elsewhere, as I shall argue in this chapter, history's plotline was even more dramatically compressed by the growing sense that early medieval Europe had been so thoroughly barbarized that it could stand in for the Paleolithic past. If one's goal is to describe the progress of human civilization, why fret about the epistemological veil that screens us from the speechless past? Far better to start with a knowable point of origin in the barbarian invasions of the fourth and fifth centuries. This view of medieval Europe, already in circulation by the late nineteenth century, became entrenched in the first generation of textbooks published in the United States in the early decades of the twentieth. The rise of medieval studies in North America from the 1920s onward owes a good deal to this reconfiguration of history's chronology. Although medieval history has long since forgotten its debt to the long chronology, echoes of the latter still linger in the textbooks devoted to medieval Europe.

As a device for plotting history, there is nothing wrong with the idea of rupture. We routinely begin our particular histories with plagues, wars, revolutions, and sudden transformations of all sorts. But no one claims that history *begins* in 1348 or 1789. The event we choose serves as a fulcrum, the pivot point of a teeter-totter. We might prefer to write our histories from a position astride the upswinging arm. But no one can afford to overlook the balance of the chronology on the other side. Yet this is exactly how historians, until recently, have mapped history. "History begins in the Near East," the distinguished authors of the *Columbia History of the World* told us in 1972.[2] Another textbook tells us that "history begins in Sumer,"[3] and a textbook widely used in the 1960s was actually entitled "History Begins at Sumer."[4] What were history students supposed to conclude from this? That our African ancestors lived without history? That early humans were biological entities without any meaningful culture? Can we really blame our students and our fellow citizens if they confuse the Garden of Eden with the irrigated fields of Mesopotamia?

One of the projects of the Enlightenment was to expose the products of human contrivance and replace them with timeless truths embedded in a natural reality. Thus, units of measurement should not be dependent on the whims of particular regions but should conform instead to universal or natural truths, an idea that eventually resulted in the meter, the gram, and the liter. This chapter engages, unabashedly, in an Enlightenment project. It seeks to expose the grip of the short chronology as a human contrivance that will dissolve in the gaze of natural reason. I am aware that a history diagrammed along the full time of human history is just another contrivance, since all questions about where to begin—with the species; with the genus; with the earth itself—are equally vexed. But my purpose is served if we can acknowledge that the short chronology is indeed a contrivance, that history need not be so limited in its span, and that something we can and should call "history" begins a long time ago in Africa.

@

Like many before and since his time, the Greek poet Hesiod (ca. 700 B.C.) was captivated by the muse of origins. To satisfy his curiosity, he invented a Golden Age of Mankind: our origin, the place where it all began. To postulate a Golden Age was to cast a jaundiced eye toward all that came after, and, in the historical trajectory that followed from Hesiod's thought, decay emerged as the dominant metaphor. Ancient and medieval historians writing in the Judeo-Christian tradition were equally captivated by the idea of a Golden Age, though theirs went by the name of Eden. Over a period of a thousand years, after the Roman Empire absorbed Christianity, historians writing in Latin and Greek became accustomed to beginning their histories in Eden. To authors like Eusebius, Gregory of Tours, and Otto of Freising, Genesis provided a necessary point of origin, an anchor by means of which they rooted their histories in time and space. The roots, admittedly, were thin and insubstantial, as authors hastened past Genesis to get to contemporary affairs. Perhaps sensing this lack of enthusiasm, the modern historians who study these texts are equally prone to skip past the preambles and go straight to the histories. But the tendency to anchor universal history in Eden was nonetheless a compelling part of medieval historiography. And though universal histories became less fashionable in early modern Europe, the impulse to begin at the beginning never wholly waned. Sir Walter Ralegh's *History of the World in Five Books,* first published in the early seventeenth century, began in Eden and worked its way down to the Roman period. Bossuet's famed *Universal History* (1681) also began the story with Genesis.[5]

The practice of writing mainstream, professional histories rooted in Eden would persist well into the nineteenth century. But even in Ralegh's day, historians and commentators like Jean Bodin (1529–96) were trying to bring a progressive element into the writing of history, a trajectory at odds with the dominant metaphor of decay. Influenced by the natural histories of the ancient world that had identified the aboriginal state of humankind as primitive, Bodin denied the existence of Hesiod's Golden Age and made much of the lawlessness and violence of the early phases of society.[6] These ideas were shared by other sixteenth-century anthropologists who proposed the idea of a progression from pastoral to agricultural society.[7] The conjectural schemes subsequently developed by philosophers, economists, and ethnographers in the seventeenth and eighteenth centuries were also influenced by the growing number of reports concerning the savage peoples of the Caribbean, North America, Tierra del Fuego, and elsewhere. In an influential argument, the seventeenth-century German jurist Samuel Pufendorf compared savage with civilized man to show how the establishment of private property marked the boundary between primitive and modern society. By the eighteenth century, there was a common understanding that humans had progressed through several economic stages—savagery, pastoralism, agriculture, and commerce were the usual suspects—and that each stage was associated with a particular set of political, social, legal, and intellectual institutions.

But how could the progressive fashion be squared with the chronological facts and descending trajectory of sacred history? The two were like the X formed by the up and down escalators in a department store. Peter Bowler has remarked that the idea that man acquired civilization in gradual stages required more time than was allowed by biblical chronology.[8] Yet in fact the authors of conjectural or philosophical histories did not necessarily offend a biblical time frame. Conjectural history, the great fashion of the eighteenth century, was a style of writing history in the philosophical mode. Freed from the obligation to work with evidence, the conjectural historians associated with the French and Scottish Enlightenments allowed themselves to extrapolate past conditions on the basis of present-day trajectories. Chronological signposts were not essential to the project. Condorcet, for example, dodged the issue of chronology by refusing to assign any dates to the stages he proposed. Others, notably the French physiocrat Baron de Turgot, were quite willing to squeeze the stages of progress into the short span of time made available by Holy Writ.[9] Adam Ferguson similarly framed the history of mankind in the limited time period allowed by sacred chronology.[10] Few saw an essential contradiction with sacred history, since no one knew how long it took societies to evolve.

The chronological conundrums were easy to square. Sacred and conjectural histories, however, were profoundly incompatible in another way, for they disagreed on history's direction. Is it from Eden downward, as proposed by Judeo-Christianity? Or from the primitive upward, the trajectory favored by conjectural historians? Yet there was a potential solution to this problem, if only one could jump off the down escalator and join the up at the point where the two cross. Embedded in the famous historical scheme promulgated by Turgot in *A Philosophical Review of the Successive Advances of the Human Mind* (1750) was a kind of biblical catastrophism, the idea that an event or events described in sacred history had wiped the slate clean and reset the clock of civilization to zero:

> Holy Writ, after having enlightened us about the creation of the universe, the origin of man, and the birth of the first arts, before long puts before us a picture of the human race concentrated again in a single family as the result of a universal flood. Scarcely had it begun to make good its losses when the miraculous confusion of tongues forced men to separate from one another. The urgent need to procure subsistence for themselves in barren deserts, which provided nothing but wild beasts, obliged them to move apart from one another in all directions and hastened their diffusion through the whole world. Soon the original traditions were forgotten; and the nations, separated as they were by vast distances and still more by the diversity of languages, strangers to one another, were almost all plunged into the same barbarism in which we still see the Americans.[11]

This, the crucial compromise, allowed conjectural history and economic stage theory to be reconciled with sacred history. Sacred history provided historians with at least three catastrophes—the expulsion from the Garden of Eden, the Universal Deluge, and the destruction of the Tower of Babel—that could be said to have returned humankind to a primitive condition. The ascent of man, as predicted by theories of progress, could begin from any of the three points.

Of these, the Deluge loomed largest in the historical imagination. An event of monstrous significance, the Deluge has seldom failed to grip the European imagination.[12] It was a prominent feature in the geological treatises of the seventeenth and eighteenth centuries and figures significantly in other writings. But the implications of the Deluge were not lost on historians and economists. In his *On the Origin of Laws, Arts, and Sciences* (1758), Antoine-Yves Goguet argued that the Deluge caused humans to forget the use of iron and other metals and return to the use of tools based on stone.[13] Ferguson, writing about how the human race had again been reduced to a few people, alluded at least indirectly to the Deluge.[14] And it was not just conjectural historians who played with the idea. Bossuet's great *Universal History* suggested how mankind was reduced to nearly nothing after the Deluge and then, by degrees, emerged from ignorance, transforming woods and forests into fields, pastures, hamlets, and towns, and learning how to domesticate animals and use metals.[15] This use of the Deluge as a resetting event in both sacred history and geology would persist into the nineteenth century.[16]

Conjectural historians, it is true, were not much interested in origins. Sacred historians like Ralegh and Bossuet, in turn, wrote much about the Deluge but were correspondingly less interested in outlining the stages of postdiluvian progress. It was Vico who, in his *New Science* (1725), most persuasively reconciled the Deluge with the theory of human progress.[17] Vico was not widely known in his own day, but *New Science* was rediscovered in the early decades of the nineteenth century, and his reputation was resurrected to a point where he and Leopold von Ranke (1795–1886) have often been called the fathers of modern history. Vico's emphasis on the Deluge was the key element of a philosophy designed to orient history around the proper interpretation of myths and legends, thereby avoiding idle speculation and armchair philosophizing. A consequence of this approach was to exclude sacred history from the terrain of the secular historian, on the theory that no documents apart from the sacred writings carried by Noah had survived the flood.[18]

Vico was clearly attracted to the idea of progress. But whereas Bodin was not interested in the Deluge, preferring instead to describe ante- and postdiluvian societies as identical in their primitiveness, Vico molded the Deluge into a powerful punctuating event.[19] The singular importance of the Deluge in Vico's history is reflected in the chronological table printed in *New Science,* which begins in the year 1656 A.M. (*anno mundi*), the year of the Deluge. In a telling phrase, Vico actually describes his work as "a new natural history of the universal flood."[20] By the light of this natural history, the Deluge was seen as a catastrophic event that forced humans into the most primitive of conditions, far more abject than anything experienced in the preceding 1,656 years of sacred history. His enthusiasm reflected in his redundancy, Vico writes in many places of a period of brutish wandering during which the three tribes of men were scattered throughout the world's forest and copulated promiscuously with mothers and daughters, unmindful of kinship. Much that Vico wrote was compatible—and designed to be compatible—with the anthropology of his day.

Far more than Turgot's, Vico's concept of historical chronology was thoroughly permeated by a philosophy of catastrophism. The dominant paradigm in eighteenth-century geology, catastrophism was not antithetical to conjectural history. Conjectural historians, concerned with process, did not trouble themselves with origins. To make their schemes work, all they needed was a set of primitive or presocial conditions. They could make their peace with the idea that a catastrophe like the Deluge had reset the clock to zero. In this view, history did not have to begin with human origins, where general historians like Eusebius or Ralegh had chosen to begin. Instead, the catastrophic paradigm authorized a history that began in the middle, on the heels of a catastrophe. The philosophy promoted so vividly by Vico, in other words, authorized the compression of historical time. This compression would persist long after the Deluge had vanished from the historical imagination.

The compression of historical time made little practical difference as long as historical time itself was of short duration. Until the discovery and acceptance of deep time in the middle of the nineteenth century, human history, as imagined in the Judeo-Christian tradition, was coterminous with the history of the earth itself.[21] Speculations on the age of the world greatly engaged ancient and medieval philosophers. Historians writing in the Judeo-Christian tradition could hardly resist the temptation to assign a date, and they assiduously combed the book of Genesis for clues. Genesis, alas, speaks of generations, not dates, and historians were forced to count generations in the manner of previous Greek, Syrian, and Jewish scholars. In the fourth century, Eusebius, bishop of Caesarea, had Adam created 5,198 years before the birth of Christ, and this was the figure used by Jerome, Paulus Orosius, and many other Christian historians. In the seventeenth century, the busy recalculations of a number of scholars resulted in estimations for the earth's age ranging from 3,700 to 7,000 years of age, though the date favored by James Ussher, 4004 B.C., soon emerged as the consensus.[22] A chronology beginning at this date was then added to the margins of English editions of the Old Testament so that readers could, at a glance, locate themselves in time. Bossuet's *Universal History* likewise provided chronologies in the margins that served to date events both by counting up, from Creation, and by counting down, to the birth of Jesus.

The chronological scaffolding generated by this computational industry was an important intellectual step because it provided a ready means for making instant comparisons between the chronologies of different civilizations. The idea was central to the work of some ancient historians and had significant influence on early modern historians.[23] In the sixteenth century, Bodin and Joseph Scaliger massaged the existing schemes into a grand system of universal time. The concordances promoted by this work suggested problems with conventional Judeo-Christian dating, for growing contact with Chinese, Indian, and Aztec civilizations exposed Europeans to timescales that were not counted in the mere thousands of years. As Paolo Rossi observes, Scaliger pointed out that Chinese cosmology went back more than 880,000 years, and in 1658 the Jesuit Father Martini found that Chinese annals, suitably transposed onto a Christian dating scheme, were reliably recording events that took place more than six hundred years before the Deluge.[24]

The great antiquity of Sumerian, Chaldean, and Egyptian civilizations was equally problematic. Work on Egyptian chronology suggested that Egyptian civilization dated back nearly to the Deluge itself, perhaps even before. How could so sophisticated a civilization have arisen in so short a time? Bodin was much troubled by these problems. The answer he and others proposed was that all non-Mosaic chronologies were either fabulous or written in the spirit of envy.[25] A second solution was to prefer the Greek Septuagint over the Hebrew Bible, since the Septuagint allowed an additional 1,440 years. In such ways, the intellectual challenge posed by lengthy Egyptian, Indian, and Chinese chronologies was, at least temporarily, absorbed and overcome.

But challenges to the grip of sacred chronology were not coming from historians alone; geology, paleontology, ethnology, and natural history also found Ussher's date too constricting. That marine fossils such as shells and sharks' teeth were found on mountaintops had always been something of a problem. One could suppose that they were just odd-looking rocks or freaks of nature laid down by a playful God. Alternatively, they were carried aloft by the waters of the Universal Deluge. Fossils embedded in rock were also a conundrum. By what process could a solid object enter another solid object? For those who admitted the natural origin of such fossils, the solution lay in the proposal that rocks formed in layers through a gradual process of sedimentation.[26] The resulting realization that layered strata represented geological time did not immediately subvert biblical chronology, since no one knew how long it took for the layers to form. Imaginative solutions were also devised for other emerging problems, such as the tilting of the bedding planes of geological strata, the discovery of strange creatures like ammonites, and the presence of humans in the New World. Even so, by the 1750s the loosening of the grip of sacred chronology had proceeded to a point where some were postulating an earth that was millions of years old, though such opinions were decidedly in the minority.[27] In his private notes, the French naturalist the Comte de Buffon played around with a date of three million years, and he argued in print for an earth some 75,000 years of age.[28] Decades earlier, Benoit de Maillet had proposed an earth more than two billion years in age.[29]

The idea of a very old earth was easily dismissed by orthodox Christian theologians and by distinguished scientists alike, for it created as many problems as it solved. Critics seldom failed to notice that mountains had not eroded away in all the time supposedly available. This particular obstacle was solved by the Scottish geologist James Hutton, who argued in the late eighteenth century that mountains were being continually uplifted and continents remade in a process that "has no vestige of a beginning, no prospect of an end." Hutton did not insist on an eternal, uncreated earth. All he claimed was that no trace of the primeval earth could have survived the endless recycling of materials. Eschewing the search for origins, he focused instead on geological mechanisms, in much the same way that conjectural historians typically avoided questions of human origins and instead focused attention on lawlike processes.[30]

Despite well-reasoned scientific objections, evidence for the antiquity of the earth continued to mount in the early decades of the nineteenth century, and the field of geology developed apace.

By the 1840s, geology's basic chronology, based on the succession of strata, had been worked out by the British geologist Charles Lyell, who published his *Principles of Geology* in the 1830s and remained a powerful advocate for the new scheme over the next forty years. Lyell's ideas were contested in his own day, and in 1868 the estimate made by the future Lord Kelvin that a molten earth first consolidated a hundred million years ago—a figure later reduced to twenty to forty million years—put an end to any ideas of an eternal earth.[31] Yet the Aristotelian idea of an eternal earth has been vindicated in a sense by the current estimate that the earth is around four and a half billion years old, easily old enough to accommodate the gradual geological and biological processes on which people like Lyell and Charles Darwin were most insistent.

Even as the field of geology was emerging as a science in the first half of the nineteenth century, antiquarians in Denmark, England, and France were excavating strata in which early human stone tools, eoliths, lay alongside extinct animals such as cave bears and mammoths.[32] The implications were obvious and had been noted since the last decade of the eighteenth century. Yet Lyell originally resisted the attempt to associate geological time with human antiquity. A British chauvinist, he dismissed the archeological evidence for man's antiquity compiled by French archeologists. A sensational archeological discovery in 1859, this time on English soil, finally convinced the geologists to support the idea that humans lived in the Ice Age. Paleontology and prehistoric anthropology sprang up as legitimate scientific disciplines in the 1860s, and the proposition that humans moved through stone, bronze, and iron ages emerged as the fundamental chronological scheme of archeology. John Lubbock later subdivided the Stone Age into old and new, Paleolithic and Neo-lithic, the latter associated with the agricultural revolution. Eth-nologists like Lewis Henry Morgan found the long chronology wonderfully liberating and took to it with great enthusiasm.[33] A crucial link in the time revolution was Darwin's *On the Origin of Species,* published in 1859, because it offered a way to link the his-tory of life and the descent of humanity to the emerging geolog-ical timescale, thereby unifying biological time.[34] *On the Origin of Species* was soon followed by Lyell's *The Geological Evidences of the Antiquity of Man* (1863) and Lubbock's *Pre-Historic Times* (1865), the three works that lie at the heart of the time revolution of the 1860s.[35]

The stages of the discovery of deep time are well known to his-torians of science and figure in the standard disciplinary narra-tives of the great historical sciences. But what were historians doing as the understanding of time was transformed in the sec-ond half of the nineteenth century? Looking back from the early twentieth century, the historian James Harvey Robinson could still reflect on the event with wonder: "Half a century ago, man's past was supposed to include less than six thousand years; now the story is seen to stretch back hundreds of thousands of years."[36] Other historians were indifferent. Yet despite the magnitude and implications of the revolution, the question of how historians ac-commodated deep time has not been seriously addressed until recently.

The later nineteenth and early twentieth centuries were the great age for patriotic histories of particular nations. In this climate, the urge to write universal histories was partially eclipsed. Even so, a good many works of general history circulated in the United States in the decades following the time revolution of the 1860s, including works imported from Europe as well as home-grown products.[37] Some of these were written for the general market. Others—a growing number—were explicitly designed for use in the classroom. Out of this pool of ideas and threads eventually emerged the narrative forms that would take shape as Western Civ textbooks, first published in the early decades of the twentieth century. In all these sources we can find clues revealing what happened to history's plotline as historians faced the challenge of deep time.

In an age when so eminent a figure as the geologist Louis Agassiz could persist in his adherence to the chronology of sacred history, it would be surprising if all historians accepted the long chronology without demur. The last edition of Royal Robbins's *Outlines of Ancient and Modern History* (1875), first published in 1830, was uncompromisingly sacred and treated Darwin as an infidel.[38] Reuben Parsons's *Universal History* (1902), written for an American Catholic audience, included an unapologetic defense of sacred history.[39] An especially significant source of resistance came from Ranke, the great German historian, who continued to affirm the truth of sacred history in his unfinished *Universal History* and argued that no history could address a time before documents. In contrast, the Oxford historians Edward Freeman and J. R. Green were remarkable for their cautious but sincere and early acceptance of the long chronology.[40] Amos Dean, in his seven-volume *History of Civilization* (1868), acknowledged the probability "that human life has existed on the planet during a much longer period than has been generally supposed," even though he perceived no investigative need to breach the barrier created by the Deluge.[41]

Rather than assess nineteenth-century historians according to the litmus test of belief, however, it behooves us to ask whether the long chronology made any difference to the framing of history, even among those who accepted it. Daniel Segal has recently argued that few late-nineteenth-century historians made a serious effort to build a meaningful historical continuum bottomed in the deep past.[42] In the general histories published before 1900, prehistory was simply tacked on at the beginning, or even reduced to a footnote.[43] What they offered, moreover, was little enough. In his important *Outlines of Universal History* (1885), one of the earliest books designed explicitly for use as a textbook in American secondary schools, the American historian George Fisher gave just a few paragraphs summarizing recent archeological discoveries.[44] In a general history first published in 1883, the Frenchman Victor Duruy, one of Fisher's sources, offered a little more. Even so, his contribution, in the 1925 English edition, amounted to no more than seven pages in a text 892 pages in length.[45] One of the most sustained efforts by a historian to summarize the discoveries of archeology can be found in the tenth edition of the *Storia Universale,* published in 1884 by the Italian general historian Cesare Cantù, who was deeply engaged with biological, archeological, and geological discoveries. The prefatory material is studded with references to scholarship on geological and prehistorical time, and Cantù devoted four chapters to the primitive world and theories about early human society.[46] But this incorporation of the paleoanthropological evidence was a curiously ironic gesture, because Cantù believed in sacred history and discussed the paleoanthropological evidence only so as to disprove it.

Cantù's skepticism aside, the problem of incorporating pre-history into the narrative was not only one of belief. It was also one of imagination. One could be open to the idea of deep history without knowing quite what to do with it. One solution to this narrative difficulty was to reimagine the European Middle Ages as a period of darkness so profound as to duplicate the social state of primitive savagery. In this new schema, ancient history stood in for the golden era of antediluvian sacred history, and early medieval Europe was transformed into the bestial and primitive world of the immediate postdiluvian age, the center of the X formed by the down and up escalators. In an echo of a Huttonian geology that eschewed the search for origins and focused instead on process, general historians of the nineteenth century found they had no need for Genesis and, like Vico, could focus instead on the progress that humankind had made since the most recent catastrophe.

The very idea of a pseudoprimitive Dark Age influenced the ways in which nineteenth-century historians framed medieval European history. The Enlightenment denigration of the European Middle Ages had made it easy to view the original inhabitants of Europe and the invaders of Rome as crude barbarians, little different from the primitive peoples that figured in conjectural histories and anthropological prehistories. Ferguson made the parallel explicit, describing the Gauls, Germans, and Britons as resembling the natives of North America in their ignorance of agriculture and their tendencies to paint themselves and wear the skins of animals.[47] Edward Gibbon himself wrote of a "deluge of Barbarians," using a word freighted with meaning.[48] These barbarians gradually came to stand in for Paleolithic man in the developmental schemes of Western history. Doris Goldstein, writing about Freeman and Green, has suggested that "their forays into what they described as the 'primeval' or the 'primitive' were closely related to their interest in the early history of the Teutonic tribes."[49] Medieval historians in the United States, deeply influenced by the idea of biological evolution and geological time, routinely referred to the early Germanic tribes using words like *primitive*.[50] They used the word in a positive developmental sense, as this 1899 paean to the era makes clear: "In the middle ages we are to see the beginnings of ourselves. We are the perfectly legitimate descendants of mediaeval men, and we have no ideas, no institutions, no manners that are not shot through and through with thread of mediaeval spinning."[51] Nineteenth-century historians were deeply attracted to the idea that progress followed on the heels of a Viconian resetting event. All that changed was the event itself: the aqueous Deluge was transformed into a deluge of barbarians.

By the turn of the century, some of the more robust intellectual obstacles to prehistory were fading. Lord Kelvin's thermodynamic principles showed that the earth had a datable point of origin that was immensely old. Prehistorical dates were circulating widely in the works of acknowledged authorities like Sir Arthur Keith, providing the chronological scaffolding on which history arranges itself.[52] The tendency to focus exclusively on the political or constitutional history of nations was being challenged by the rise of social and economic history, fields that focused on how people lived in the past, not just on how they were governed.

In the wake of these changes, the 1910s and 1920s saw some remarkable attempts to bridge the gap between prehistory and history. In 1913, the English historian James Bryce spoke enthusiastically about the possibility of a chronological expansion of the historians' terrain.[53] In 1916, the Berkeley historian Frederick Teggart suggested that "the historian has come to see that there is no hard and fast boundary between 'historic' and 'prehistoric' times, between 'historical' and 'unhistorical' peoples; the history of Man includes man everywhere and at all times. . . . Anthropology and History differ only in so far as each represents the use of a special investigative technique."[54] Around the same time, Robinson was arguing forcefully for a historical understanding that would embrace the Paleolithic, and he castigated his peers for their failure to make the mental switch:

> There may still be historians who would argue that all this has nothing to do with history,—that it is "prehistoric." But "prehistoric" is a word that must go the way of "preadamite," which we used to hear. They both indicate a suspicion that we are in some way gaining illicit information about what happened before the footlights were turned on and the curtain rose on the great human drama. Of the so-called "prehistoric" period we, of course, know as yet very little indeed, but the bare fact that there was such a period constitutes in itself the most momentous of historical discoveries.[55]

If the time revolution of the 1860s had caused the bottom to drop out of history,[56] "prehistory and its living representatives were a means of 're-bottoming' history." This is how Segal has characterized the result of Robinson's unprecedented engagement with the long chronology.[57] In this schema, the primitive conditions of the Paleolithic, serving as a convenient measure for our subsequent progress, are an essential element of the story of Western Civilization.

There is much truth to this argument. The paragraph or two devoted to prehistory in nineteenth-century works like Fisher's *Outlines* generally grew to a chapter or more in the textbooks and professional histories published in the United States after the 1920s.[58] Yet when Robinson actually applied this idea in his own textbook, *An Introduction to the History of Western Europe,* first published in 1903, the results were curious. Consider the question Robinson posed at the very outset of the book:

> One of the most difficult questions that a historical writer has to settle is the point at which he is to begin his tale. . . . How far back shall we go to get a start? Modern research seems to show that man was a wandering, hunting animal for hundreds of thousands of years before he learned to settle down and domesticate animals, cultivate the soil, and plant and reap crops.[59]

So where did he begin? The answer is surprising: the European Middle Ages. Eschewing the need to return to the Paleolithic bottom, Robinson argued that, since our civilization has descended directly from the fusion of Roman civilization and medieval Europe, there is no particular need to go any earlier.[60] Recapitulating this argument in *The Ordeal of Civilization* (1926), Robinson noted that "the development of our present civilization began with the first inventions and findings-out of mankind, of which no records remain." This was the great Viconian conundrum: how to study an age without documents? "Fortunately," Robinson went on to say, "we can take up the story with the decline and break-up of the Roman Empire."[61] Subsequent passages reveal Robinson's assessment of where medieval Europe belongs on the scale of civilization:

> It seemed for a few years as if the new German kings . . . would succeed in keeping order and in preventing the loss of such civilization as remained. But no such good fortune was in store for western Europe, which was now only at the beginning of the turmoil which was to leave it almost completely barbarized, for there was little to encourage the reading or writing of books, the study of science, or attention to art, in a time of constant warfare and danger.[62]

Much like nineteenth-century historians, Robinson sought to find the primitive in medieval Europe so as to have a more recent foundation on which to build history's narrative of progress. Despite Robinson's engagement with the long chronology, in other words, he ultimately arrived at a fundamentally Viconian solution, where the events of the Dark Ages stand in for the Deluge.

As Segal has noted, Robinson never really overcame the idea of rupture, the idea that some gulf separates us from the Paleolithic. With rare exceptions, textbooks and general histories published over the twentieth century followed more or less in Robinson's footsteps.[63] In these works, authors sometimes sought to define what it was that made civilization "history." In the process, they came to the conclusion that the Paleolithic simply was not historical.

In the nineteenth century, *prehistoric* meant "undocumented." A new shade of meaning was added in the twentieth, when prehistoric came to mean a time before history, as if history had not moved in the eons before civilization. Current in some anthropological circles around the turn of the century was the belief that progress itself was highly unusual—authors like Henry Sumner Maine and Walter Bagehot had spoken of stationary societies and "fixity." Several decades later, Oswald Spengler wrote of a culture in stasis as being caught within a "historyless" period.[64] Ideas such as these, when applied to the deep past, constitute the myth of Paleolithic stasis. This myth configured humanity's deep past as a grim and changeless era. The authors of a world history textbook for use in Catholic secondary schools, published in 1958, conveyed the idea nicely:

> Our imagination fails us when we try to see in the mind's eye the uncounted generations of Paleolithic people. We know what men have proved capable of accomplishing—their sciences and arts and great civilizations. Why, then, did they live for so long in the wilderness? It appears as if some great calamity had fallen upon human nature itself, as if some sentence of banishment and damnation had been laid on man by his Creator.[65]

Paleolithic stasis, in this admittedly atypical view, was the result of the Fall. But what broke the stasis and set man on the move? Rather than catastrophe, some general histories of the twentieth century proposed the idea of a catalyzing event that introduced progress or direction into a society hitherto without history. Mott Greene characterizes the argument in this mordant way: "At some point a leap took place, a mutation, an explosion of creative power—the 'discovery of mind,' or the 'birth of self-consciousness'—interposing a barrier between us and our previous brute, merely biological existence."[66] For John Hoyland, the author of *A Brief History of Civilization* (1925), the events that brought humankind out of the "darkness" included the warming of the earth's climate as well as the arrival of the Aryan race on the scene.[67] Hermann Schneider waffled between environmental changes and the fortuitous blending of human stocks.[68]

An especially important catalyzing event was the invention of writing. Eighteenth-century historians were not particularly sensitive to the invention of writing as a historical event, since the Word was considered the gift of God. By the nineteenth century, however, the invention of writing was beginning to figure prominently in historical accounts.[69] In 1928, Geoffrey Parsons introduced his chapter on the dawn of civilization in this way: "After 100,000 years of savagery and 10,000 years of barbarism the beginnings of writing and of civilization appeared at the eastern end of the Mediterranean."[70] Schneider identified the discovery of the art of writing and working in metal as crucial events in Near Eastern history.[71] Writing, in later accounts, was thought to have allowed humankind to preserve valuable learning for posterity and thus, for the first time, permitted human civilization to build upon itself in rapid Lamarckian fashion.[72] Historians like Vico and Ranke had long argued that writing made the past knowable. The belief in writing as a catalyzing event was a much more profound concept. Writing, in this view, actually put civilization on the move and created history out of the historyless Paleolithic. The catalyzing events described in these accounts are secular. Nevertheless, they function in the narrative in a fashion identical to the infusion of God's grace. I make no claim, would in fact resist the claim, that the authors of these accounts were crypto-creationists. The problem lies in the grip of the narrative itself, whose rhythms and patterns were left essentially unchanged as the sacred was translated into the secular.

In the same way that the chronology of the sacred histories of the nineteenth century persisted in the general histories of the twentieth, so too did sacred history's geography carry over from one era into the next, as the Garden of Eden was translated into Mesopotamia. Eden was not always in the Middle East. In medieval Europe, virtually all observers associated the Garden of Eden with the Far East. Eden formed part of the lure of the East, and some of the great *mappaemundi* even illustrate the garden hovering there at the top of the map, roughly in the spot where Japan or China would now be found. Over time, however, the Garden of Eden shifted westward, toward the Near East, where both Bodin and Vico were inclined to place it. Armenia was the location preferred by the church historian George Smith in his *Patriarchal Age* (1847).[73] In Smith's case, the reasons for this shift are especially interesting. Armenia, he noted, is where Noah and his sons settled after the Deluge. In this vision, the Ark, scarcely drifting at all on the waters of the Deluge, settled on Mt. Ararat after the flood subsided. Smith was insistent on Armenia because it was close to the geographic roots of the Indo-European peoples—and hence better suited to Smith's purpose, which was to argue that the historical splitting of the Indo-European linguistic family was identical to the Confusion of Tongues.[74] Twentieth-century history and archeology would soon arrive at a consensus that Mesopotamia was the birthplace of writing. The Sumerian origins of writing joined with the relatively new myth of a Mesopotamian Eden in confirming the Near East as the cradle of humanity. The rise of Mesopotamia is palpable. General histories and textbooks published in the later nineteenth century typically had history begin in Egypt, then considered the oldest civilization.[75] In most post–World War II textbooks, however, Mesopotamia supplanted Egypt as the point of origins.[76]

The deep gulf separating the Stone Age from civilization, backward Africa from progressive Mesopotamia, was humanity's Rubicon. Crossing it at some point late in the Neolithic era, just before the invention of metallurgy, humanity entered on the road to civilization, creating history in the process. The Neolithic Rubicon performs a narrative function eerily similar to the Viconian Deluge. There are some obvious differences. The Deluge was a resetting event, plunging humanity into the primitive conditions demanded by conjectural history. The Neolithic Rubicon was a passage from stasis to progress. But both sit astride the buffer zone between nonhistory and history. Both act as a rupture, generating a discontinuous narrative.

By this analysis, the Paleolithic "bottom" to the narrative of Western Civ was a false bottom. Robinson was earnest in his desire to integrate the Paleolithic into the stream of history, but his own texts were perfectly content to use the European Middle Ages as the Western world's point of origin. But even as Robinson was perfecting his textbooks, others were having a go at rebuilding the narrative of history and coming up with very different results. In the 1920s, the reading public was fascinated by the vertiginous prospects of deep history. Some measure of this fascination can be found in the phenomenal success of H. G. Wells's *The Outline of History*, whose first edition was published in 1919.[77] From his opening chapter, Wells rooted history in deep geological time, even astronomical time, and devoted far more attention to the Paleolithic and Neolithic than other histories of his time. Moving continuously from geological and biological time to historical time, the narrative does not postulate a rupture. Several books and series published in the wake of *Outline* were equally ambitious and equally seamless. A remarkable exemplar is a ten-volume series called *The Corridors of Time*, published in 1927.[78] Beginning with a volume entitled *Apes and Men,* the series develops a natural history of humanity that runs down to the agricultural revolution and beyond. In *The Stream of History,* a general history published in 1928 that moved from the origins of the earth to the twentieth century, Geoffrey Parsons devoted 142 pages, a quarter of the total, to prehistory. These and other works entered the space first opened by Wells.[79] The modern-day descendants of this narrative include trade histories written by Jared Diamond and others whose disciplinary affiliation is not with history.[80]

As William T. Ross has pointed out, *Outline,* with its frank Darwinian message, was aimed at a middlebrow audience "obstinately unwilling to subordinate itself to any older 'blue-blood' elite."[81] The response was immense: the work sold 150,000 copies in its initial British edition and 500,000 copies in the subsequent U.S. edition. The work's appeal lay in the message that biology, not genius, was responsible for getting us where we are today.[82] This was an explicit attack on the university-educated political elite who were inclined to explain history's progressive direction as a function of 6,000 years of careful political stewardship. Political elites were not necessarily anti-Darwinian. Instead, they favored the older narrative, suitably shorn of its sacred underpinnings, for the political myth it conveyed—leaderless, Paleolithic man was doomed to live in a world without history; properly submissive to the benevolent rule of far-seeing and learned elites, mankind may ascend the ladder of civilization.

The captivating possibility of Ross's argument is that the historians responsible for writing and teaching the first generation of Western Civ textbooks had political motivations for placing the Paleolithic on the other side of a gulf. Adopting the long chronology, after all, might invite the dangerous idea that political hierarchies emerged as the result of natural or Darwinian processes. To believe this would be to doubt the civilizing function of education; the blessing that is writing; even the beneficent role of academia itself.

@

By the early twentieth century, most professional historians had abandoned sacred history. Yet the chronogeography of sacred history and its attendant narrative of rupture has proved to be remarkably resilient. History still cleaves to its short chronology. The otherwise meaningless date of 4000 B.C. continues to echo in our histories.[83] Authors still use the narrative device of rupture to create an artificial point of origin, reducing the Paleolithic to the status of a prologue to history, humanity's "apprenticeship." And history's point of origin is still Mesopotamian, or even more recent than that, given how the myth of the medieval origins of the modern world has embedded itself in the historical community. First told by Robinson, the myth has been peddled industriously by medieval historians who understandably desire a fair share of the curriculum and all the resources that go with it. Yet in this scramble for resources, it is the Paleolithic that gets left out of the history. A cynical comment, perhaps, but one that suggests how the exclusion of the Paleolithic did not derive just from the failure to break the plot of sacred history. There has also been resistance.

TWO

Resistance

In the well-known critique of ahistorical anthropology offered in his *People of the Mediterranean* (1977), John Davis commented wryly on how the anthropologies of his day were prefaced, almost obligatorily, with a few pages of history, often no more than three or four.[1] Because the past provided no informants, it was a world unknowable to the anthropologist, and so it could be safely left to the historians. He could have said much the same about how some of the general histories written in the 1960s and still in print in the 1970s contemplated the deep past of paleoanthropology. The pages or short chapters dedicated to the Paleolithic in these books do not lack a sense that the period deserves some coverage. What they lack is conviction. Key phrases appearing in chapter titles and headings—"The Threshold of History," "The Birth of Civilization," "Out of the Darkness," "The Step into History," "Prologue"—hint at the rupture that separates prehistory from real history. The facts about this era are known by paleoanthropologists, among whose conversations and debates the historian is no more than an eavesdropper. Here and there, one finds arguments explaining why the other side of Eden does not quite count as history; why history came to be made, and came to be knowable, only with the rise of civilization:

> [History exists] because generation after generation men have kept records, both intentional and unintended ones. . . . In the first chapter of this book we speak of prehistoric man, that is, man before he had begun to keep any self-conscious records.[2] (1964)

> To understand any era of the past one must be able to penetrate into the minds of its inhabitants. This is an ever challenging, yet extremely difficult task, to which the historian should bring sympathetic imagination and a wide knowledge of the passions of man; if he is to have any success, there must also be adequate written records as well as physical objects. Such records are available only for the past five millennia of human existence and then only for certain areas. This period is the historical age proper, the era of civilization.[3] (1965)

> A culture can endure only if the knowledge necessary for its survival is passed on from generation to generation. Early peoples relied on information transmitted by word of mouth—an undependable means of communication. But as towns and cities grew up and cultures became increasingly complex, methods for keeping records were devised and systems of writing were created. To many authorities, the development of writing is a prerequisite to civilization.[4] (1965)

> Neolithic culture marked a great advance in human destiny, but not the ultimate fulfillment. The small isolated village, the limited technology, the routine imposed by nature, the narrowly conceived social system, and the restricted intellectual horizons characteristic of Neolithic society combined to inhibit further advances. Men had to discover a new ambience in order to improve their condition. Such a leap forward occurred during the fourth and third millenniums before Christ. . . . The urbanization of life in the Near and Far Eastern river valleys constitutes the crucial

event inaugurating the history of civilization in the proper sense of the term.[5] (1966)

In the several centuries before 3000 B.C. there came into being the twin kingdoms of the Nile, equipped with bureaucratic systems, owing allegiance to central authority and poised, quite unconsciously, on the brink of history.[6] (1967)

These are among the latest and the last of a series of passages that go back to the dawn of the time revolution. What this genealogy indicates is that it was not the inertia of sacred history and the problems of plotting alone that have delayed the reception of humanity's deep history. There was a certain degree of resistance, a lingering unwillingness to contemplate the dark abyss of time. Historians no longer think this way.[7] But when resistance was active—when, in the late nineteenth and early twentieth centuries, some historians were alive to the implications of that abyss—the exclusion of the deep past was motivated by genuine intellectual doubts and uncertainties. Their resistance absolved historians of the need to read deeply in the paleoanthropological evidence. This resistance is now dormant, but its legacy—a few dutiful pages on the Paleolithic, a sense that this is not the province of history—continues to shape our texts and our curricula.

Since arguments for the exclusion of deep history circulate today in the form of ghost theories rather than cogent intellectual positions, it is difficult to know quite how to expose them. There is no smoking gun. There are no figures from the past to demonize or to poke fun at. One must gather together the wisps of a ghost theory, giving the whole an intellectual coherence it never had, before one can set about the task of dismantling it. The whole enterprise smacks of setting up a straw man. And what do we gain by exposing the resistance to deep history? Why not just *get on* with it? But one might just as well ask why historians of women thought it necessary to explore the historiographical grip of patriarchy even as they undertook the task of writing a women's history. Histories, like all products of disciplinary knowledge, are made in the context of what their own frames will allow. It is the frames that one must stretch and bend.

One of the most prominent obstacles to the incorporation of the deep past centered on the ways in which historians imagined the evidence appropriate for the study of history. Since the seventeenth century, when schemes for lengthening the age of the earth first began to circulate, the "time beyond history" was dismissed as unknowable. "All of that time was unknown and concealed," remarked Philippe Le Prieur in 1656.[8] Giambattista Vico's method denied the possibility of approaching the time before the Deluge via the products of vernacular human language, since all vernaculars postdated the Deluge. Nineteenth-century archeologists spoke of the fog that obscured their vision of the pre-Christian era. John Lubbock summed up the philosophy of those opposed to prehistoric archeology in the mildly caustic opening paragraph of his *Pre-Historic Times* (1865):

> The first appearance of man in Europe dates from a period so remote, that neither history, nor even tradition, can throw any light on his origin, or mode of life. Under these circumstances, some have supposed that the past is hidden from the present by a veil, which time will probably thicken, but never can remove....

Some writers have assured us that, in the words of Palgrave, "We must give it up, that speechless past."⁹

That speechless past: no other phrase could capture so well the skeptical attitude toward the possibility of studying time beyond the veil.

The singular problem was the absence of documents, which by the end of the nineteenth century had become the sine qua non of the professional historian. It was not always so. When universal education was implemented in the United States earlier in the century, historians saw fit to offer manuals of historical understanding. Documentary evidence figures significantly in these manuals but does not crowd out other forms of evidence. In his 1885 textbook, George Fisher counseled young historians on the necessity of having facts, in the form of either direct or indirect testimony. Such testimony included written records such as registers, chronicles, inscriptions, and literature but could also include oral tradition, material structures such as altars, tombs, and private dwellings, and language, using the techniques of comparative philology.¹⁰ Yet with the wave of professionalization that swept the country in the last two decades of the century, the document became ever more central to historical epistemology, the system that defined how historians could know things. This move was a vital element of professionalization, since it removed documents from the gaze of the vulgar masses. Only experts, the new professional historians, could be trusted to ferret out the true meanings of authors and offer correct interpretations of texts. To invent an author with complex motives was to create arcane knowledge that only scientific historians trained in seminars could be trusted to interpret accurately.

History's professionalizing agenda was motivated by the same disciplinary impulses that were transforming other fields of inquiry.[11] Among professionalizing historians, however, the documentary ideology was at least partially linked to a desire to distinguish the realm of history from the realms of archeology and anthropology, and hence to demarcate the time of history from the time of prehistory. That a documentary epistemology could serve to exclude deep history can be seen in the figure of Leopold von Ranke.[12] Toward the end of his life, Ranke undertook a monumental task: a *Weltgeschichte,* or *Universal History,* intended to tell the full story of history as Ranke saw it in the 1880s. In the remarkable opening paragraph of this work, Ranke expressed his reluctance to breach the veil of prehistory:

> History cannot discuss the origin of society, for the art of writing, which is the basis of historical knowledge, is a comparatively late invention. The earth had become habitable and was inhabited, nations had arisen and international connections had been formed, and the elements of civilization had appeared, while that art was still unknown. The province of History is limited by the means at her command, and the historian would be over-bold who should venture to unveil the mystery of the primeval world, the relation of mankind to God and nature. The solution of such problems must be intrusted to the joint efforts of Theology and Science.[13]

In this epistemological stance, Ranke was joined by his near contemporaries, the French historians Charles Langlois and Charles Seignobos, whose *Introduction to the Study of History,* first published in English in 1898, was described by Frederick Teggart almost three decades later as "the most important 'introduction' available to students in the English language."[14] Contemplating the evidence appropriate to history, Langlois and Seignobos observed that "[t]he historian works with documents. Documents are the traces which have been left by the thoughts and actions of men of former times. . . . For want of documents the history of immense periods in the past of humanity is destined to remain for ever unknown. For there is no substitute for documents: no documents, no history."[15] Similar sentiments were proffered in other guides and manuals. "Historians get their knowledge from written documents," remarked V. A. Renouf in 1909. "No history of any country can be written unless its people have left some such record of their activities."[16]

No documents, no history. An important feature of Vico's *New Science,* this epistemological stance was repackaged by Ranke and others in the nineteenth century and promulgated as a basis for scientific history. Now one can, with Herbert Butterfield, point out that Ranke was trying to preserve the realm of history from the speculations of philosophers.[17] But it is important not to lose sight of the fact that Ranke, like Vico, accepted the truths of sacred history. Early chapters of *Universal History* echo the sacred histories of the seventeenth and eighteenth centuries. Ranke's firm belief that "the course of history revealed God's work," in Peter Novick's phrase, is well known.[18] In other words, Ranke arguably promoted writing as the sole reliable basis of historical knowledge not just because he sought to place history on a scientific footing but also because this was the only way he knew to exclude prehistorical artifacts from historical reckoning and thereby dodge the vexed theological questions created by biology and archeology.

There can be no written documents from the Paleolithic and Neolithic periods. How serious is this obstacle to the writing of a

deep history in the twenty-first century? The answer to this depends on how you choose to define a document.

Scrambling for a metaphor to describe how natural historians
conduct their research, the Comte de Buffon, one of the great
philosophers of the eighteenth century, reached for the image of
a text. Natural historians, he tells us, are people who "rummage
through the archives of the world."[19] It is an arresting image: the
idea that the birds, beetles, soils, rocks, all the objects in the gaze
of the eighteenth-century natural historian were lined up on so
many shelves, ready to be retrieved and studied. Several decades
later, Charles Lyell treated the geological record as a library or an
archive. Lyell's idea was subsequently cribbed by Darwin in a
well-known passage from *On the Origin of Species,* where he
viewed the natural geological record "as a history of the world
imperfectly kept, and written in a changing dialect; of this history we possess the last volume alone, relating only to two or
three countries. Of this volume, only here and there a short
chapter has been preserved, only here and there a few lines."[20]

Nineteenth-century archeologists were equally taken by the
idea. The title of Daniel Wilson's *The Archaeology and Prehistoric
Annals of Scotland* (1851) evokes the image of the early medieval
annalistic chronicles; a little later, Lubbock wondered why prehistoric antiquities were not regarded as "pages" of ancient history. Harold Peake and Herbert Fleure, in their natural history
of humankind of 1927, described the geological record in vivid
terms as a number of volumes organized into two series, the first
of which, the Azoic, survives only as "a few pages, badly crum-
pled, scorched, and burnt," all that is left of the last two volumes
of the series.[21] The metaphor remains a commonplace to this day.
Most recently it has surfaced in the work of population geneti-

cists, who compare DNA to ancient parchments on which the history of the human race is written, and evolutionary psychologists, who view behavioral traits as archives.[22]

The use of the metaphor reveals a telling epistemological claim. The great historical disciplines, including geology, evolutionary biology and ethology, archeology, historical linguistics, and cosmology, all rely on evidence that has been extracted from things. Lumps of rock, fossils, mitochondrial DNA, isotopes, behavioral patterns, potsherds, phonemes: all these things encode information about the past. The remarkable success of these sciences over the past century and a half has shown how meaningful histories can be written on the basis of these things. By referring to them metaphorically as documents, the other historical sciences lay a claim for an equivalence, in meaning and value, between their "documents" and the documents consulted by historians. That they engage in metaphor and circumlocution is not a symptom of the poverty of their claims. It is merely a reminder that the English language does not have a word for the category that consists of all things that encode information about the past. So what shall we call these things, if not documents? *Artifact* could do, except one balks at the idea of describing a gene or a phoneme as the product of handiwork. *Remains* cannot help suggesting dusty bones and ruins. Perhaps the most serviceable word is simply *trace,* whose added attraction lies in its deep pedigree. "The facts of the past are only known to us by the trace of them which have been preserved," remarked Langlois and Seignobos, who went on to distinguish between "material traces" and "written descriptions."[23]

A trace is anything that encodes some sort of information

about the past. As Paul Connerton has put it, traces are "the marks, perceptible to the senses, which some phenomenon, in itself inaccessible, has left behind."[24] A few moments of thought will be enough to convince you that the concept is an empty one, since almost everything around us, from an echo of the Big Bang to the smallest bit of sandstone, bears some historical trace, the mark left behind by some phenomenon that is no longer accessible to us. Yet some traces are more revealing than others, and these merit the embrace of a name. Ocean cores, microscopic pollen, conodonts, basalt: all carry echoes of the past embedded in their isotopes, their colors, their patterns of mineralization. From these echoes histories can be built. Some traces, such as fossils, rocks, and manuscripts, inform us by virtue of being contemporary to the events whose histories they encode. But traces need not be old to carry historical information. A phoneme, uttered today, is a living fossil, though the lineage fades into oblivion after a few thousand years. So is DNA. Although population geneticists do occasionally extract DNA from ancient remains, they more commonly work with modern DNA borrowed from the inside of a cheek or from a drop of blood. Modern DNA is uncannily similar to an edited text. It consists of lines of code, written in an alphabet of four letters, that faithfully reproduce an original. Like a text, it carries information that can be read by future generations. It must be read to have any meaning. The only difference—and to some this will be important—is that DNA is not the product of anyone's intention. A dependence on documents, if philosophically justified, would limit history to the short chronology. But if we accept that a document is just one kind of trace, we are led to the position that documents merely add to the sources of the past. A powerful claim, and one that opens doors to the possibility of a deep history. Yet how secure is it?

©

The first edition of Robert H. Labberton's *Universal History* was published in 1871, shortly after the time revolution. Like many of his contemporaries, Labberton suffered from mild vertigo when contemplating the abyss of time, and so, withdrawing from the brink, he sought to explain why history should be limited to the short chronology. This is what he came up with: a society can be subject to the gaze of history only when the society itself has a historical consciousness.[25] This was scarcely a pressing concern for him. The argument occupies no more than a few lines and is revealing only because he thought it necessary to respond in some way to the challenge of time. The idea itself did not belong to Labberton; like any meme, it popped up elsewhere—across the Atlantic, for example, in the work of the great French historian François Guizot, who arrived at this dictum: the keeping of written memorials of deeds and destinies is the beginning of history, since they reveal "sentiments which testify to the superiority of man over all other creatures." From this Guizot spun a conclusion to which Labberton would have subscribed: these sentiments, the desire to transmit a legacy, foreshadow the immortality of the soul. Why is this? Well, on a moral level, the desire for immortality is indistinct from the desire to be remembered fondly by history. The idea that future generations are watching you, according to Guizot, acts to spur your own moral development. Thus, in the consciousness of history, we find the roots of morality and human altruism and hence the beginning of history.[26]

There are shades of Hegel here, shades of the idea that history has a beginning that springs from the masculine desire for recognition. (These histories really were about *men*.) The meme continues to pop up. "History is *conscious* history," remarked Oswald Spengler. "The knowledge of goals, possibilities, means; the memory of victories and defeats; the hope for happiness; fame as a form of *personal* immortality—all this distinguishes history from mere events, *having* a history from mere endurance of fate, *making* history from mere indistinctive behavior."[27] In 1951, the idea that history begins with the consciousness of history was recapitulated in the twenty-fourth edition of Karl Ploetz's *Auszug aus der Geschichte:* "Prehistory embraces the period before humankind wrote its own history."[28] And then again, a little later, a remarkable expression found in *The Columbia History of the World* (1972): "History exists only in a persisting society which needs history to persist."[29]

Ranke, Langlois, and Seignobos had made a material claim: the unwritten past is unknowable. Labberton and others contributed a wholly new dimension to this claim. Whenever a society has reached a point where it creates its own histories or strives, through archives, to transmit the thoughts and sentiments of men down through the ages, it has achieved self-consciousness and entered the realm of history. In the same way that an organism without self-consciousness cannot be said to have an autobiography, so too a society without self-consciousness cannot be said to have a history. It is a sense of history, the stream of time, that transforms a motley assortment of ape-men into a human society.

"The beast lives *unhistorically,*" Friedrich Nietzsche observed in 1874, prosaically contemplating cows in a pasture.[30] By this argument, the consciousness of history was one of the catalytic devices that propelled humans across the Neolithic Rubicon, demarcating an era of timeless bovinity, the static world of the Old Stone Age, from a progressive humanity, now made complete with both past and future. This is why one occasionally finds the assertion that history begins with the Greeks, for the Greeks had Herodotus.

Assessing the value of different kinds of traces, historians have parted ways from archeologists and other students of human history by implying that the traces valued by the discipline of history are superior to others by virtue of being deliberate and conscious inscriptions.[31] The vast majority of traces, after all, are accidental preservations. They convey historical meaning, but they do so without purpose or intent. Most human artifacts, perhaps especially the objects found in ancient trash heaps, are also accidental preservations. No one searches for intention in the making of a coprolite. The inscriptions, monuments, and documents favored by historians have a different feel to them. Documents, as Langlois and Seignobos said, contain a record of the thoughts and actions of men. Other traces cannot make this claim so easily. In addition, documents were *explicitly* designed to record information about the past. In the words of the authors of *The Illustrated World History* (1935), archives constitute "conscious records," by which they appear to mean records showing evidence of conscious thought.[32] Deliberate archives reveal the awareness of past and future that many historians need to convince themselves of a society's historicity and moral direction.

This issue was significant because the scientific impulses of the late nineteenth century assumed that one aim of documentary analysis was to ferret out an author's meanings. As Langlois and Seignobos put it, "A document only contains the ideas of the man who wrote it. . . . We thus arrive at this general rule of method: the study of every document should begin with an analysis of its contents, made with the sole aim of determining the real meaning of the author."[33] This was an attitude fully in keeping with a style of literary analysis focused on authorial intentions, a style that was especially prominent in the later nineteenth century. If there is no author and no meaningful thoughts to uncover, there can be no history. This would be enough to exclude the vast majority of traces that are accidental preservations. This was especially so in Langlois and Seignobos's era, when many historians accepted the dictum that history is the biography of great men. The very possibility of history is excluded if we cannot name the leaders who acted as progressive forces.

So let us examine this complex of ideas regarding the history-making nature of documents. Seen from a present-day perspective, the claim that a society must have a written history or deliberate archives in order to be historical does not hold up well to scrutiny. We would not deny historicity to medieval European Jews or to Aztecs merely because their oppressors very nearly succeeded in destroying all their archives, though we might admit that their histories are now much more difficult to write. In a different vein, we do not deny historicity to the Incans or to the people of Great Zimbabwe because they never recorded history in writing. Neither do we deny historicity to the vast majority of premodern Europeans who have never kept records, let alone histories. Peasant societies have rarely generated written chronicles, and not all of them have been mindful to preserve other forms of written record. Do these societies become historical only when a historian or archivist living in a city fifty miles away happens to take notice of them? As another example, is early medieval Europe considered historical because a very few members of its population were literate clergymen? Or was it a world that was 99 percent historyless and 1 percent historical? Does the percentage of historians and archivists have to achieve a certain density for a society to become historical, or is one historian enough? These are ridiculous questions, but they nonetheless hint at the tortured logic generated by the argument that a society must have once generated documents to be held within the gaze of history. We can certainly claim that we are able to write the histories of the Incans and of medieval peasants on the basis of the written observations of others. But if we are going to admit that a meaningful history of an illiterate society can be written using the observations of others, then I for one would prefer the writings of modern archeologists to those of contemporary conquerors and clerics. I am not especially troubled by the fact that the archeologists and biological anthropologists did not experience, firsthand, the events and patterns they describe. The veil of time undoubtedly obscures their vision, but no more than the twin veils of cultural misunderstanding and self-deception that cloud the accounts of eyewitnesses. In light of these arguments, deep history is a natural extension of historiographical trends that began in the mid-twentieth century. The goal of the social history of this era, after all, was to uncover the world of the people without history.[34] This move was seconded by branches of world and postcolonial history that sought to apply the same logic to colonial peoples deemed historyless before the arrival of the Western colonial and imperial enterprise. The grip of the political has been significantly weakened; so too the grip of European civilization. All that remains for us to shake off is the grip of sacred history.

Written documents are not essential to the writing of history. But is history essential for the constitution of society? The claim that "history exists only in a persisting society which needs history to persist" suggests that people without their own histories do not constitute a society, since a society has to be aware of its past and its future in order to hang together. Like an individual, a society has to have a memory as well as goals and aspirations. History is the measure of a society's self-consciousness. But, even if we accept this principle, it does not permit us to insist that this history take written form. What mattered to Guizot was that a desire for remembrance, coupled with a belief in the afterlife, supplied humanity with a moral compass. As far as deep history is concerned, we cannot rule out the possibility that Paleolithic populations had a sense of history or a desire for immortality in this sense. Cave paintings can be taken as evidence for a desire to transmit something to future generations. The initial discoveries of cave paintings in the 1870s and 1880s were troubling for exactly this reason, for they posed a serious challenge to those who doubted the humanity of Paleolithic humans. The capacity to create art was seen as a symbol of a higher worldview—evidence for the thinking, feeling human who was so difficult to detect in the eoliths and bones that had hitherto dominated the archeological world.[35] Graves and grave goods also betray a similar sort of historical sense. As with cave paintings, part of the shock of discovering Paleolithic graves—both those of Neanderthals and those of modern humans—derived from the fact that the existence of graves implies a belief in an afterlife, which in turn implies a desire for the same sort of immortality that comes from the keeping of histories.

Far more significant than either of these is the possibility, even the likelihood, that Paleolithic humans had oral histories. Since the researches of Alfred Bates Lord and others, we have come to realize the lasting role of memory as a medium for recording all sorts of information, including historical information. Once again, medieval European history is illustrative in crucial ways. Dozens or hundreds of historical epics, originally oral in form, have survived from the period because clerics were instructed to write them down. What has survived is surely but a tiny fragment of a vast historical literature that circulated in oral form among the military aristocracy. We can only guess at the histories once remembered and told among peasants. If our purposes are similar to Guizot's, it cannot matter that these oral histories were semifabulous, that the twelfth-century written versions of *The Song of Roland* or *Raoul de Cambrai* contain only dim echoes of the real Carolingian events they purport to describe. Roland's heroism and Raoul's single great flaw would inspire, or deter, all who listened. All such histories and epics make their listeners aware of the past and mindful of the future. This, as many have pointed out, is the function of myth.

Equally significant is the fact that we routinely use our memories to record all sorts of information that is functionally equivalent to the kinds of evidence housed in archives. This archival function is one of the array of functions embraced by the term *social memory,* as proposed by James Fentress and Chris Wickham, and has been shown to have been of considerable significance in medieval European society.[36] Modern trial systems rely hopefully on the principle that witnesses will provide reasonably accurate memories of events and circumstances. Biologists and evolutionary psychologists have pointed out that animals routinely keep track of information regarding the altruistic or self-serving behavior of other members of their species.[37] Humans exchange this sort of information through gossip, building or breaking political coalitions in the process and rewarding or ostracizing the parties involved.[38]

The keeping of history, the remembrance of heroes and ancestors, the tracking of credits and debts: these are all important functions of language. Even if modern linguistic capability and the neural pathways necessary for symbolic thought are no more than 50,000 or 60,000 years old, as some have claimed, one could still argue for a history considerably older than what is conventionally conceded by the chronological grip of sacred history.[39] I could make my peace with this claim. As it happens, however, I do not hold with the idea that a consciousness of history is a prerequisite for historicity, preferring to join with others in believing that history is something that *happens* to peoples, things, and organisms, and is not *made* by them. I shall return to this theme a little later. But to the extent that historians consider the consciousness of history a prerequisite for history, they shall have to consider beginning their histories, in a serious way, with the invention of language, not writing. And depending on how one defines language, this could take us back nearly two million years, when the voice box first began to descend to a point where it was capable of making the range of sounds considered necessary for symbolic language.

To acknowledge the likelihood of oral histories in Paleolithic societies and the continuing role of memory and orality in Postlithic societies is to begin to realize that documents did not really matter all that much in the making of civilization, despite persistent claims to the effect that writing first set us on the move and created history out of the nothingness of our biological past. Few historians have been troubled by the obvious incongruities of this argument. Agriculture, villages, towns, even cities and empires arose without the benefit of writing. The earliest forms of cuneiform writing consisted of clay tablets recording market transactions and tax records with none of the moral, political, or legal lessons for future generations that Guizot had imagined. These were mnemonic devices, no better and no worse than a string tied around the finger or the rather more sophisticated sets of knots created by the Incans. The tablets circulated as bills of exchange, carrying a symbolic value as money rather than a historical value as something-to-be-preserved. Their symbolic function served, the tablets were simply thrown away in the trash. Above all, the great religious texts and myths deemed essential for the binding of society, texts that can be read as making moral statements, circulated in oral forms long before they were written down. To the extent that they had or have any catalyzing qualities, moreover, they catalyzed as oral texts, not as written documents. Even after being written down they *still* circulate, and still have their greatest influence, as oral texts, precisely because oral texts are freer to contain the meanings that societies with changing needs want to attribute to texts. Much the same holds for archives. If the information that circulates in present-day society could be quantified, we would find that the vast majority of data bits that inform our daily activity are remembered, not written. The insistence on the written is a patronizing deni-

gration of the oral, a persisting and blind denial of the fundamental role of memory as an archival and historical medium in
all Postlithic societies.

@

"A society can be subject to the gaze of history only when the society itself has a historical consciousness." Even if we choose to accept Labberton's claim, we can defend the idea of a deep history
on the grounds that early societies had oral texts and therefore the
historical and moral consciousness demanded by him and by
Guizot. Although these oral texts no longer survive as such, we
can use other traces to piece together the faint outlines of the history and moral consciousness of Paleolithic ancestors. Compared
to the hearty stew of modern history, it makes for a weak broth.
But at least it is history. There is no reason to allow ourselves to be
caught in Labberton's trap, however. His claim, and the claim
made subsequently by Ranke and others, depends on the idea that
"conscious" records generated a history qualitatively different
from, and superior to, a history based on unintentional preservations. It is fair to admit that written documents add richness to
history. But as most historians recognize, documents are not necessarily used only for what authors intend to put in them. Some
of the richest historical information comes from documents that
are made to reveal the information they unintentionally possess.[40]
There is very little distinction between documents and the sorts of
unintentional traces examined by archeologists and geneticists
when the information is handled in this inferential way.

Surveying the various kinds of traces that could serve as the
objects of historical attention in 1885, Fisher added language to

the list, claiming that "language is a memorial of the past, of the more value since it is not the product of deliberate contrivance." He was referring to extraordinary discoveries that had been made in recent decades by students of the Indo-European language family. But especially interesting is his claim about language's value as a historical source. Histories, chronicles, legends: these are all deliberate contrivances. Speakers of languages, in contrast, are wholly unaware of the histories to which they contribute whenever they use words and subtly alter phonemes, spellings, and syntax. Philological analysis is all the more reliable precisely because we do not have to erect filters for sifting out bias. As Fisher knew, authorial intentions are problematic precisely because authors are not neutral conveyancers of ideas, events, and images. Instead, they shape, twist, mold, and deceive.

Ranke and his disciples were intensely aware of these problems. Ranke's well-known concern about narrative forms the basis of his emphasis on nonnarrative documents. Given all the problems of interpretation, historical manuals written around the turn of the nineteenth century were insistent on the need to erect filters against the problems of authorial manipulation.[41] Whether these historians succeeded in their efforts is another question. Writing barely a generation after the Rankean revolution first swept through the practice of history in the United States, Teggart expressed deep skepticism about the scientific method and the documents on which the method was based: "The unsupported affirmations of one man concerning the actions and motives of an opponent would not be accepted in the ordinary affairs of life, yet historians . . . end by admitting any statement which does not happen to be contradicted by another accessible document."[42] Yet this criticism does not gainsay their awareness of the problem. The filters also extended to the very archives that were legitimate objects of historical inquiry. In a letter written in 1927 to a fellow historian, J. Franklin Jameson, the founding editor of *The American Historical Review,* rejected social history on the grounds that "you do not have definitely limited bodies of materials, handed down by authority, like statutes or other manageable series, but a vast blot of miscellaneous material from which the historian picks out what he wants."[43] In this particularly radical claim, only documents *intentionally* preserved can have meaning. The rest is just aimless sediment that has precipitated out of the lakes and streams of social patterns and human actions.

As Fisher had perceived, however, there is a great deal of value in the aimless sediment. Authored texts are deliberate contrivances, subject to bias. We can erect filters against the bias, as Langlois and Seignobos sought to do. But we can also study the sediment, for there can be no human bias in things that are not the product of intention—excepting, of course, the biases that interpreters bring to the traces they contemplate. In many areas of premodern history, archeology is sometimes used as a control device, precisely because one does not have to worry about erecting filters against authorial bias.[44] Often the archeological evidence corroborates the written evidence, but sometimes it does not. Genetic evidence—and I think there are good reasons to treat genes as if they were potsherds—has suggested that most modern Hungarians are not of Magyar lineage, giving the lie to chroniclers who described a Pannonia laid waste by the campaigns of Charlemagne and subsequently repopulated, from scratch, by Magyar invaders.[45] Leaping over the centuries, consider the history of the Jamestown settlement in 1607. Sources written by the colonists themselves made it possible to write a history of "inept and indolent English gentlemen" who came looking for easy wealth, unlike the stern and industrious Calvinists who settled in Massachusetts Bay. But recent archeological research has revealed industrious people adapting industriously, if ineffectually, to their difficult environment.[46]

Nondocumentary traces like genes and potsherds provide valuable checks on the written word. But historians have long since been aware that documents, too, possess many features that are not the product of intent. Freudian theory, transported into the philosophy of history, gave historians reason to search for deeper meanings beyond superficial appearances and the chimera of authorial intent. Liberated by this transformation in historical epistemology, historians could use documents for more than their superficial purposes or meanings.[47] Texts carry meanings that are intended, but they also carry information that just happens to be there, in the margins of intent. Writing for a high school audience in 1926, the historian Henry Johnson phrased the issue in this especially insightful way:

> In general, two kinds of sources are distinguishable: (1) those that bear some evidence of conscious intent to transmit information; and (2) those that have come down to us as mere relics or survivals of past conditions or events. . . . Some sources may be regarded either as conscious or unconscious testimony, that is, either as traditions or remains, according to the point of view from which they are considered. A newspaper, for example, contains conscious representations of conditions and events; it is at the same time not only a direct material remain, but, even as a report, an unconscious reflection of the tastes, the interests, the desires, and the spirit, of its day.[48]

If it is the center of meaning that draws your attention, it is legitimate to inquire into an author's intention. But if you are drawn to the unintended meanings or the accidental preservations, the author, in effect, disappears, and you are left with a text that must be decoded in a different way. This is the logical extension of a line of inquiry introduced by Michel Foucault when he sought to describe an archeology of knowledge. As Franco Moretti and others have shown recently, a similar kind of methodology can be very useful in the effort to decode the literature of the past.[49] In his work on the early medieval economy, Michael McCormick has vividly illustrated how much can be extracted from texts handled as if they form archeological strata.[50] Here we find a historical epistemology in which words serve as the potsherds from which we may tease out the contours of the age.

In the course of my own specialized research on the city of Marseille in the fourteenth century, I have read several thousand notarized contracts—debts, loans, bills of sale, testaments, marriage contracts, house sales, and so on. It is possible to read these acts for what they intend to convey: that in 1348, for example, Bertran Auriol sold to Bernat de Batut a house located on the Street of the Tannery for the sum of twenty florins. But we can never actually know whether truth or deceit lies behind any of the claims we read. Isnart Bres says he is a citizen of Marseille. Guilelma Brunella tells the notary that her husband is dead. I suspect these claims are true, but they are not necessarily so. In some cases, as in the simple loan, we know or at least suspect that the claims are not true. Given the concerns about usury, it is likely that notaries wrote up loan contracts in such a way as to hide the actual amount of the loan by including the amount of interest in the stated sum.

But one does not have to read notarial evidence only for the intended facts. Notarial acts contain all kinds of sedimentary deposits, information that has drifted into the document without the notary or the clients really being aware of it. The proportion of different kinds of notarial acts relative to one another can shift dramatically over the course of decades and centuries. For example, in a Moretti-type move, a chart surveying all notarial acts extant from thirteenth- and fourteenth-century Marseille would reveal that family-related acts—dowry acts, testaments, guardianships, and so on—grew as a proportion of all acts, showing how family relations were gradually being penetrated by legal and contractual understandings. This mode of analysis is identical to the way an archeologist would interpret the remnants of African red-slip pottery in late antique strata. Or consider the cartographic grammar that embeds place-names in notarial acts related to property transfers. Over the course of the later Middle Ages, one sees a marked change in the spatial vocabulary used by Marseille's notaries. But there is nothing here that is authored in the way imagined by Ranke, Langlois, or Seignobos. Although the changing vocabulary reveals the creation of a new spatial imagination, notaries had no intention of imposing this imagination on the city and can hardly be said to have been aware of what was going on. Equally telling is the choice of spatial prepositions used in property transactions. Over time, prepositions such as *above, below,* and *beside* gradually gave way to cardinal directions and numeric devices for locating people and property. This trend, with its Enlightenment quality of reasoning whereby relative measurements gave way to universal or natural measurements, is not something that notaries would have been aware of. Like any philological fact, the information is present without anyone intending it to be there. The list of sedimentary facts could go on: ideas about time or dating; patterns in the identification and labeling of people; attitudes toward goods and possessions; and so on.

This absence of intention or even awareness means that we can trust the facts that emerge from this analysis in just the same way that we can never really trust the facts intentionally conveyed by notaries and their clients. The unintended meanings found in all documents are like sediments that have precipitated out of solution. Gather up that sediment. Add water and stir. What you have now is something resembling the original solution, what the French might call a *mentalité,* and from this we can write our histories. Notice that, whenever we read documents for their sediment, we interpret them in much the same way that a paleontologist would interpret a tooth, or a population geneticist a strand of DNA. We search not for the meanings that an author chose to leave behind but rather for the information that was accidentally or unintentionally preserved inside that little trace of the past. As this analysis suggests, documents bearing intended meanings cannot be seen as qualitatively superior to nondocumentary traces. Nor are the intended meanings superior to the word-sediment that figures in every written document. To acknowledge the importance of all forms of sedimentary traces is to collapse the distinction between intentional and unintentional preservations that history in the Rankean vein—history that sought to decode the meanings of authors—had so carefully erected.

To suggest that historians still interpret documents in the way recommended by Langlois and Seignobos is to erect an especially flimsy straw man, a mere caricature of a caricature. The point of this analysis is precisely to show that few, if any, historians today would insist that history depends on this documentary epistemology. Yet even though we have abandoned all the beliefs that originally justified a scientific history based on the analysis of documents—the belief that history is made by great men, that history consists of analyzing documents in an effort to discover motive and intention—we sometimes cling to the idea that historical analysis must begin with documents. A deep history considers all traces that are relevant to the writing of history. Rather than Ranke's epistemological rupture, demarcating the unknowable from the knowable, we should imagine a cone of increasing evidence, swollen but not fundamentally transformed in the past five thousand years by the addition of writing.

So much for the absence of Paleolithic and Neolithic documents. Yet the resistance to an undocumented history has not been exclusively epistemological in nature. There were, and are, other ways to justify the gulf between history and prehistory. Once again, I excavate the deep past of the modern discipline of history in an effort to unpack the layers of thought that informed previous resistance to the possibility of deep history.

In early efforts at framing the narrative of Western history, the idea that a society must be aware of its own history was closely associated with the idea that history should address only the formation of nations. Fisher made this argument in 1885:

History is concerned with the successive actions and fortunes of a community; in its broadest extent, with the experiences of the human family. It is only when men are connected by the social bond, and remain so united for a greater or less period, that there is room for history. It is, therefore, with nations, in their internal progress and in their mutual relations, that history especially deals. Of mere clans, or loosely organized tribes, it can have little to say.[51]

In 1909, John Bagnell Bury elevated this to a more systematic philosophy, arguing that anthropology dealt with pre-social humans, whereas history "deals only with the development of man in societies."[52] Bury argued that the characteristic feature of society was the "differentiation of function" or division of labor, evidently assuming that primitive societies had no such division of labor. In light of the anthropology of his own day, still influenced by the idea of primitive promiscuity or by the idea that history began when status, or natural family bonds, gave way to contract and other forms of artificial connection, this assumption was not entirely unwarranted.

One need not contest this particular point with a great deal of energy, since virtually all historians now acknowledge the legitimacy of family history and other forms of social history that pay attention to groups much smaller than nations. But beyond that, recent archeological research has demonstrated the existence of late Paleolithic villages and towns with hundreds of people subsisting on a hunter-gatherer economy. In pre-contact California, these late Paleolithic villages boasted a spectrum of trades as well as complex political hierarchies.[53] This is vital. It proves that complex political organization did not arise solely from agriculture, still less from the invention of writing.

Bury and others identified the origins of history with the origins of political societies because political history, in their day, was the center of historical inquiry. Embedded in this stance, however, was another idea: that humans only become human when they cease to live as solitary individuals. The fantasy that humans used to live solitary lives, like orangutans, has an ancient lineage in the Western tradition, going back at least as far as Thomas Hobbes and Jean-Jacques Rousseau. Vico made this a key feature of his depiction of life right after the Deluge. The switch to group living was a sign of civilization because—there are shades of Guizot here—humans gave up their selfish individualism and learned to subordinate their own desires to the greater good. In so doing, they shed their biological status as animals and, for the first time, became fully human. It was civilization that made humanity, not humanity that made civilization.

This argument, that history began when biology gave way to culture, became a prominent feature of twentieth-century general histories. Consider Hermann Schneider's general history of world civilization, first published in German in 1927 and translated into English in 1931:

> There have been man-like creatures of the human breed (prehumans, ape-men) for tens of thousands of years, nay, hundreds of thousands of years, before the Ice Age. Human beings proper have existed only since the end of the Ice Age; only then did apeman develop into man on the road to civilization. . . . Herein man surpasses the brutes; no animal before him ever took that step: here is the dividing-line between brutes and men.[54]

Almost half a century later, Arnold Toynbee, in a posthumous work, suggested that victory over natural selection in the past 10,000 years has been man's true achievement.[55] In the words of J. M. Roberts, author of *The New History of the World:* "Human history began when the inheritance of genetics and behaviour which had until then provided the only way of dominating the environment was first broken through by conscious choice."[56] Or in the slightly different version by William McNeill, in the first edition of his *World History:* "When cultural evolution took over primacy from biological evolution, history in its strict and proper sense began."[57] This has been an attractive argument because it proposes a workable solution for the vexed question of where to begin. History, according to this argument, began at exactly that moment when humans ceased to be animals and started being humans. The moment, moreover, is reasonably datable, since it can be identified with the emergence of civilization and the birth of a culture that accelerates.

In the next chapter, I shall discuss the widespread belief that the accelerating or Lamarckian nature of human cultural evolution obviates any need for recourse to Darwinian explanations. But the very proposition makes sense only if other animals do not have history. I have no intention of quarreling with Nietzsche on the issue of whether cows have a sense of history, though others may want to point out that many animals have culture, transmit that culture within subpopulations, and recognize that other population groups have different cultures. But to admit that other animals have no sense of history is a quite different thing from claiming that animals cannot be held within the embrace of history. Displayed prominently at the American Museum of Natural History in New York City is a natural history of horses. It is a remarkable history, illustrating profound changes in body size as different equine species adapted to different ecological niches. We see the stutter-steps whereby the original three-toed horses lost two of their digits. By any measure, there is history in this display. The difference is that horses do not make their own history. This brings us back to the concerns dimly expressed by Labberton: history can be history only when people are conscious of having it. Natural history, obviously, does not require an awareness of history on the part of the subjects. To write a natural history of the earth is to imagine that all the events of the past four and a half billion years could have been captured by a video recorder capable of tracking events in all their minutiae. The film, alas, has now been lost. To be more exact, it is streaming away from the earth at the speed of light and would be very, very difficult to pursue, capture, and resolve. Happily, however, the passage of events remains embedded in various traces that were left on earth, and from these traces we can get a sense of what is imprinted on those photons of light. To take the stance of the video recorder is to hold that history is a narrative of things that have happened in the past.

So which is it to be? Should history follow the video-recorder style of natural history? Or is history something that has to be made by people to count as history in the strict and proper sense?

In his influential course of lectures What Is History? delivered at Cambridge University in 1961, the historian E. H. Carr took aim at the very idea that history is made by the great figures of the past. "What I will call the Bad King John theory of history—the view that what matters in history is the character and behavior of individuals—has a long pedigree. The desire to postulate individual genius as the creative force in history is characteristic of the primitive stages of historical consciousness." Several pages on: "Everyone knows today that human beings do not always, or perhaps even habitually, act from motives of which they are fully conscious or which they are willing to avow."[58] Few today would care to defend the obvious target of Carr's reproof, the idea that history is the biography of great men. But Carr was also getting at something else—namely, that the absence of full consciousness of motive means that any history written only from what the sources actually say is an exercise in self-deception. "It defies all the evidence to suggest that history can be written on the basis of 'explanations in terms of human intentions' or of accounts of their motives given by the actors themselves, of why, 'in their own estimation, they acted as they did.' "[59] It is the unintended outcomes that have great force in history. But since they are unintended, they cannot so easily be found in documents. All genuine historical evidence must be dug out of sediment.

Like other philosophers of history, Carr wrestled with the problem of presenting this conundrum. We all imagine ourselves acting with intention and motive in everyday life. How can the sum of these intentions produce trends or patterns that cannot be seen as intentional? He evoked Adam Smith and other figures who proposed laws that transcend human choice. But the point is obvious enough. Every time you brake on the interstate to avoid hitting the car in front, you do so intentionally. But in certain traffic conditions, standing waves that mimic the ripples in a stream are created as the product of the sum of individual actions. Human behaviors, likewise, conform to broad statistical patterns. Roughly 32,000 people each year commit suicide in the United States. Each and every one is the result of individual circumstances. But in some statistical sense, the global number is roughly predetermined. Next year, roughly 32,000 people will not escape the cruel demands of statistical probabilities. Carr was writing as a social historian, and social history is not to everyone's taste. Yet social history is a strict and proper style of doing history.

What has been little noted is how the macrohistorical perspective of social history dovetails with that of natural history. In both cases, the historians involved are reluctant to attribute agency to the large populations they analyze or claim direction for the history they are writing about. We write about historical populations as if they had little more awareness of history than horses.

Of all the forms of resistance to the writing of a deep history, or at least those that have precipitated in written forms, the claim that recent history follows an accelerating, Lamarckian pattern is the only one that has legs. Few historians, I think, will defend the claim that documents are the only measure of history; that a society must have a sense of history for it to be a legitimate object of the gaze of history; that history must address political societies; that 4000 B.C. marks the boundary between animal society and human society. Yet many historians are deeply committed to the idea that humans, by virtue of their capacity to transmit their experience to future generations, are in some sense the authors of the changes that happen to their societies. I cannot make this claim about horses, and I am not convinced that such a claim can be applied to the peoples of the Paleolithic in any authoritative way. As the most active source of resistance to the idea of a deep history, it deserves special treatment: hence, the chapter that follows.

Nevertheless, of all the obstacles to the writing of a deep history, the most unforgiving will undoubtedly be that of indifference. "Sure, I have no objections to the prospect of a deep history," runs the response. "At any rate, as long as *I* don't have to do any more reading." There is little one can do about over-specialization, and it would be hopeless to try to bully people into engaging seriously with the long chronology. As the two final chapters of this book will make clear, another obstacle is scientific literacy. I can, and will, offer my own description of that fascinating place where history intersects with biology and neurophysiology, but this is a mere palliative, a set of signposts, and cannot replace a long and sustained engagement with the relevant literature. For this to succeed, historians will have to become more scientifically literate, and biologists and physiologists, many of whom have ceased to be historically minded, will have to learn to think again with history. This chapter alone cannot overcome the many forms of inertia or indifference. What it can do, I hope, is generate discussion about whether any of the epistemological arguments against deep history bear the weight of scrutiny.

THREE

Between Darwin
and Lamarck

The Whiggish histories discussed in the first chapter were, with few exceptions, providential and triumphal accounts of man's elevation from some primitive condition.[1] Their authors commonly gave ultimate credit to God or divinity but were also prone to give praise and blame to leaders and innovators. In either case, historians believed that the course of human progress was directed by a thinking mind, a style of reasoning that Daniel Dennett has characterized as "John Locke's Mind-first model."[2] A particularly vivid expression of this belief can be found in George Fisher's *Outlines:* "There are laws of historical progress which have their root in the characteristics of human nature. Ends are wrought out, which bear on them evident marks of design. History, as a whole, is the carrying out of a plan: '... through the ages one increasing purpose runs.' " Fisher goes on to quote more from St. Augustine: "God can never be believed to have left the kingdoms of men, their dominations and servitudes, outside of the laws of his providence." And finally, Fisher arrives at the nub of the issue:

The progress of society has been inseparably connected with the agency of eminent persons. Signal changes, whether wholesome or mischievous, are linked to the names of individuals who have specially contributed to bring them to pass. The achievements of heroes stand out in as bold relief in authentic history as in the obscure era of myth and fable. Fruitful inventions, after the earlier steps in civilization are taken, are traceable to particular authors, exalted by their genius above the common level. So it is with the literary works which have exerted the deepest and most lasting influence. Nations have their pilots in war and in peace. Epochs in the progress of the fine arts are ushered in by individuals of surpassing mental power.[3]

Implicit here is the belief that these eminent persons were inspired, in some fashion, by God. This is how God's providence was enacted.

Fisher's stance is interesting not because the man himself was a leading theoretician in nineteenth-century historiography. It is interesting because Fisher, both as an author of a textbook and as a president of the American Historical Association, was typical of those who shaped the early decades of a history curriculum that in turn has shaped generations of historians and students in North America. For late-nineteenth-century historians steeped in this mode of thinking, one of the difficulties posed by prehistory lay in the fact that it was impossible, in the absence of documents, to locate those special individuals whose agency was responsible for historical progress. As discussed in the previous chapter, this was one of the many points of resistance to the possibility of a history that incorporated the Stone Age. But even if historians, in later decades, gradually shed the idea that history is little more than the biography of great men, the discipline of history has not entirely shaken off the theory of directed evolution: the idea that someone's brain, whether divine or human, has shaped the pathways of history. It is true that the idea of directed evolution has been almost entirely evicted from the works of professional history that circulate in history's inner sanctum: in seminar rooms and conference halls, among faculty and graduate students. But in textbooks and other works intended for students or for a more general audience, the idea is still present, often surfacing in the form of a telling metaphor or image.

Consider, for example, the works of history that have used the metaphor of the seed. Five or six thousand years ago, we are told, the "seeds of civilization" were planted in the gardens of Mesopotamia. Since then, according to the hundreds or perhaps thousands of authors who have used the metaphor across the twentieth century, this hardy and adaptable seed has taken root and flourished in a multitude of environments. Romans carried the seed with them in their conquests. The medieval Christian church preserved it during the barren Dark Ages. European conquerors and colonial traders planted the seed in fertile colonial lands. The seed has itself evolved, forming new genera and species as it ramifies in metaphorical discourse. Thus, it has been possible for a recent author to claim that the idea of the separation of church and state in U.S. constitutional thought came from a seed that was planted during the European Middle Ages. Also planted in medieval Europe was the seed of the idea of human rights, not to mention those of intolerance, hatred, and bigotry. Try a casual keyword search in a full-text electronic library. You will see how medieval Europe, in the hands of twentieth-century historians, came to be conceived of as an especially fertile seedbed for good or for ill. What better way to justify allotting a portion of the curriculum to so abstruse a topic? Historians of other eras have made much the same claims. Use of the metaphor is especially pervasive among the popular writers who operate on the fringes of the world of professional history: those who contribute to travel guides, newspaper columns, movie scripts, encyclopedia entries, blogs, and any of the multitude of other venues where historical thinking can be found.

History, like any discipline, like any system of thought, is constrained by the metaphors at its disposal. In the general historical imagination common to professionals and hacks alike, it is not biology alone that sets the metaphorical framework. Architecture claims its share of the metaphorical edifices built up by historians. Warfare has its devotees. But even if biology is not, as I suspect, the most favored supplier of metaphor, it certainly ranks near the top. What is more, biological metaphors bear a distinguished pedigree, rooted as they are in the freshly Darwinized soil of nineteenth-century Western historical thought. Historians like Henry Adams and Herbert Baxter Adams promoted the idea of the Teutonic germ in their seminar at Johns Hopkins precisely because history had lost both Providence and a Kantian telos. They knew that history's apparent direction, the sense that institutions experience growth and change while nonetheless preserving some essential or perduring form, needed to be explained in some other way. Although the two Adamses may have pushed the image to an unworkable extreme, the underlying metaphorical complex they helped build nonetheless persisted. More than a century of fidelity to and faithful recapitulation of this metaphorical complex demands explanation. Metaphors, as George Lakoff and Mark Johnson have argued, are much more than stylistic flourishes that add color to otherwise tepid prose.[4] Metaphors do much of our thinking for us. Evoking whole fields of thought, they communicate complex ideas and images with extraordinary efficiency. So just what kind of work has the seed been doing in the historical imagination?

Seeds are magical. They carry their own metabolic energy and grow according to sets of invisible instructions contained within them. Although they may require a helping hand from time to time, they always know where they are going, for the form toward which they strive is written in the original code. The metaphor of the seed renders human cultural change as an ontogeny, the process whereby an individual is born, then passes through childhood and adolescence before coming to maturity and old age. This process is guided by the instructions contained within the seed, a kind of cultural DNA. In some cases, authors suggest that these instructions take the form of constitutions or similar documents routinely assigned in Western Civ courses: Hammurabi's Code, the Corpus iuris civilis, the Magna Carta, the Declaration of the Rights of Man.[5] Students dutifully read these fragments of historical DNA and, unless they are warned otherwise, ascribe genius to their makers. When applied to any historical trend, from the rise of civilization to the separation of church and state, the metaphor of the seed allows us a comfortable illusion of understanding change while dodging the vexing question of why the change happened.

Used in the teaching of Western Civ, the metaphor of the seed explains why the past is relevant to the present. But this justification comes with a heavy cost, for it denies that non-Western cultures have any relevance. Seedless, these cultures were doomed to a timelessness broken only when they were absorbed into the expanding cone of historicity created by Western expansion, col-

onization, and imperialism, becoming fertile ground for Western seeds. World histories break the dominance of Western Civ
by exporting the model to other countries. These histories discover non-Western counterparts to Europe's experience that also
led to political centralization, trading networks, systems of
thought and education, and moral values. World historians thus
break the history up into a multitude of gardens but replicate the
conundrum in the process. The problem lies in the fact that, although our ideas of historical causality may have eschewed God
and the genius of great men as the driving force behind civilization, our narratives, insofar as they gesture at the seed, have not
escaped a subtle principle of planned growth.

Biology is a natural source for historical metaphor. Confus-
ingly for historians, biology offers two processes that describe
growth: ontogeny and phylogeny. Only in the case of ontogeny is
the shape of the organism determined in part by a blueprint.
With phylogeny, there is no blueprint. If lineages appear to head
in certain directions, it is only because organisms are doomed to
pursue the Sisyphean goal of optimal design in a changing environment and are limited in their options by their own evolutionary history. Yet it is easy to get the two processes muddled, because phylogeny carries so powerful an appearance of intentional
design. Imagine how the evolution of any biological adaptation—say, the panda's thumb—would appear if captured by
time-lapse photography. Transported backward many thousands of years, the camera takes a shot of the radial sesamoid on
the wrist of a proto-panda. The shot is repeated every millennium, using the wrist of one of the panda's descendants, until we
reach the present day. Viewed in sequence, these frames would
reveal a bump growing ever more thumblike, to the point where

giant pandas now use their opposable sesamoid "thumbs" to manipulate bamboo. Seen on film, the panda's thumb—like civilization, like the idea of democracy or human rights—would
look for all the world like something that grew from seed and
knew where it was headed. Yet we know that this is an illusion,
perhaps inspired by our own predisposition to view any complex
structure as if it were the product of someone's or something's intention. What is more, had the selection pressures promoting the
evolution of the thumb in panda phylogeny come to a sudden
end, the growth of the radial sesamoid would have stopped with
equal abruptness. These kinds of stutter-stops are common
enough in the paleontological record, and equally common in the
human cultural record, though the lesson is often forgotten. The
illusion of teleology is generated because ongoing selection pressures, coupled with biochemical and morphological constraints,
squeeze adaptations down relatively narrow and often converg-
ing pathways. It is a powerful illusion. Applied to history, the illusion has tripped up more than one observer.[6]

It is here, in the potential confusion between ontogeny and
phylogeny, that a deep history has to take a stand in favor of phylogeny. An ontogeny necessarily begins at a point of conception
or germination: in the narrative of sacred history, the Garden of
Eden. In contrast, the deep history of humanity has no particular beginning and is certainly driving toward no particular end.
To the extent that we think we can discern any direction to
human culture, that process can be guided only loosely by human
design or intent. Among historians, this observation is not controversial, suggesting a terrain on which historians and biologists
can meet. Some evolutionary theorists, in fact, are eager to think
with history, and historians may well find much that is useful in

recent evolutionary theory and figure out ways to contribute to its ongoing elaboration. The models that have emerged in the past two decades have relevance for any field of Postlithic history. Yet as this chapter will suggest, they are even more essential for a deep history, which necessarily denies the existence of any rupture separating a slow, biological, Darwin-driven Paleolithic era from an accelerating, cultural, Lamarck-driven Postlithic era.

@

In the eighteenth century, the French naturalist Jean-Baptiste Lamarck (1744–1829) promulgated a theory of evolution that included the possibility of the inheritance of acquired characteristics. Later, in the nineteenth century, this relatively minor principle in Lamarck's overall model was elevated to a central dogma of neo-Lamarckian evolution, which proposed that all organisms inherit characteristics acquired by their parents. The hackneyed example is the ancestor of all giraffes, who, by stretching for leaves, acquired and then passed on a slightly longer neck to all subsequent giraffes. If giraffes really did stretch their necks, of course, they did it without any particular intention apart from a desire to reach tasty leaves. But humans do things for a reason, and social scientists found it tempting to incorporate intentions or goals into Lamarckian theories of culture. For contemporaries, the problem with Darwinian evolution was that it had some difficulty explaining the obvious chasm between the higher and the lower animals as well as the rapid rates of change that seemed characteristic of human evolution. Such was the prestige of biology in late-nineteenth-century social thought that neo-Lamarckian evolution, with its associated tag, the "inheritance of acquired characteristics," was readily brought into history and the social sciences. Neo-Lamarckism, as adopted by such figures as Lester Ward, an important figure in the early years of American sociology, allowed for the conscious and hence more rapid betterment of human races as the result of human actions. Ward believed in a form of Lamarckism wherein organisms were responsible for willing their own biological destinies.[7] In an age when societies were viewed as organisms, the idea was easily applied to the rise of civilization and labile enough to influence imperialists and social workers alike.

By the turn of the century, neo-Lamarckism was on the wane in biology. Carl Degler has argued, very plausibly, that the decline of Lamarckism led to the rise of the eugenics movement: if you cannot improve the less fit through Lamarckian social services, then you had better prevent them from breeding, lest their progeny swamp the world.[8] Yet in the 1920s and 1930s an approach to culture suggesting that favorable characteristics can be transmitted through learned habits and customs surfaced in the form of cultural anthropology and behaviorism.[9] A leading figure was A. L. Kroeber, who, in rejecting social Darwinism, spoke of "another evolution . . . in which use modification [Lamarckism] *is* permanent and transmittal of the acquired exists. . . . This non-organic process of evolution is that of civilization, of human accomplishment."[10] Lamarckism also influenced a number of important social scientists of the era, including the economists Friedrich Hayek and Herbert Simon.[11] Historians, perhaps less inclined to inquire so deeply into this issue, accepted Lamarckian principles without much demur, though it is unusual to find explicit affirmations of Lamarckian evolution among historians.[12] In his What Is History? lectures, E. H. Carr observed that "it is a presupposition of history that man is capable of profiting (not that he necessarily profits) by the experience of his predecessors, and that progress in history, unlike evolution in nature, rests on the transmission of acquired assets."[13] This was a casual observation, and one that he thought needed no defense.

By voicing a parenthetical skepticism about man's capacity to profit from experience, however, Carr showed himself to be distinctly tepid about the idea that the inheritance of acquired characteristics inexorably leads to improvement in the human condition. To believe this would be to believe that history unfolds according to the agency of far-seeing individuals who know exactly which traits to build up and pass on to future generations. This was not an idea that Carr wished to have any truck with, since it was the essence of the "Bad King John" theory of history he so adamantly opposed. The argument, in fact, worked the other way around: if there *has* been progress, then that progress can be explained by virtue of the inheritance of acquired assets. A dozen, a hundred, a thousand people might produce a whole stable of good ideas, but humankind is not necessarily capable of profiting from any of them. The men who built the nation of Iraq out of the wreckage of the Ottoman Empire in the wake of World War I had the idea that a nation-state and its institutions can transcend the bloody ethnic divisions of the past. This is a fine and noble concept. Had the experiment succeeded, it would have been a perfect example of a whole nation profiting from an acquired asset. But merely having the idea is not sufficient to guarantee its success. The dozens, the hundreds, the thousands of good ideas out there all have to undergo some sort of selection process. That process is what history is all about, whether it is a history of political successes or a history of failures, a history of the technologies that transform or a history of the technologies that fall with a thud.

Carr himself was silent on the sort of selection mechanism that operated here, and this is not surprising, because by 1961 the intellectual Cold War was in full spate and the barrier between the social sciences and evolutionary theory was as high and as impenetrable as the Berlin Wall. Earlier in the century, social scientists had decided, reasonably enough, that culture follows a Lamarckian process. Yet in the wake of August Weismann's discoveries, which were interpreted as proof that the genome could not be altered by experience, they were told somewhat sniffily that Lamarck could have no place in biology and should also be excluded from a scientific sociology. Who could blame Carr and other historians if they concluded that biology had no lessons to teach them? This is quite apart from the natural revulsion toward the horrors engendered by social Darwinism, the eugenics movement, and National Socialism. So although in this passage Carr appears to have been on the verge of creating a dazzling synthesis showing how Lamarckian processes of transmission are, ultimately, subsumed within or embraced by Darwinian processes of selection, he was never able to take the final step, and he left the thoughts incomplete. Only now, in the field of cultural evolutionary studies, are they finally coming back together again.

The apparent incommensurability of Lamarckian and Darwinian processes has been used to justify the existence of a rupture in history's basic chronology. As I noted in the previous chapter, some historians have hinted that history begins when humans ceased being animals and became people. The problem with this argument is that humans were not created as a plaything of the gods, like Prometheus, formed of clay and a spark of heavenly fire. Over the course of the twentieth century, it was becoming ever more clear that humans evolved slowly from apes—in punctuated fits and starts, admittedly, but incrementally all the same. So historians found it necessary to identify a different factor. Culture alone would not do, since the existence of tools and cave paintings showed that Paleolithic humans had culture. But what they did not have was a culture that *accelerates.* Darwinian evolution, in the conventional view, always follows a modest pace behind climatic and ecological changes, which in turn typically alter at a slow or rhythmic pace—leaving aside collisions by asteroids or other natural disasters of similar immensity. What evolution does not do is go haring off by itself in directions wholly unnecessary for simple ecological adaptation. Only a logic of directed evolution can explain the accelerating nature of human culture, for if we can recognize which traits are superior, we should be able to anticipate the outcome of the slower process of natural selection and get the jump on biology. As one historian has remarked, in a passage worth contemplating a second time: "Human history began when the inheritance of genetics and behaviour which had until then provided the only way of dominating the environment was first broken through by conscious choice."[14] In a move that would have disconcerted Carr, the inheritance of acquired characteristics, in this model, has been subtly blended with intentionality. Lamarckism, as I noted earlier, is innocent of intentionalism. Giraffes do not consciously intend to grow longer necks as they stretch for leaves. They are just hungry. But intention is too tempting an explanation for the accelerating nature of recent cultural evolution, not least because it gives pride of place to the brain and the human faculty for reasoning.

The idea that recent cultural acceleration was associated with historical rupture has been seconded by at least one evolutionist:

> Cultural evolution has progressed at rates that Darwinian processes cannot begin to approach. Darwinian evolution continues in *Homo sapiens,* but at rates so slow that it no longer has much impact on our history. This crux in the earth's history has been reached because Lamarckian processes have finally been unleashed upon it. Human cultural evolution, in strong opposition to our biological history, is Lamarckian in character. What we learn in one generation, we transmit directly by teaching and writing. Acquired characters are inherited in technology and culture. Lamarckian evolution is rapid and accumulative. It explains the cardinal difference between our past, purely biological mode of change, and our current, maddening acceleration toward something new and liberating—or toward the abyss.[15]

It was in eloquent passages like this that Stephen Jay Gould made his stand on the limits of biological reasoning. He did not attempt to date this transition, but a telling clue indicates the line of his thought, and that is his reference to writing. Cuneiform tablet in hand, we stand with Gould on the banks of the Tigris and Euphrates in the fourth millennium B.C., contemplating the rupture that demarcates the time of biology from the time of history.[16]

@

The suggestion that humanity is distinct by virtue of possessing a culture subject to Lamarckian evolution is more problematic than it may appear. The glitch lies in the fact that humans are no longer considered to be the only species to possess culture. The idea that other animals have culture has been circulating for nearly three decades and has reached a point of media saturation that partially obscures the challenge created by the fact of animal culture. Although early studies focused on the apes and monkeys who make tools and wash sweet potatoes, culture does not end with primates. Birds' songs and migration routes are learned and transmitted culturally rather than genetically.[17] Some groups of dolphins manipulate sponges to protect their noses while foraging and teach the practice to offspring.[18] The crows of New Caledonia clip twigs to create hooked tools that are used to retrieve insects from crevices.[19] As with chimpanzees, the types of tools used by crows vary from one group to the next, suggesting that the very use of tools is transmitted through culture.

Although the cultural transmission of these practices has a Lamarckian quality, because the transmission involves social learning rather than genes, no one, to my knowledge, has argued that the traits in question are the product of intentional design. They evolved, surely, through a process of blind variation and selective retention. Pursuing their shy and retiring meals, ancestral crows presumably fabricated tools of extraction, each of which was subtly different. Some of the shapes proved more functional than others in extracting particular bugs from particular crevices. As a working hypothesis, let us suppose that the corvine lineages that fashioned those tools slightly out-reproduced other lineages; in this way, the design gradually fixed itself as a cultural trait wherever those particular bugs and those particular crevices predominated. Patterns like this show how Lamarck will always be dogged by Darwin, for it matters not one whit how traits are acquired and transmitted if natural selection continues to sift out the adaptive traits and finds a way to reward the lineages that transmit them. This is what Carr was reaching toward in 1961, with a model of historical change that banished intention while acknowledging a place for Lamarckian acquisition.

If we admit that cultural traits among animals can be selected according to a principle of blind variation and selective retention, it stands to reason that we can find this pattern in early human cultures as well. In the area of tools and technology, the plenitude of human experimentation supplies the variation on which natural selection can act. Consider the Folsom people of North America some 13,000 years ago. It is possible that Folsom hunters understood exactly what they were doing when they first invented spear points (smaller and thinner than the previous generation of Clovis points), whose concave design opened large wounds in bison and caused the animals to bleed to death. Yet it is just as likely that Folsom spear points evolved through an adaptive process identical to natural selection. A Folsom hunter skillfully shapes a number of points, all of which vary slightly one from the other. No copy, after all, can ever be exact, and artisans naturally tinker with designs. Used on bison, a fairly new food source, several prototypes open especially large, blood-letting wounds and are therefore slightly more likely to serve as models for the next generation of points. I can even think of a just-so story that would explain how this could have happened without Folsom hunters being fully aware of the superior blood-letting ability of certain points. Folsom hunters, wielding these points, probably did not kill their prey on the spot. Instead, the animal bled to death as it fled. The hunters just followed the trail. If a point stuck in the animal but did not cause it to bleed to death rapidly enough, the point would not be recovered: the animal would escape to die elsewhere, taking the spear point with it. Well-designed points that lodged themselves in the animal and subsequently killed it, or those that fell out along the way, were recovered and were available to serve as prototypes for the next generation. The incremental (albeit rapid) evolution of Folsom point technology suggests a process driven by random variation and selection more than explicit design.

Perhaps a skeptic could admit Darwinian processes in early human cultural evolution while still adhering to Gould's idea that Lamarckian cultural evolution has now supplanted Darwinian cultural evolution. The difference, the claim would go, lies in rapidity. The point at which Lamarck replaced Darwin is that point of rupture where human culture began its maddening acceleration. Later in this chapter I shall address the question of whether evolution by natural selection is necessarily slow. Here, another issue presents itself. Since we have to admit an important role for Lamarckian processes in Postlithic societies—it would be difficult for a watch to evolve without some express selection of attributes by watchmakers—does that necessarily mean that all Darwinian processes have been excluded? In other words, can we leave blind variation and selective retention completely out of the picture once we turn from Paleolithic societies to Neolithic and Postlithic societies?

In 1959, around the same time that Carr began to write the lectures he would soon deliver at Cambridge University, the University of Michigan anthropologist Leslie White decided it was time to rehabilitate nineteenth-century theories of cultural evolution that had been out in the cold for so long. In *The Evolution of Culture,* White wrote explicitly of his desire to cast off the antievolutionist perspective he had learned as a graduate student.[20] This, as it turned out, was one of the first of a trickle, then a stream, then a veritable flood of cultural evolutionary studies.

In the recent literature, the model is now taken for granted, a sort of "well, of course culture undergoes selection" frame of mind, and debate has come to center on the precise mechanisms of cultural evolution.[21] Some authors are more adaptationist than others, focusing on cultural traits that have been selected because they allegedly contribute to biological fitness. The ancient Central American custom of treating maize with lime, a practice that releases niacin and an essential amino acid and thereby staves off pellagra, is the sort of thoroughly adaptive cultural trait that gets cited in the literature on cultural ecology. It is not always easy— infanticide does not, at first blush, appear to increase fitness— and no one, to my knowledge, has been rash enough to argue that all cultural traits are necessarily adaptive. Drug abuse, for example, is a widespread cultural practice that defies any and all adaptive arguments. Here, the concept of memes or culturgens that inhabit the minds of their hosts and evolve purely for their own interests, like junk DNA, have been offered. In a similar move, Robert Boyd and Peter J. Richerson have pointed out how human credulity—a necessary component to any system of transmission through learning—necessarily leads to the accumulation of maladaptive ideas.[22] Adaptation, maladaptation, or selfish meme: whatever the description, there is a large community of biologists, archeologists, cultural and physical anthropologists, economists—the boundaries between the disciplines fade significantly when the authors operate within the embrace of evolutionary theory—whose work has been stimulated by the idea that human behavioral traits, transmitted through culture, have evolved through a process of blind variation and selective retention.

It is important not to overlook all those occasions where one finds evidence for some kind of planning and design. Yet, as Luigi Luca Cavalli-Sforza and M. W. Feldman remarked, "many innovations, however purposeful and intelligent they may seem to their proponents and first adopters, may not turn out to be highly adaptive, at least on a long-term basis."[23] Or in the lapidary phrasing suggested to me by David Sloan Wilson: "Even intentions become a form of blind variation when they interact with other intentions and produce unforeseen consequences."[24] This is why, as later events were to show, the League of Nations ultimately proved incapable of creating a workable Iraq. The law of unintended consequences necessarily obscures the foresight of visionaries. Alternatively, with enough visionaries and sufficient variation among their visions, we can always be sure that someone's prediction is going to prove accurate.

Family history provides an example of how certain patterns studied by historians can be understood within the embrace of a theory of undirected evolution. Family historians have long noted that family forms and inheritance patterns in agricultural societies often seem to be adapted to particular land-use systems.[25] Stem families and the practice of primogeniture, for example, are characteristic of regions of arable farming in medieval and early modern Europe. Partible inheritance, in turn, is typical of mixed-used land. No one suggests that family forms are genetically wired. Instead, patterns of inheritance and domestic arrangements, over the thousands of years during which Europeans have practiced agriculture, have converged on solutions that appear to have been tuned to specific environmental conditions. At some point these patterns may become fixed in custom

or law and thus acquire the appearance of conscious or deliberate cultural transmission. A biological analog could be the Bald-
win effect, the process whereby adaptive cultural traits in animal
populations may, over time, fix themselves in genes.

This fixing of traits in custom is somewhat problematic for
overly simplistic Darwinian theories of cultural evolution, since
fixed customs can act as a brake on natural processes of cultural
evolution. Recent studies of ecological catastrophes—on Easter
Island, in Moche, Peru, in Greenland—have suggested how
human cultural traits can have spectacularly unadaptive consequences.[26] Similarly, when people move they sometimes carry
with them a culture that shows little sign of wanting to adapt itself to the new environment. Richerson and Boyd call this "cultural inertia" and emphasize it as part of their ongoing efforts to
persuade biologists and evolutionary psychologists that culture
actually does matter. They cite a number of analyses showing
how people living in the same environment can have very different cultural and institutional histories, suggesting how culture
can provide multiple solutions to environmental pressures.[27] Culture, in other words, is not so finely tuned to a specific environment as rigid adaptationist models would hope to find.

The autonomy of culture has suggested itself to other observers. Lying near the heart of William Durham's imposing synthesis, *Coevolution* (1991), is a powerful model of evolution developed by Clifford Geertz in two articles first published in the
1960s and later reprinted in his influential *The Interpretation of
Cultures* (1973). Geertz's goal was to find ways in which the
strange and the particular, the subject of ethnographic research,
could be made to reveal what he called "enduring natural

processes." To finesse this apparent paradox, he proposed two ideas:

> The first of these is that culture is best seen not as complexes of concrete behavior patterns—customs, usages, traditions, habit clusters—as has, by and large, been the case up to now, but as a set of control mechanisms—plans, recipes, rules, instructions (what computer engineers call "programs")—for the governing of behavior. The second idea is that man is precisely the animal most desperately dependent upon such extragenetic, outside-the-skin control mechanisms, such cultural programs, for ordering his behavior.[28]

In a metaphor that surfaces several times in Geertz's writing, these control mechanisms are like genes, and they do for humans what genes do for lower animals.[29] Phylogenetically, they actually replaced genes as the determinants of human behavior. Control mechanisms, according to Geertz's model, did not just appear once humans were biologically complete. Instead, they evolved in synchrony with human biological evolution. Even more than that, they formed part of the environment of adaptation of the Pliocene and Pleistocene epochs. At first, the influence was small: australopithecine culture consisted of little more than tool use, protolanguage, and hunting, all of which were processed by the relatively small australopithecine brain. But as human culture grew more complex, it came to serve an ever more prominent role in the hierarchy of environmental influences on human phylogeny. Culture was the crucial force in determining the expansion of the forebrain, and selective advantage was conferred on those most able to take advantage of culture. For Geertz, the key feature here is that there is no single culture. Man is suspended in webs of significance he himself has spun, and culture is those webs. But any culture will do. Dobuan, Javanese, Hopi, Italian: they all provide the control mechanisms on which humans are now cognitively dependent, having cast off genetic controls on behavior. And because any culture will do, the cultures themselves need not have anything in common, thus obviating, in Geertz's view, the need to search for human universals. Here we have an explanation for the conundrum posed by Richerson and Boyd: how can different cultural systems flourish in the same environment?

The idea that culture supplanted genes as a control mechanism is fully in sympathy with Gould's argument that biology gave way to culture with the advent of civilization. Geertz, however, places this transition in the very deep past. It is not by accident that I chose to cite his reference to the Pliocene and Pleistocene eras of the geological timescale. In this context, it is worth noting that the Pleistocene, the Ice Age, was an era of rapid climatic shifts, with at least twenty major oscillations in temperature—an era, in other words, in which it is easy to imagine how selection pressures might have favored flexible cultural solutions, though figuring out how to test the hypothesis is another matter entirely. The key thing to bear in mind is that culture as a whole is adaptive, an observation that frees us from the necessity of arguing for the adaptive nature of specific cultural traits. If Elliot Sober and David Sloan Wilson are right, it is the possession of culture that allows group selectionism in human societies, since culture enables a vital biological asset: altruism.[30] Their mathematical models show that population groups of any species that practice altruism will outcompete groups that do not. The problem with altruistic groups, however, is that they are susceptible to freeloaders. Culture in human societies overcomes the biological problem of the freeloading individual who would otherwise corrode the practice of altruism. The model proposed by Sober and Wilson is tantalizingly susceptible to a Geertzian perspective, since the particular forms adopted by any given culture are irrelevant as long as the culture, seen as a set of control mechanisms, manages to enable altruistic behavior.

@

Some biologists have developed their own ideas about how to apply Darwinian thinking to human cultural evolution, and one of the most prominent of these, first proposed by Richard Dawkins, centers on the meme.[31] A meme is simply an idea that propagates itself in human minds, a cultural trait that "may have evolved in the way it has simply because it is *advantageous to itself*."[32] Since this is a difficult concept, introductions to "memetics" often begin by offering a list of all things that can be deemed a meme. The list provided by Dennett is as good as any: "arch, wheel, wearing clothes, vendetta, right triangle, alphabet, calendar, the *Odyssey,* calculus, chess, perspective drawing, evolution by natural selection, impressionism, 'Greensleeves,' deconstructionism."[33] The list goes on and ends up embracing virtually every idea, practice, or melody that anyone has ever thought or whistled. Suicide, for example, can be a meme. So can celibacy. As the analysis develops, however, we really only hear about memes-as-ideas. The memes-as-things, such as arches and wheels, more or less disappear from the radar screen or else get turned into blueprints or recipes. Ideas "possess" people's brains in a way that wheels do not and therefore, apparently, are more appealing: you can speak of a meme as a body-snatcher, replicating itself with little regard for the adaptive fitness of the brain it is currently occupying. The not-necessarily-adaptive quality of memes, a central element of memetic theory, shows that memes are quite unlike the adaptive cultural traits discussed by Durham.

The use of the idea of the meme, at least in Dawkins's hands, has been partly rhetorical: it has forced readers to confront their most cherished ideas regarding human culture and, in so doing, opened them up to the idea that genes replicate for themselves and not, on some philosophical level, for the good of the body they happen to inhabit. Another claim made for the meme is that it could help explain why we do things that we do not like doing and that are not even in our best interests. Supporters of memetics are rarely able to resist mention of the catchy tune you just cannot shake from your head—their dependence on this catchy image is itself a perfect illustration of the point they are trying to get across—and like to think that the idea can also explain any number of more seriously maladaptive practices. In this regard, they share common ground with evolutionary psychologists.

The idea of a meme, an apparently human contrivance that has a life and lineage of its own, is an interesting one. One concern, as suggested above, lies in the fact that memetic theory actually makes it hard to see human cultural traits as biologically adaptive. In a thoroughly counterintuitive way, the more that memeticists emphasize the body-snatching meme, the more they remove history and the social sciences from the purview of Darwinian theory. How can we explain the cultural practice of celibacy? Well, it is just a meme that is replicating itself. There is no need to test whether it might be adaptive. It is just there, like a piece of junk DNA, and cannot be explained.

A second concern arises from the fact that memes do not have to control the body they inhabit. You can think of celibacy without being celibate, in much the same way that you can have an unexpressed gene for blue eyes. As Dennett puts it, the meme of celibacy can be present in the brain without being "in the driver's seat."[34] The meme for celibacy, by this account, does not even care whether it is expressed or not. More to the point, the meme is "expressed," following Dennett, not when I behave celibately but when I just happen to mention the idea to someone else. Is this idea useful when it comes to explaining celibacy as a social fact? If memes don't have to do anything to qualify as memes, they have retreated to so ethereal an ontological status that we really do not need to take them seriously.

Nevertheless, there is something useful about the idea that certain ideas—call them memes if you will—can "possess" the brain. In *The Extended Phenotype*, Dawkins has developed some compelling ideas regarding the ability of organisms to manipulate the body states of other organisms.[35] Certain species of parasites that hijack the neural pathways of their hosts provide the classic examples in biology, but the principle extends to other kinds of interactions, such as birdsong. What Dawkins is arguing with memes is that ideas, too, can affect neural pathways. This stands to reason, and I think most historians would admit the possibility—perhaps even insist on it. Suitably transposed, Dawkins's insight forms the basis of my arguments, discussed in the last chapter, regarding the mood-altering consequences of human cultural traits. Here, my chief concern with the idea of memes is that we not lose sight of the possibility of agency or function. If the idea of celibacy circulated in medieval Europe, as it did, then it served someone's interests—in this case, the interests of military aristocrats with too many sons and daughters and not enough estates and dowries. The church, likewise, did not want to see its patrimony spiral away into the hands of the legitimate children of clerics, and it insisted on celibacy so as to disinherit the many illegitimate children of the clergy. In this case, it is not particularly helpful to argue that celibacy arose simply because the idea was advantageous to itself.

@

In a paragraph quoted earlier, Gould suggested that the very rapidity of human cultural evolution reveals Lamarckian processes at work. It is an idea to which some historians are deeply committed. As one author of a textbook used for teaching Western Civ courses remarked: "One is struck by the fact that the *rate* of change has been increasing sharply. . . . During the last 1% or so of the human experience, the rate has increased with a speed that, by comparison with previous times, can only be described as fantastic."[36] The minuscule rate of change so commonly ascribed to Paleolithic humanity was the rate deemed typical of biological organisms experiencing slow, aimless Darwinian evolution, what one author has called "the genetic slow march."[37] Consider the image presented in the fifth edition of *A History of Civilization: Prehistory to 1715* (1976): "During those long, long centuries the advance of the human animal was enormously slow."[38] A line or two later, we learn that the era was dominated by technological stasis: "It was by stone weapons and tools that early man lived for hundreds of thousands of years." So nothing, in fact, did change. As I noted in an earlier chapter, Western Civ textbooks published before 1970 often include no more than a few pages on the Paleolithic. These pages do not narrate a story of change. They offer, instead, a verbal diorama, like the display of a primitive tribe found in the American Museum of Natural History, describing an unchanging, historyless socioeconomic order—the hunter-gatherer lifestyle, based on primitive stone tools and dominated by the relentless struggle for survival.[39] It was difficult to avoid viewing the era with an unjaundiced eye. As late as 1979, a textbook described the state of Paleolithic humans in this way: "Since their lives were often 'solitary, poor, nasty, brutish, and short,' their responses to troubles and dangers were filled with fear."[40]

Yet the reasoning deployed here is not entirely sound. Gould made the simple though understandable mistake of measuring the speed of evolution on a human scale. Darwinian evolution is not, in and of itself, naturally slow. It follows a rhythm dictated by the rapidity of generational turnover and thus modulates its pace according to the reproductive cycle of the evolving entity. Compared to humans and other mammals, bacteria and fruit flies reproduce very rapidly. Facing significant adaptive pressures created in artificial laboratory conditions, both sets of organisms can undergo profound genetic modification over the course of several thousand generations, which amounts to just a few months or years. Human cultural innovations, the evolving "entities" I am concerned with here, are generated by slowly reproducing humans and not by fruit flies. But cultural innovations do not have to follow the human reproductive cycle of twenty to thirty years between generations. Consider, again, the phylogeny of the Folsom spear point. A new generation of Folsom points did not come into existence every twenty or thirty years. It happened every time a hunter knapped a new stone, on the order of weeks or months. Nearly 13,000 years ago, selection pressures on the tools being used by Folsom hunters were becoming intense, given the extinction of all species of slow-moving megafauna and the need to exploit fleet bison as a major food source. In these conditions, the rapid generational turnover of Folsom points allowed their blood-letting ability to evolve at a rate much faster than human evolution would have allowed.

The same observation operates in other realms not involving material objects. In the realm of language, for example, a phenotype of the word *father* is created every time someone uses the word, a rapidity of generational turnover that makes it easy to understand how, in the space of a few millennia, the Indo-European root word *pəter* evolved into *pater, vater, father, père*, and so on. Gould himself provided one of the classic examples of Darwinian evolution in a cultural, nongenetic setting. Over the decades, Disney artists created new phenotypes of Mickey Mouse, doing their best to stay as true as possible to the original type. The generational turnover was rapid, given the frequent production of comic books, cartoons, and movies. Yet with each new generation of Mickeys, the artists unconsciously introduced minuscule variations in Mickey's braincase, ears, eyes, and nose. Those phenotypes with slightly neotenic or childlike features proved more appealing to artists, readers, and audiences, and the trait spread accordingly, transforming Mickey in a matter of decades from a sly trickster to a wide-eyed innocent.[41] Human cultural evolution exceeds the pace of human biological evolution not necessarily because it follows a Lamarckian process but because the generational turnover of cultural traits is so much more rapid.

So why do we always get a sense of "acceleration" while contemplating certain human cultural achievements? Perhaps it was impossible to "accelerate" what someone, in 1920, might have thought of as Mesopotamia's natural evolution toward a nation-state. But as Carr understood, when a good idea *has* worked, then most of us feel it necessary to acknowledge that some trait has been not only intentionally created but also deliberately transmitted. We want to acknowledge Lamarck. Does this just mean that Darwinism and Lamarckism operate side by side, in autonomous realms? That some patterns require explanations in terms of guided inheritance, whereas others need to be acknowledged as the product of blind variation and selective retention? This seems reasonable enough. Even so, it may ultimately be more rewarding to develop a unified theory of cultural evolution, one that does not even bother to segregate the realm of Darwin from the realm of Lamarck. This is exactly what Boyd and Richerson have recently put forward. The complex elegance of their model defies a simple summary. At its heart, though, lies the simple point that we need to acknowledge a fundamental difference between processes that operate at different levels, what historians might call the microhistorical and the macrohistorical. At the level of the individual, decisions are susceptible to guided variation and biased transmission, allowing human cultural traits to build on each other. Boyd and Richerson insist on this point, for this is exactly what separates human culture from the culture of other animals. Complex cultural patterns or technologies, however, are not created instantaneously. Instead, stepwise improvements—*adaptive nudges* is the term they offer—gradually build more complex adaptive entities:

> Even if most individuals blindly imitate with only the occasional application of some simple heuristic, many individuals will be giving traditions a nudge in an adaptive direction, on average. Cultural transmission preserves the many small nudges, and exposes the modified traditions to another round of nudging. Very rapidly by the standards of ordinary evolutionary time, and more rapidly than evolution by natural selection alone, weak decision-making forces generate new adaptations.[42]

Does this acknowledgment of rapidity lead Boyd and Richerson to embrace the idea of a recent historical rupture? Not at all, for the model is grounded in the observation that the ability to have culture is itself an adaptation and, historically, was the product of the rapid climatic fluctuations of the Pleistocene, oscillations that placed a premium on cultural flexibility.[43] As far as deep history is concerned, in other words, the model offers a tight, logical way to embrace the Paleolithic and the Postlithic in a continuous historical narrative. We can also admit to the folk wisdom that suggests that things have accelerated since the Neolithic revolutions. As Cavalli-Sforza and Feldman have pointed out, the growing density of Neolithic populations enhanced occasions for the horizontal transmission of cultural traits—from cousin to cousin, friend to friend, colleague to colleague.[44] Durham, in turn, notes that Postlithic human societies faced enormous new challenges to fitness: the emergence of new diseases was but one of many selection pressures particular to the new ecology that humanity created for itself. In the case of malaria and other new diseases, the selection pressures were so intense that certain populations underwent a genetic response. But cultural traits, he argues, can also help mitigate the effects of emergent diseases. The apparent rapidity of recent human cultural evolution is a consequence of the enormity of the selection pressures that human cultures have faced and are facing. Previous human cultures did not evince a similarly accelerating pattern merely because the selection pressures were not so intense.

These are strict adaptationist arguments. As befits someone who follows elements of a Geertzian model, however, Durham is open to the idea that some cultural traits do not necessarily improve human fitness. "Some traits of culture," he argues, "in some fashion, by their effects, reinforce their own persistence and spread; others do not and eventually disappear for that reason."[45] It would be wrong, in other words, to assume that all cultural traits must contribute to Darwinian fitness, because sometimes the fitness to which they contribute is, oddly, their own. Thinking this way means that we sometimes have to consider evolution from the point of view of the thing evolving. Is an adaptation a thing that rides on humanity, like our upright posture or cognitive brain? Or is an adaptation its own organism, complete with its own traits and attributes, operating in an ecosystem consisting of the human brain and human behavior? In the case of the Neolithic revolution, did humans domesticate horses and wheat? Or was it the other way around?[46] The idea that we must sometimes take the perspective of things is strikingly congruent with Arjun Appadurai's observation that we need to acknowledge that things have their own social lives.[47] To draw parallels between current trends in evolutionary theory, on the one hand, and the new history of goods, on the other, is to gesture at potential points of attachment between Darwinian models and current historical fashions. It is to suggest how historians often work with models that are compatible with Darwinism, explicitly discounting the goals and intentions of rational actors in the process.

@

Although philosophers of history like Carr stigmatized the idea that intentions matter in history, it is often the case that they creep in through the back door of the historical narrative. This is what the metaphor of the seed has allowed us to do in our histories of Western Civilization. It is not always easy to find intentionalist perspectives in historical arguments, and it is uncharitable to suggest that they are forever lurking somewhere in the background. Yet they occasionally rise to the surface and offer themselves as legitimate targets for Darwinian arguments. By way of example, consider the rich vein of sociological and anthropological literature, influenced by Benedict Anderson's *Imagined Communities,* that has emerged in recent years.[48] The branches of this literature that interest me most have focused on the ways in which the discourses developed by record-keeping bureaucracies serve to frame people and things. State bureaucracies necessarily classify the subjects of their gaze, and this intellectual project of classification can have social consequences. Anderson himself observed this process in his analysis of how the keepers of the Indonesian census, merely by deciding that citizens must have ethnic labels, created ethnic identities where none had existed in quite so clear a fashion before.[49] In such acts of classification, record-keepers engage in what the sociologist James C. Scott has called a "state project of legibility and simplification."[50] Classification, of course, can be mere convenience.

When populations exceed the memory capacity of bureaucratic agents, it makes sense to develop impersonal identity categories that can be used to define any person or thing. But classification can also be seen as an instrument of the state.[51] As Bernard S. Cohn and Nicholas B. Dirks observed, "The legitimizing of the nation state proceeds ... by constant reiteration of its power through what have become accepted as natural (rational and normal) state functions, of certifying, counting, reporting, registering, classifying, and identifying.[52] Scott phrases the role of state interest in classification in these terms:

> How did the state gradually get a handle on its subjects and their environment? ... [P]rocesses as disparate as the creation of permanent last names, the standardization of weights and measures, the establishment of cadastral surveys and population registers, the invention of freehold tenure, the standardization of legal discourse, the design of cities, and the organization of transportation [seem] comprehensible as attempts at legibility and simplification. In each case, officials took exceptionally complex, illegible, and local social practices, such as land tenure customs or naming customs, and created a standard grid whereby it could be centrally recorded and monitored.[53]

It is a captivating model. Absorbing its lessons, you will never again fill out a bureaucratic form without being aware of the act of power that is involved when you are forced to define yourself according to someone else's identity categories. Yet when I first began to work with this model some years ago, I was troubled by the evident inconsistencies. For example, it is hard for anyone to imagine that bureaucrats themselves had any awareness of the transformative processes they were initiating. It is easy to attribute agency to the state but very difficult to locate this agency in any thinking individual.[54] Were Indonesian census-takers aware that their classificatory schemes contributed to state power? If we balk at attributing to them a Machiavellian intelligence, then how exactly did the schemes emerge? This was not the only problem. Surveying record-keeping practices from late medieval Europe, it is possible to identify trends in bureaucratic standardization that look like precursors to the trends described by Anderson and Scott. Yet this is not a period in which most sociologists would be comfortable talking about a "state." Unless we decide to find a state where one has not been thought to exist, we have to find another way to describe the evolution of bureaucratic categories.

Consider, for example, the verbal mapping of property sites in written records, the rather improbable subject of my own specialized research to which I alluded in the previous chapter.[55] By the twelfth or thirteenth century, a flourishing economy in many regions of western Europe had created a sizable market in property, consisting of urban houses and workshops as well as rural estates and lands. By the fourteenth century, property transactions were among the most common sorts of records kept by public notaries, the semiprivate legal agents responsible for recording legal contracts in Mediterranean Europe and, increasingly, in the north as well. In all late medieval archives, there are tens of thousands of surviving property transactions—a fragment of an aboriginal total that once numbered in the hundreds of thousands, if not millions. It was, in short, a rich ecosystem for the evolution of verbal cartography.

In the thirteenth century, at least in the city of Marseille, there was a great deal of variety in the grammar of space—not the toponym, but instead the way the toponym was fixed in space. In one record, for example, a house might be described as being located "under the Change"; in another, the very same house might be located on "the street of the Change"; whereas a third might speak of "the island of the Change" (where "island," *insula,* means a city block). In still other records, the notaries or their clients might eschew landmarks, streets, and city blocks altogether, speaking instead of trade-based neighborhoods such as the "Cobblery" or the "Smithery," areas of production and sociability where artisans and shopkeepers plied their crafts. In biology, we might find a similar diversity in an animal population where there was no selection pressure fostering sameness in plumage or coloration or some similar trait. Yet the diversity in the grammar of verbal cartography was impermanent. Across the ensuing centuries, one can discern a slow and fitful process whereby property sites based on streets began to crowd out all other types of addresses. By the sixteenth century—a century before the emergence of cadastral-type maps with fixed street names and two centuries before the emergence of the numeric address—around 90 percent of all addresses in Marseille were defined in terms of streets. Much the same trends hold for the personal addresses that sometimes appear in identity clauses. The trend in Marseille, incidentally, does not match trends elsewhere, for although virtually all west European addressing strategies eventually converged on the street as the most basic cartographic unit, the trajectories were different in other cities—in London or Winchester, for example, where the parish acted as the major category of spatial awareness into the sixteenth century.

Charting this process is one thing; explaining it is another.

The perverse problem is that the street, as a device in carto-graphic grammar, can be thought of as promoting the political interests of the notaries, the record-keepers of late medieval so-ciety in Mediterranean Europe. Notaries, after all, are only nec-essary where there is no trust. You did not need a notary to lend money to a family member, a friend, or a protégé. Yet the street, as an architectonic grid imposed on a city, dissolved the neigh-borhoods and solidarities that had hitherto shaped urban socia-bility. If you can persuade a client that he lives on the New Street, you are suggesting to him that he does not live in the Fruitery or the Smithery, self-sufficient neighborhoods or centers of urban sociability that might have less need for notarial services. Given this political interest, it is tempting to attribute agency to notaries. Yet it is impossible to find any sources suggesting that notaries were even dimly aware of the potential benefits of a street-based nomenclature. The homogenization of the landscape, moreover, was a gradual process, with many fits and starts. It is impossible, in short, to attribute any awareness or intention to the notaries.

So how did the grammar evolve? The answer, I argued, lies in the conversations that lay behind the act of notarizing a property transaction. When a buyer and seller decided to exchange a house, they came before a notary who asked them, pro forma, for the essential details: the names of the clients, the sale price, the name of the lord, the tax owed, and, of course, the description and location of the property. The variation in cartographic gram-mar that is still a major characteristic of fourteenth-century records shows that people had different ideas about how to de-fine the space in question. But, though buyers and sellers might have this conversation several times over their life spans, notaries engaged in these conversations dozens, if not hundreds, of times per year. Categories emerged naturally in this conversational field, and the notary, as the steward of these conversations, naturally had the greatest influence over the field's evolution.[56] The accelerating market in property in late medieval Europe ensured that the conversational field particular to urban cartography was gradually expanding. In the circumstances, it is easy to appreciate how a very slight and unacknowledged preference on the part of the notaries for a street-based grammar would gradually fix itself in the conversational field. One can posit an evolving form that promotes the political goals of the notaries without having to attribute any purpose or intention to the notaries themselves.

This model applies well to the more-or-less stateless world of late medieval Marseille. But I think it might help us understand how bureaucratic templates evolve even in societies with states. Reading the literature on bureaucratic schemes of classification, in fact, one finds that most authors refrain from building conspiracy theories. Sociologists and historians do not attribute too much in the way of Machiavellian cunning to the bureaucratic agents who devised forms. In the case of the Indonesian census, the racial categories described in the form reflected new ideas about race that were circulating in colonial societies—thus, not the wholly aimless drift we can see in the case of spatial nomenclature in late medieval Marseille. It would not be wise to eliminate Machiavelli from all our habits of political analysis. What these evolutionary models allow us to do, however, is to avoid the temptation to allow the "state" to take the narrative function hitherto assigned to God, or Providence, or the genius of great men. We do not have to accept the idea that states do all the thinking. We do not have to assume the existence of a designer when we see the appearance of design.

○

To adopt any nongenetic Darwinian perspective on human cultural evolution—coevolutionary, neo-Geertzian, memetic—is to minimize the role of genius and forethought in recent human history and abandon Locke's Mind-first model. It is to suggest, moreover, that the transmission of information through writing did not have quite the catalyzing effect imagined by an older generation of Lamarckian-style historians. Writing obviously made a difference. Yet when humans replicate cultural institutions, they do not follow a written template and they never create exact copies. The resulting variation, however slight, allows for new adaptations to emerge without anyone willfully directing the process. It is only too human to read purpose into the past, and it is comforting to imagine that things have happened for a reason. But to cling to this idea is to cling to providential history.

As Boyd and Richerson have shown and as other evolutionists have acknowledged, there is no need to abandon all recourse to guided variation and biased transmission. I think it is possible for states to become aware of the power of the categories they use. Yet, as with cases like the Internet, the intentions of the original designer, to whatever degree they are achieved, can be utterly dwarfed by the unintended things that happen as we adapt to the ecology that has emerged from someone's tinkering. Examples discussed in this chapter suggest how some of the most important cultural achievements of the Postlithic era have been shaped by blind variation and selective retention. And this becomes important for the two final chapters, where I shall set about the task of historicizing recent breakthroughs in our understanding of the brain and, in the process, suggesting just how much Postlithic cultural evolution has been shaped by human neurobiology.

FOUR

The New Neurohistory

Humans, as animals, are part of the natural world and subject to natural selection. Our genus has been around for more than two million years, and our particular species for more than a hundred thousand. Until the Neolithic revolution, natural selection acted primarily on foragers, gatherers, and hunters who lived in relatively small and widely dispersed bands on the African savanna, later throughout the world. Many of the things characteristic of our bodies and brains—upright posture, gut size, speech—emerged as adaptations for this ancestral ecology and lifestyle. Still others reflect a deeper primate or vertebrate legacy. Yet as we have seen in previous chapters, the short chronology of the standard historical narrative of the twentieth century was built on a rigid Cartesian distinction between mind and body: the body may be old, but the mind, for all intents and purposes, is young. This is why the standard historical chronology used in cultures influenced by Judeo-Christianity, beginning as it did around 4000 B.C., could afford to ignore humanity's deep history.

But we cannot dispense with the brain's history quite so easily. Current theories suggest that our large brain did not evolve to solve the relatively simple problem associated with tool use, much less the problems posed by the hunt. Instead, the large human brain evolved over the past 1.7 million years to allow individuals to negotiate the escalating complexities posed by human social living. This is still what we use the brain for today—most of the time, at least. And then there are all the noncognitive features of the brain. Many of the things we do are shaped by behavioral predispositions, moods, emotions, and feelings that have a deep evolutionary history. These body states are not ghostly things flitting mysteriously through consciousness. Recent work in neuropsychology and neurophysiology has shown that they are physiological entities, characteristically located in specific parts of the brain and put there by natural selection. Some of them, including emotions, are relatively automated, no different from the other areas of life governance—basic metabolism, reflexes, pain, pleasure, drives, motivations—that are routinely handled by the brain in all hominoids. Most, perhaps all, are also associated with an array of hormones and neurotransmitters such as testosterone and other androgens, estrogen, serotonin, dopamine, endorphins, oxytocin, prolactin, vasopressin, epinephrine, and so on. Produced in glands and synapses throughout the body, these chemicals facilitate or block the signals passing along neural pathways. They induce the somatic states revealed on and in our bodies and help determine how feelings actually feel. We share virtually all of these chemicals with other animals, though the nervous system of an iguana, say, will not necessarily use testosterone in the same way ours does. In a sense, each of these chemicals has its own natural history.

This chapter and the next explore the possibility of a history informed by some of the recent findings of neuropsychology and neurophysiology. The existence of brain structures and body chemicals means that predispositions and behavioral patterns have a universal biological substrate that simply cannot be ignored. This is the principle that lies behind the neurohistorical approach, an aspect of the "biological turn" alluded to by Michael Fitzhugh and William Leckie.[1] The neurohistorical approach embraces the recent interest in cognition as well as all histories that emphasize noncognitive aspects of the brain, including the history of emotions. But to acknowledge the physical or neural reality of moods and predispositions is not to adopt a crude genetic determinism. Even less does it invoke the illusory search for an essential human nature engineered by natural selection in the distant past, a stance that can only lead to a simpleminded history-without-change.

First of all, as I will illustrate in this chapter, the behaviors that are shaped by predispositions and emotions are often plastic, not hardwired. Basic social emotions are almost certainly universal. Nonetheless—the point is almost too obvious to bear repeating—they do different things in different historical cultures. Take disgust. All humans, like other primates, are normally capable of being disgusted. The facial expressions associated with disgust and probably the physiology as well have a high degree of human universality.[2] Yet the things that may disgust one person will not necessarily disgust another and will rarely disgust an infant. Writing of his visit to Tierra del Fuego, Charles Darwin noted the mutual disgust generated by an encounter with a native. The native was unmistakably disgusted by the look and feel of the cured beef that Darwin was eating—insofar as Darwin could interpret his facial expressions, that is to say. Darwin, in turn, could not finish his meal, disgusted by the fact that a dirty savage had presumed to touch his meat. Same disgust, different object. A neurohistorical perspective on human history is built around the plasticity of the synapses that link a universal emotion, such as disgust, to a particular object or stimulus, a plasticity that allows culture to embed itself in physiology. By the same token, the universal capacity to feel disgust can be exploited in ways that are unique to a given culture. The medieval female saint who ate lice and licked pus from infected wounds and leper sores knew, on some level, just what sort of effect she would have on those who watched. Other cultures use disgust in very different ways. Given the plasticity of such emotions as disgust, the interaction between universal cognitive or physiological traits and particular historical cultures is never simple.

Second, the universal capacity to have an emotion or a feeling does not necessarily mean that the neurophysiological state necessary for that feeling will ever arise in a given individual. The hormones prolactin and oxytocin are deeply associated with paternal caregiving, for studies have shown that certain male animals—mice, sea horses, scrub jays, tamarins—will experience elevated levels of prolactin while caring for their offspring.[3] So could doctors simply inject deadbeat dads with prolactin in an effort to get them to care more for their children? Naturally, it is not that simple, because the father in question also has to have a brain that is receptive to these hormones. The primatologist Sarah Blaffer Hrdy reports that brain receptors for oxytocin, one of the "peace and bonding" hormones, are typically more numerous in species where males bond with their mates and participate in rearing offspring. But if such receptors are not hardwired in humans, if they have to be formed through development and experience, if cultural norms militate against them, then fathers will not necessarily have the neural equipment to process injected prolactin and oxytocin. So, yes, as humans, all men have (or had, as children) some of the biological equipment necessary to bond with their own children, but for whatever reason—perhaps cultural, perhaps biographical—the bodies of deadbeat dads cannot easily generate or use the hormones that undergird the bonding process. The social effects of hormones like prolactin are never human universals. They are particular to given cultures and individuals.

Third, the body states generated by activities of the brain and the endocrine, even those induced by wiring set in place by culture, normally cannot dictate behavior.[4] Instead, they provide a backdrop of feelings against which people evaluate situations, make decisions, and do things. To this extent, they bear striking similarities to the control mechanisms or cultural programs, loosely described by Clifford Geertz, that allow individuals to place constructions on the events through which they live.[5] Human behavioral norms, suitably internalized, allow one to ignore or override the predispositions one may have toward doing things or the emotions experienced while doing them. Few people cave in, on the spot, to the feelings of lust they might occasionally have toward someone who is not their partner. By the same token, people often choose to do things that their predispositions tell them not to do. The fact that some people like to climb cliffs or watch horror movies shows how intoxicating it can be to stimulate our natural sense of vertigo and terror. Using Joseph LeDoux's term, we like to "modulate" our emotions—though some of us, surely, are more prone to these kinds of behaviors than others.[6] For those who do enjoy it—adolescents spring to mind—the reward for such behavior is the thrill provided by the

wash of epinephrine (adrenaline), dopamine, serotonin, endorphins, and other neurochemicals that flood the body and brain.
In a curious way, as these examples suggest, humans are often
predisposed to play around with, sometimes even violate, their
own predispositions. But the ability of the will or culture to determine behavior independently of the automated emotions and
predispositions does not mean that we can safely leave body
states out of our analysis of culture or history. First of all, it is not
always that easy to avoid the automated responses. One holds as-
cetic figures in awe precisely because it is difficult to make yourself lick plague pus. Second, the signals generated by the predisposition or the feeling have done something to human behavior
whether they are accepted or overridden. Neither climbing cliffs
or watching horror movies would have developed as human
practices in the absence of vertigo and terror.

Seen this way, moods, emotions, and predispositions inherited
from the ancestral past, where they evolved at the intersection of
human biology and human culture, form a structural backdrop
for many things we do and have done. They are interesting for
how they tease or suggest. They are also interesting for how they
are violated, manipulated, or modulated. And this is precisely
where it becomes so important to think with neurohistory. Although the fact is not widely known among historians and is
generally overlooked by psychologists and biologists, cultural
practices can have profound neurophysiological consequences.
Key elements of human economic, political, and social activity, as
I shall be suggesting here and in the final chapter, emerged precisely because humans possess relatively plastic or manipulable
neural states and brain-body chemistries. The effect of the Neolithic transformation, in this neurohistorical perspective, brought

about the conditions necessary for a rapid increase in the range of economic, political, and social devices that serve to modulate the body states of self and others. New devices continued to evolve throughout the ensuing millennia of the Postlithic period. These devices range from religious liturgies, sports, education, novel reading, and military training, all of which stimulate the production or reuptake of neurochemicals and create or remove synapses and receptors, to the agricultural and economic practices that promote commerce in chemicals like alcohol, caffeine, and opiates, which alter body chemistry in a more direct fashion.

To make these arguments, or even to make them comprehensible, this chapter seeks to locate that space where history can be informed by some of the recent developments in biology, neurophysiology, and cognitive science. The last decade of the twentieth century saw the publication of an extraordinary number of works devoted to the question of the brain, and the research continues. This work was the fruit of very real advances in the understanding of the brain made possible by new technologies, notably computed tomography, magnetic resonance imaging, and positron emission tomography, as well as emerging theories or understandings, such as those regarding the modularity of the brain or the nature of the endocrine. No one would claim that the riddles of the brain are anywhere near to being solved, and there is much disagreement among workers in the field. Even so, it is fair to say that a new dimension has been added to the rather sterile nature-versus-nurture debates that have dogged thinkers for several thousand years. A deep history demands that we acknowledge a genetic and behavioral legacy from the past. Yet recent trends in biology and neurobiology have emphasized the degree to which organisms are built by the interaction of genes, environment, and random developmental noise, to the point where there can be no nature without nurture and vice versa, as every right-thinking observer has long suspected anyway.

@

Few people are bothered by the idea that characteristics of the body, such as shape of the nose or color of the eyes, are influenced by genes, though not everyone is aware of the degree to which environmental influences, including nutrition, chemical influences, and upbringing, help determine how some traits are expressed. The proposal that behavior has a genetic component, however, has not met with universal acclaim, at least among social scientists. The impulse to argue that a behavioral trait may be just as much an adaptation as a physical trait can be traced back to Darwin himself, though the modern field known as ethology, the study of animal behavior, normally traces its ancestry to a 1937 paper by the biologist Konrad Lorenz.[7] The modern synthesis between Darwinian biology and Mendelian genetics was only just getting under way when Lorenz published this paper, and the field of ethology did not begin to develop in earnest until the 1960s.

A basic principle of a major strand of ethological research is that behavioral traits can be explained as adaptations to past environmental circumstances and, as adaptations, must be located in the genes. Richard Dawkins describes a study of black-headed gulls who remove eggshells from the vicinity of the nest shortly after their chicks have hatched.[8] According to the authors of the study, Nikolaus Tinbergen and others, the most likely explanation for this behavior is that sunlight flashing off the white insides of eggshells attracts the attention of crows and other predators. Over the millennia, black-headed gulls with a genetic tendency for keeping their nests clean slightly outreproduced their slovenly peers, causing the gene to spread among the population of black-headed gulls. In theory, natural selection could have solved the problem of flashing eggshells in several different ways. The outside of eggshells in some species are often speckled or colored so as to provide camouflage from predators; it is not inconceivable that the insides could have developed a similar kind of camouflage. Yet for whatever reason, perhaps because the necessary minerals were not available in the gulls' diet, natural selection arrived at a behavioral rather than metabolic solution to the problem of eggshells that winked in the sun. This, at least, is how the reasoning goes.

An ethological approach like this does not assume that behavioral traits will necessarily remain adaptive. Climate and geology are constantly changing, and ecosystems therefore change in subtle and not-so-subtle ways. Since microevolution, the fine-tuning of traits within a species, necessarily follows a step or two behind environmental change, a situation can emerge whereby an adaptation is no longer so adaptive for the organism's current environment. This is sometimes called a time lag or, in Paul Ehrlich's vivid expression, an "evolutionary hangover."[9] One can easily imagine a zoo with an aviary of black-headed gulls, all of whom scrupulously clean their nests, unmindful of the fact that crows are incapable of penetrating the fence surrounding their living space. The energy is wasted, but the gulls just cannot help it. In any species, it is possible that currently observable behavioral traits are nonadaptive or even maladaptive because they were adapted for an earlier environment.

The disposal of eggshells is just a behavioral trait and has little or no social impact. Ethology becomes sociobiology when it focuses on adaptive behaviors that contribute to the formation of animal societies. Such behaviors typically include devices for communicating, marking territory, choosing a mate, and creating dominance hierarchies: the stuff of animal sociability. There is little doubt, among biologists, that these behaviors have a genetic component. But what about humans? According to the historian Carl Degler, the possibility of a human sociobiology, indeed the word itself, has been around since at least the 1940s. It surfaced initially not just among ethologists but also among psychologists and cultural anthropologists, and it spread later into the fields of political science and economics.[10] In Margaret Mead's *Male and Female* (1949), Degler observes, ethological perspectives on human sexual characteristics play a role in distinguishing traits acquired biologically from those acquired culturally. By the 1950s, Alfred Kroeber was calling for a study of human nature through comparison of human and animal behavior.[11] Yet despite the early anthropological component to human ethology, the very term *sociobiology* became inextricably associated with the 1975 publication of E. O. Wilson's text of the same name, largely because of the monumental nature of the biological synthesis he put together.[12] Most chapters of *Sociobiology* dealt with biological perspectives on insect and animal society, though in a final chapter Wilson allowed himself to speculate on the application of sociobiology to human psychology and human society. Human sociobiology had been around for several decades. It was Wilson who brought the field into the popular consciousness.

In the ensuing years, the field of human sociobiology became associated, at least in the eyes of some social scientists, with a set of noxious ideas regarding the inferior nature of racial minorities, social inferiors, women, and the mentally retarded that had been around, in one form or another, since at least the nineteenth century. Up until the 1920s or 1930s, such ideas lay at or near the heart of intellectual inquiry in many fields of history, biology, anthropology, psychology, the eugenics movement—virtually all the human sciences, in fact. The grip of the various theories of innate and hereditary difference, at least in American social science, began to slip in the 1920s and 1930s. Fields as diverse as Boasian cultural anthropology and behaviorist psychology acknowledged the fact that humans do differ—no anthropologist could ever fail to notice the remarkable differences that exist between human cultures, and a similar situation holds for psychologists and their human subjects—but practitioners chose to explain the difference in terms of culture, education, and upbringing. In the 1960s and 1970s, the emergence of sociobiology and related theoretical moves, including rational choice theory in economics and political science, marked the return of the theory of innate difference, this time based on genes.

That sociobiology was hijacked by pop science writers and neoconservative politicians on behalf of theories of innate and heritable difference was, in many respects, a curious development. The theoretical core of sociobiology is neutral on the question of whether there are innate racial or sexual differences among humans. The underlying biology, as Degler points out, could easily have been interpreted as promoting the essential sameness of all human beings, as it was by American anthropologists like Kroeber and Ruth Benedict. In 1983, Claude Lévi-Strauss noted wryly that sociobiology in France was linked to leftist arguments seeking a return to Rousseauian ideas about natural man, whereas in the United States it was associated with neoconservative doctrine.[13] To argue that behaviors are "genetically programmed," as Wilson once suggested, may be offensive to some ears and is probably wrong, at least insofar as computer programs generate automatic or predictable results rather than complex behavioral patterns. Yet the argument is not even remotely racist or sexist, for one can use it to argue that all humans are programmed in essentially the same way and that any variation is the result of culture—as Wilson, following a path carved out by Mead, argued in his 1978 book *On Human Nature.*

Yet no one these days is so naïve as to imagine that science is impervious to social and political persuasion. "Darwinism," as Daniel Dennett puts it, "has always had an unfortunate power to attract the most unwelcome enthusiasts—demagogues and psychopaths and misanthropes and other abusers of Darwin's dangerous idea."[14] The theoretical neutrality of sociobiology certainly proved no obstacle to neoconservative politicians and pop science writers who, for one reason or another, delighted in using the authority of science to "prove" the hereditary basis of racial, sexual, and social difference. This was the feature of sociobiology that proved most objectionable to many social scientists, psychologists, and biologists, who saw in it an attempt to revive social Darwinism and the eugenics movement.[15] The idea of behavioral plasticity, after all, had been central to many strands of American social scientific and psychological thought since at least the 1930s. Key aspects of governance, social policy, and medicine were and are organized around the idea that education, social services, training, and therapy can help individuals escape the structural constraints that prevent their social or economic advancement or their psychological and physical health. The sociobiology of the 1970s and 1980s was interpreted by some observers as part of a neoconservative effort to limit government-funded social services and to naturalize the harsh inequalities of the social order.

Among most historians, the general attitude toward sociobiology was indifference rather than outright hostility, since few historians in the 1960s and 1970s, with the possible exception of figures like Fernand Braudel, Arnold Toynbee, and William McNeill, were thinking along biological lines anyway. All the same, as Gabrielle Spiegel has pointed out, it is no coincidence that cultural history emerged almost simultaneously with sociobiology: although poststructuralism has deep roots in twentieth-century thought, it was also a ready riposte to the essentialism of biological difference postulated by pop sociobiology.[16] Following poststructuralist currents found in many humanistic disciplines, cultural historians typically deny that there is anything essential or primordial about things like race or identity. By the same token, there is not anything "normal," like a normal monogamous heterosexuality. In the absence of any core or essential human behaviors, it is impossible to write history as if it were moving toward some perfectible state, like the nuclear heterosexual family, or perhaps away from some imagined paradise. Nor can history say whether one construct is better than another. This is a moral decision, not a historical one.

Oddly enough, this is exactly what biology says. Darwinian natural selection, after all, has a fundamentally *anti*-essentialist epistemology. That is the whole point. Species, according to Darwin, are not fixed entities with natural essences imbued in them by the Creator. Nor do morphological entities have essential identities, since one animal's leg may be another animal's flipper.

Is it a jaw bone? Or is it an ear bone? The answer depends on whether you are interrogating a reptile or a mammal. Recent trends in biology, moreover, have stressed the importance of acknowledging the wide variation that can exist among members of a given population group. The reasoning is complicated. David Buller, for example, has summarized the perspective in this way: "[A] consistent result of mathematical models of frequency-dependent selection is that balanced proportions of alternative phenotypes, rather than just single phenotypes, turn out to be evolutionarily stable." Translated, this means that natural selection does not homogenize the individuals of a species. Buller offers the example of a particular marine crustacean (*Paracerceis sculpta*) whose males come in three different body types—small, medium, and large—and three corresponding mating behaviors. The large males maintain harems. The small males sneak past their guard and copulate with the females whenever they can. The medium-sized males are perhaps the most interesting of all. In the spirit of cross-dressing or wearing drag, they mimic the female courtship display so well that they actually fool the dominant males into bringing them within the harem, where they then proceed to enjoy themselves.[17] Given this state of affairs, the search for a normal crustacean nature and body type is futile. And so it goes for the equally futile quest to identify "human nature." Here, as in so many areas, biology and cultural studies are fundamentally congruent.

Some of the arguments against strong versions of biological determinism did not come from historians and social scientists alone. They also came from other evolutionary biologists and geneticists challenging the theory on its own turf. The most obvious objection to sociobiology, in 1975, was that no one had ever found a gene for any behavioral trait, so the field of sociobiology at that point was a series of conjectures rather than a testable scientific hypothesis. Sociobiology was associated with the adaptationist perspective that arose with the modern synthesis of Darwinian evolution and Mendelian genetics: all traits, even behaviors, are adaptations, and all adaptations are coded in genes. Given this intellectual mapping, one did not actually need to find the gene: it just had to be there. But supposing the synthesis itself was misguided?

In an influential article published in 1979, the paleontologist Stephen Jay Gould and the geneticist Richard Lewontin questioned the adaptationist philosophy that underpinned population genetics in general and the field of sociobiology in particular.[18] Gould and Lewontin did not dispute the primacy of adaptations. What concerned them was the lack of standards governing how adaptationist stories could be told. Moreover, they challenged the idea that all traits, including behavioral traits, must be adaptive. They called this the Panglossian paradigm, from Voltaire's Dr. Pangloss, who argued, among other things, that noses were designed to hold spectacles. To take a particularly salient example: humans use their brains for a great many things that cannot easily be explained as the product of natural selection. Language may be adaptive, but surely the cognitive abilities that allow us to compose music, play chess, or engage in theoretical physics are just by-products of some other natural process that caused the human brain to grow so large and complex. They cannot have been selected for per se. Such behaviors are "exaptations," a neologism coined by Gould and Elizabeth Vrba in an equally important 1981 article.[19] An exaptation is a trait, like the large cognitive brain, that evolved to serve some function but subsequently became available for entirely different purposes. Sexual desire, for example, is adaptive with regard to its procreative function, but many primates have figured out that sex can be fun regardless of whether it produces offspring. In certain species, especially bonobos and humans, non-procreative sexual play has come to serve important social functions. Adaptive as far as reproduction is concerned—which is why sexual desire evolved in the first place—sex is "exaptive" with respect to its ability to create and maintain social bonds. In other essays, Gould saw the brain as serving an extraordinary number of exaptive roles in civilized societies, in addition to its continuing adaptive functions.

One of the most interesting exaptations characteristic of human behavior and culture is the very fact that humans take an interest in modulating their brain-body states. Many animals do this to a certain degree. Horses who get bored or lonely while isolated in a paddock sometimes take pleasure in startling themselves. A lively snort causes a chemical feedback that induces a startle reflex and an exciting wash of neurochemicals. Birds who flock around trees bearing fruit that is somewhat past its prime and eat the alcohol-laden fruit have found a way to ingest, rather than manufacture, a mood-altering substance. Cats are drawn to catnip. None of the behaviors induced by these chemicals is particularly adaptive. In the case of drunken birds, the behavior is downright dangerous. They do it just because it is fun. Humans, as one might suspect, are particularly interested in fun, and the degree to which humans stimulate brain-body chemistry through the ingestion of natural toxins and alcohol or through sensory input is, like many things humans do, unparalleled in the animal world. The human brain-body system did not evolve "for" the purpose of being stimulated or manipulated. The feelings that wash through your body when you read a particularly good novel or watch a powerful movie are entirely exaptive. The exaptive capacity of the human brain-body system to be modulated by behaviors of this kind is central to the idea of neurohistory. Behaviors and the institutions that accompany them are crucial components of any human culture, though the institutions clearly vary from one culture to the next. The human capacity to have culture, to this extent, has been built on neurophysiology.

A different kind of nonadaptation is the spandrel, a trait that came along for the ride, as it were, because it was morphologically or metabolically linked to an adaptive trait. The male nipple, a nonfunctional trait, is a particularly salient example: it exists only because certain basic fetal structures are built before the fetus is subject to the wash of testosterone that turns a fetus with XY chromosomes into a male. Using the same basic principle— and following an argument first proposed, as it happens, by Mead and later developed by Donald Symons—Gould suggested that the clitoris is a spandrel.[20] Recent research on the upsuck function of the female orgasm has suggested that the argument may be wrong, but the reasoning remains vividly instructive.[21] As Symons argued, the clitoris and the penis are built from the same morphological entity. As the process of natural selection imbued the penis with the capacity to give its owner sexual pleasure, the clitoris, morphologically linked to the penis, also picked up a degree of sexual sensitivity. Gould did not deny that this particular spandrel could be and subsequently was used for adaptive purposes. All he denied was that the clitoris evolved *for* the purpose of giving women sexual pleasure.

The exaptationist perspective promoted by Gould, Lewontin, Vrba, and other paleontologists and geneticists was not developed solely for the purpose of challenging biological determinism or pan-selectionism. Along with the theory of punctuated equilibrium—the idea that species evolve in a geological instant and then remain essentially unchanged throughout the remainder of their evolutionary history—exaptationism represented a concerted and largely successful attempt by paleontologists to enter into Darwinian debates. But the challenge to biological determinism was always there, and it served as the goad that inspired the whole exaptationist edifice. If exaptations and spandrels are common—if it is difficult to figure out which traits are adaptations and which are spandrels or exaptations—then it becomes pointless to speak of a gene "for" such and such a trait. On a strict reading, there can be no gene "for" playing chess or doing nuclear physics; reverse engineering will never allow one to discover the "function" of such traits. One could conceivably say that there is a gene or set of genes that, in this particular environment, happen to allow someone to be good at chess, but the gene (if there is one at all) did not evolve under that particular selection pressure.

Over the past quarter century, the debates between adaptationists and exaptationists have been, at times, bitter and frequently descended to the level of pointless name-calling.[22] Both groups position themselves as the lonely voice of truth. For the adaptationists, this truth is a Darwinian and secular truth, assaulted on all sides by fuzzy anti-Darwinian thinking, accusations of doing beanbag genetics, and the rising tide of religious fundamentalism. The exaptationists, in turn, see a world seduced by the idea that all traits are fixed in the genes—predestination, if you will, in biological garb. To an outsider like me, it seems clear that exaptationists, in their ongoing effort to educate the public about the pitfalls of pop sociobiology, have sometimes misconstrued or overdrawn the adaptationist program. As some geneticists have pointed out, the modern synthesis does allow for the things emphasized by paleontologists.[23] Of course geneticists write about genes, but that does not mean they deny environmental influences on how those genes get expressed in bodies. At the same time, it is likely that geneticists, in their enthusiasm to talk about adaptations, simply had not paid enough attention to spandrels, exaptations, and punctuation. As Niles Eldredge has pointed out, moreover, geneticists were more than a little snooty about allowing paleontologists to dine with them at the High Table of Darwinian theory, and the modern synthesis suffered accordingly.[24] The exaptation, frankly, is a lovely idea, and I am glad it has a name. And as Henry Plotkin has noted, it is an especially useful device for thinking about human culture.[25]

One result of the exaptationist assault on the modern synthesis is that biologists have generally become a little more careful about postulating genes "for" such and such a trait, which was always a convenient shorthand for something that everyone knew was much more complex. Such hesitancy is especially appropriate where behavior is concerned. Molecular biologists often write this way, since it is not wholly illegitimate to speak of a gene "for" blue eyes or sickle-cell anemia. It was never likely, however, that a simple kind of one-to-one association could work so easily for behavioral or cognitive traits. Among other things, the math does not hold up. It has recently been suggested that the human genome consists of fewer than 30,000 genes or cistrons—the estimates change on a regular basis but the figure is accurate enough as a ballpark estimate. Maybe half of these genes manufacture the particular proteins that build brain cells. Given the immense repertoire of human behavioral traits—there are several thousand facial expressions alone, each of which is associated with a different combination of feelings or emotions—nobody could make the mistake of assuming that one gene could code for one particular synaptic configuration associated with a specific behavioral trait.[26] It makes sense to assume that natural selection used some genes to build the life-regulating elements of the nervous system and perhaps others to engineer key traits like a theory of mind or linguistic capacity, but it used the remaining genes to build a plastic brain capable of learning the necessary array of behavioral traits and coding them in synapses.

Facial expressions, of course, are not all that profound. Things are different where fundamental features of human social behavior are concerned: deep grammar, theory of mind, even altruism. Here, recent studies, using advances in molecular biology, are beginning to identify the particular genes or polymorphisms associated with cognitive patterns.[27] Once again, however, it is likely that the neural predispositions have to be triggered in some way. Genes alone are not enough to build deep grammar or a theory of mind in the absence of specific developmental experiences. These developmental experiences are not only environmental; they are also cultural. In this way, culture can actually be wired in the human body. Since cultures change, human psychologies, in principle, can differ greatly from one era to the next.

To appreciate this point, it is helpful to understand how the body is built. The human body consists of about 350 different kinds of cells—skin cells, brain cells, liver cells, and so on. Each cell in the body contains exactly the same genetic information, in the form of twenty-three pairs of chromosomes. Here is the paradox: skin cells and brain cells start with precisely the same information, so how on earth do they end up being so very different in type? The problem is distinctly similar to the problem faced by naturalists trying to explain how social animals living in large colonies know what jobs to perform. Though it was once possible to imagine the existence of a divinity who ordered all social tasks, established a social hierarchy, and guided social progress, few practicing historians or political scientists actually believe this nowadays. In the same vein, no naturalist would imagine that any ant or termite queen has the capacity or even the will to order the hundreds or thousands, even millions, of workers that make up the colony. Moving down a step to the molecular level, there is certainly no queen cell that guides the process of cellular differentiation. So how does differentiation take place?

In the case of both cells and social insects, the answer lies in chemical signals.[28] No cell, by definition, contains a specific set of instructions telling it to develop into a neuron or a skin cell. Instead, cells figure out what to do based, more or less, on their location in the developing embryo. As cells divide and begin to form the gastrula, the hollow sphere of several thousand cells in three layers that is an early embryo, the cells that happen to be located on the outside figure out, from the chemical signals they are receiving (or not receiving), that they are going to be ectodermal cells: skin, nails, hair, or brain; there is no way of knowing their fate just yet. The inner cells, the endoderms, figure out likewise that they are going to be the lining of the throat, stomach, and intestines. The mesoderms get to be everything in between. That much is reasonably clear. Why chemical signals subsequently encourage ectodermal cells located on a specific part of the gastrula to curl up and form the hollow tube that will be the central nervous system, whereas others are persuaded to become toenails or calluses, is perhaps less obvious. But the fact that a complex creature eventually emerges from the exchange of simple chemical signals is not, in fact, terribly surprising. Mathematical studies have shown how considerable complexity can arise from the successive iteration of a few simple rules and processes. The extraordinary social complexity of social insects is a case in point, since it is created by means of just a few pheromones and other signals exchanged among the members of the colony.

Since the genetic instructions within cells are all exactly the same, bodies and brains cannot, therefore, be built by genes alone. Strictly speaking, they are built by interactions between cells. Nor is the interaction itself guided solely by genetic information contained in cells, as one might imagine, for development is shaped both by environmental influences and by something that geneticists call "developmental noise," the entirely random influences that shape the phenotype, the actual entity built by genetic instructions.[29] Moreover, you must have a reader, the specific cellular machinery necessary for reading the amino acids off the sequence of nucleotides that form a strand of DNA. Although DNA is sometimes called self-replicating, a chromosome, like the score for a symphony, does not actually do anything. It just sits there. To turn the score into a symphony, as Dennett points out, you need musicians, musical instruments, a conductor, air to transmit the sound waves, and so on. The same is true for a chromosome. Using Dennett's neat analogy, the conceptual flaws that mar the science behind *Jurassic Park* lie not just in the difficulty of assembling dinosaur DNA (though that is problematic enough). What is really missing is a dino-DNA reader.

Given an appropriate reader and the metabolism to go with it, a unit of DNA will code for nothing more complicated than a sequence of one-dimensional amino acids. Through a process that is not well understood, these amino acids are then folded to form a three-dimensional protein—or in some cases several possible proteins, depending on the type of cell involved—whose molecular shape determines what it can do. From here, it is a long, long step toward phenotypic traits. Any number of intervening chemical influences can alter the ways in which those proteins are expressed as traits. Many of the chemical signals necessary to the developmental process are released by the fetus itself. The developing gonads, to take the best-known example, release the hormones that usually provide an XY fetus with male sex traits and an XX fetus with female traits. In roughly one in every 2,500 births, a different set of hormones is produced, sometimes for no discernible reason. As a result, XY babies are born with vaginas or micropenises, and XX babies are born with enlarged clitorises.

Other chemicals capable of influencing development can be absorbed across the placenta, and sometimes the effect is pernicious. Ingested toxins have an obvious impact on fetal brain structures. Obstetricians routinely advise pregnant women to avoid alcohol and tobacco for just this reason. Recent studies have suggested that pregnancy sickness was an adaptation to the toxins present in meat.[30] These toxins would have been particularly dangerous in the fifth to twelfth weeks of pregnancy, the weeks during which key portions of the fetal brain are built, and so women's bodies evolved to be particularly sensitive to potential toxins during these weeks. Severely malnourished mothers unable to ingest enough folic acid in the first trimester are more likely to give birth to babies with spina bifida and cerebral palsy.[31] The stress to which subordinate female baboons are routinely subjected by dominant females encourages them to give birth to males, a subject to which I shall return in more detail in the next chapter.[32]

The environmental or cultural impact on genetic expression continues long after birth. Human infants are born with a cortex containing ten billion neurons and possibly hundreds of trillions of synapses. Trillions of synapses are subsequently created by experience during the years of juvenile synaptic plasticity, and they continue to be created and maintained throughout adulthood. According to the theory of neural Darwinism, it is not even necessarily experience that lies behind the formation of neural pathways. Instead, synapses are formed entirely at random, and only those that are subsequently used and prove useful actually survive.[33] The neurons that are not used, perhaps several hundred million per person, are simply discarded in a process that begins in children around the age of eight and continues through the teen years and beyond. It has long been known that young children whose parents read to them perform better in school, and recent studies have shown that the effect of reading can be located on the synaptic level. The same is true for playing a musical instrument or doing art, and future studies will surely add to the list. On the other side of the coin, children born with cataracts and hence blind at birth will not achieve normal vision if the cataracts are not removed fairly soon. The problem is that the synapses of the visual cortex will not develop without visual stimulus. More grimly, abandoned or severely abused children are prone to suffer from sociopathic or dissociative disorders as adults, and brain scans suggest that these disorders are locatable on the synaptic level. As noted earlier, it is possible that some kinds of social skills, such as the theory of mind notably absent in autistic children, have distinct genetic components.[34] But even so, the lesson of interactionist approaches to genes and environment suggests that many social skills and social pathologies have both genetic and environmental components. They may be fairly hardwired in an adult, and for that reason may prove resistant to therapies of all sorts, though therapies, often enough, do work. But the synaptic wiring itself may be the product of education, experience, and environment, laid down primarily during the individual's juvenile development.

What all this means is that genotypes do not code for phenotypes in some simpleminded, one-to-one fashion. Since the 1980s or so, virtually all biologists, adaptationist or otherwise, have acknowledged this point, the truth of which is patently obvious to any gardener. It is true that no one starting with a human genotype will ever grow up resembling a chimpanzee or a zebra; the developmental process is not *that* flexible. But at the level of behavior, there is more developmental plasticity, more room for cultural influence, than imagined by pop sociobiology and even mainline evolutionary psychology. Evolutionary psychology, a field I will discuss in more depth in the next section, posits the existence of cognitive modules that are akin to computer programs. A number of neuroscientists (by no means all) accept the idea of a modular brain, perhaps encompassing the five senses, language, and maybe a few other components. Evolutionary psychology, in contrast, argues for massive modularity:

hundreds of thousands of modules that were engineered by natural selection and reside in all human brains. Yet the implication of developmental accounts is that modules, even if they exist, do not just show up automatically. Instead, they must be triggered by environmental circumstances before they can be expressed. Experiments done on monkeys have suggested that a fear of snakes will not develop unless young monkeys are exposed to snakes or, according to one experiment, are given live insects like crickets or grasshoppers in their food.[35] The fear of snakes, if it exists at all as a predisposition, may exist as a genetically informed potential that will not be expressed in synapses unless triggered by experience.[36]

Juveniles have a surfeit of neurons, according to this view, to allow for such wiring should it become necessary. This makes eminent sense: why waste metabolic energy nourishing neurons if their synapses are not going to be used? In this vein, one wonders just how many potential synaptic connections were lost to members of the civilized world when their ancestors abandoned a foraging lifestyle and settled in villages, towns, and cities. Anyone who has seen an African tracker scan a featureless plain and locate a distant pride of lions, invisible to everyone else in the car, will appreciate the impoverished nature of the synapses in his or her own visual cortex.

Although the biological camp appears divided, substantial agreement actually exists on most of these issues. The differences often lie in the things that people choose to emphasize. Those who favor interactionist or developmental systems approaches to the understanding of genotypes and phenotypes sometimes do so with an enthusiasm that overemphasizes the environment at the expense of genes. It is undeniable that environment shapes the phenotypic expression of genes. Yet it is important to bear in mind that, if genes cannot express themselves in generally predictable ways, natural selection has nothing to act on. Domestic cattle are smaller and gentler than their wild ancestors, and this is presumably because the Neolithic pastoralists of the Middle East killed and ate the larger and more obstreperous animals and bred the smaller and more passive ones. Yet this process would never have taken place if certain cattle genes did not code for body size and temperament in a fairly predictable way. The developmental systems paradigm should not be an excuse for bringing blank-slate behaviorism in through the back door. The trick, here as in all things, is to get the right balance between genetic and developmental perspectives.

How should historians approach these ongoing developments in biology? One proposal to historicize human biology, at least in some fashion, has come in the form of evolutionary psychology.[37] In a sense, the emergence of the field of evolutionary psychology in the late 1980s and 1990s showed that Wilson was correct when he predicted in 1975 that biological influences would come to shape the field of psychology—or at least partially correct, since many academic psychologists today remain skeptical of the idea that evolutionary biology has much to offer them. Evolutionary psychology seeks to repair a serious theoretical flaw that dogged the field of sociobiology from its inception. Pop sociobiologists were quick to claim that genes shaped behavior but could offer only vague ideas about how genes actually did so. Wilson wrote speculatively of a science-to-be that he labeled "neurobiology," tacitly acknowledging that no one had as yet made any progress toward building such a science. This is what evolutionary psychology has tried to do. The basic premise of the field, as noted earlier, is that genes shape behavior not directly but through the cognitive modules they build in the brain. These cognitive modules are like computer programs. In theory, if one could map the neural networks of the brain, one could actually see these programs in the form of vast, interconnecting sets of neurons. Here is the evolutionary or historical component: these modules were engineered by the process of natural selection acting on humans in the ancestral environment. Some modules, like basic fears, urges, and other predispositions, are identical to those found in primate or mammalian brains and indeed derived from them. Other modules, like deep grammar, emerged more recently and are unique to humans. According to evolutionary psychologists, all have remained largely unchanged since the origin of the species some 140,000 years ago.

This is the central historical contribution of evolutionary psychology, even if, in its unchangingness, it does not seem very historical. The historicity of evolutionary psychology comes from the idea that cognitive modules are like fossils—indeed, the fossil metaphor surfaces from time to time in the writings of evolutionary psychologists. Like fossils, modules were laid down in the strata of the brain a long time ago and preserved against the ravages of time. With the right sort of experimental techniques, we can dig them up and use them to figure out what the ancestral society was like. Are you, like most people, somewhat scared of the dark? Our distant ancestors must have been scared of the dark. Those who acted more cautiously at night managed to outreproduce their fearless peers, and this slight selection pressure resulted in the cognitive module for fear of the dark that you eventually inherited. Enough evidence for the prey status of early hominins[38] has now been collected to show that australopithecines and archaic humans actually had good reason to be scared of the dark. Here, at least, the findings of evolutionary psychology seem to dovetail with the archeological evidence.

Evolutionary psychology is based on the idea that the brain is an enormous computer program with many subprograms. The computational theory of mind, according to some of its proponents, does not necessarily require a Darwinian perspective. The actual programs can be exaptations or, alternatively, programmed through upbringing. Evolutionary psychologists insist that modules have an evolutionary history, however, because they are eager to invoke the ethological concept of the time lag or the evolutionary hangover. The idea is simple: the modern brain is optimally adapted to an ancestral society located in the savannas of East Africa and is not especially well adapted to modern social and demographic conditions. Civilization evolved so recently that natural selection has not yet been able to fine-tune the brain to the new environment. Nowadays there is no reason to be scared of the dark and plenty of reason to be scared of fast cars. Unfortunately, we are stuck with the modules we have or do not have. Other, more serious social and psychic problems stem from a similar environmental mismatch. The married man who takes up with a young mistress may damage his reputation, alienate himself from his children, set back his career, increase his level of stress, and perhaps reduce his overall fitness as a denizen of the modern world, but the idea is that he cannot help it: the behavior is preprogrammed—or so the argument goes. Or consider the teenage girl who kills her newborn baby. Such behavior not only gets her in trouble with the law but also seems inexplicable in strict Darwinian terms. Hrdy, however, has argued that maternal infanticide was not uncommon in ancestral African societies.[39] Among modern hunter-gatherers, few women, especially young women, are able to raise a child successfully in the absence of two things, namely, a husband and the social standing necessary for generating other social networks that can supply economic support. By invoking the concept of a time lag, by suggesting that originally adaptive traits persist as maladaptive practices, evolutionary psychologists, working in the manner of Sigmund Freud, have tried to explain behaviors that otherwise seem inexplicable or pathological.

All this has a certain appeal, and few biologists would ever want to deny that the brain itself is an evolutionary adaptation. All the same, the strong version of evolutionary psychology associated with the work of John Tooby, Leda Cosmides, and others has attracted a great deal of criticism. For starters, though the computational theory of mind has attracted some support among cognitive scientists, even the most sympathetic observers must admit that the theory's evolutionary component is in a rather conjectural state. Jerry Fodor, an early and vocal exponent of the idea of cognitive modularity, once expressed doubt that there is a meaningful evolutionary component to it.[40] Another obstacle is that it is difficult, if not impossible, to prove that modules (if they exist) are programmed by genes and not by culture. Most work in evolutionary psychology is achieved through the process of reverse engineering—you look at the trait (such as fear of the dark) and then try to imagine the evolutionary context in which it might have been adaptive (predation by leopards). It is easy to make mistakes. The well-known evolutionary psychologist

David Buss has argued that mate selection choices, as revealed through personal ads and other indicators, show a female bias toward older, financially secure men and a male bias toward younger, attractive women.[41] Women, it seems, seek mates who are good providers, whereas men only want sex. As it happens, recent research has suggested that this model is not correct when it comes to real spousal choices. Personal ads, as you might guess, do not really capture a representative slice of the population. But even to argue that this is a cognitive module engineered long ago by natural selection, it is necessary to assume that a similar mate-selection pattern held true in the past. This is not certain. Studies done by the anthropologist Kristen Hawkes and others suggest that men in certain tropical or subtropical hunter-gatherer societies do not make terribly good providers. Successful hunters tend to distribute meat equally among all members of the band— such generosity enhances their prestige, among other things— and the extra bits to which they are entitled they sometimes distribute to lovers rather than wives.[42] It has long been known, moreover, that in many African foraging societies the women provide a significant proportion of the calories. Husbands are useful, according to Hrdy, but even more useful are the allomothers (mothers, sisters, daughters, sometimes brothers or male lovers), who all contribute to the task of raising a child.[43] It is doubtful, therefore, that ancestral African women were as economically dependent on their husbands as Buss's model seems to suggest. In fact, heavy female dependence on male providers was arguably a recent development, the product of agricultural systems based on male labor, a characteristic pattern in most non-African agrarian societies. Buss claims to be finding the remnants of ancient practices fossilized in human cognition. What he may be seeing are new cultural patterns that arose outside of Africa only within the past 10,000 years.

More problems with evolutionary psychology arise from the basic assumption that the biological inheritance of cognitive modules is the whole story. Consider the following scenario—admittedly speculative, but nevertheless instructive. Let us assume that there is a module for recognizing social subordination in appropriate settings and responding accordingly. It is a reasonable assumption, since recognizably similar behavioral patterns are common in virtually all primate societies. Among humans, it is common to find situations in which social or political subordinates, in the presence of their superiors, unconsciously speak with a higher voice, carry a submissive grin on their faces, and laugh immoderately at the bad jokes made by those above them. Now, if the parents' subordinate status can shape the synaptic configurations of their children, both before and after birth—again, a reasonable conjecture derived from primate studies—then a subordinate frame of mind can be inherited within a lineage. But notice the key feature of this inheritance: though it ends up being at least loosely wired in the brain, the configuration is inherited culturally, via development, rather than genetically, via the genes. In small-scale ancestral human societies where hierarchical differentiation was severely limited, the subordination module, though present, may have been moribund. But imagine what happened with the rise of great agricultural societies and the immense political and social hierarchies that resulted. Culturally inherited subordination would now be felt among a far wider spectrum of the population—in effect, among all slaves and peasants, members of tributary societies, and other dependent or marginal groups, possibly including most women. Certain forms of political display evolved precisely to encourage the psychic effect of the module. Thus, whereas it may be true that there is a subordination module and that the module has not changed in significant ways since the ancestral past, the historical process of political centralization vastly increased the expression of the module in human populations and may have done so at the expense of other equally powerful modules, such as altruism. I shall discuss this kind of hypothetical approach to the impact of the Neolithic revolution on basic human psychology in the final chapter. Here, it is only necessary to point out how a neurohistorical approach suggests the possibility of significant changes over time in the social distribution of cognitive modules as an effect of cultural, not biological, inheritance.

Another recent critique of evolutionary psychology arises from neurophysiologists concerned by the overemphasis on cognition. Antonio Damasio has argued that a great deal of "thinking" actually gets done by means of brain-body chemistry interacting with the nervous system, not neural activity alone.[44] Think of the bored horse. The horse cannot say to himself, "I feel like getting startled" and, by virtue of the thought, get startled. Instead, the horse has to fool his own nervous system. He does so by mimicking the conditions that would naturally cause a startle reflex: the widened eyes, the sudden sound. The horse's brain then analyzes these signals and reaches the instant conclusion: wide eyes, sharp sound . . . gosh, there's something startling out there. A signal is then sent through the sympathetic nervous system to the adrenal gland, which releases a jolt of epinephrine— all this happens in the blink of an eye—and the epinephrine in turn causes the startle reflex. As Damasio has argued, experiences are constantly being mediated through brain-body chemistry; there is no thinking that is independent of the feedback mechanism linking sensory input, body chemistry, the body map, and neural activity. Curiously, the will can intervene in this process. Studies have shown that people with a set smile on their faces are more prone to laugh at jokes than people carrying a frown. At the very least, Damasio's work has shown that it is not enough to propose the existence of cognitive modules: one has to include chemistry in the equation. But the ready manipulability of body chemistry weakens the grasp of cognitive modules.

One of the most devastating critiques of evolutionary psychology has come from David Buller, a philosopher of biology, who has unraveled many of the field's claims from the inside out. Three features of his critique stand out. The first centers on a point discussed earlier: that natural selection in no way works to homogenize psychological traits. Different behavioral types, as it turns out, are typically (not necessarily) associated with stable polymorphisms, that is to say, different alleles of a gene that are capable of producing different psychological phenotypes. So how does this apply to humans? According to Buller:

> By the best estimates, humans are genetically polymorphic at 20 to 25 percent of all loci. That's a significant amount of genetic variation, and it would be truly remarkable if none of that variation underlies adaptive psychological variation, since comparable degrees of genetic variation underlie adaptive variation in other species. So the odds are very good that there are *some* polymorphic psychological adaptations in human populations. It just remains for empirical research to discover what they are.[45]

Since this is the sort of claim that may raise some hackles, let us be absolutely clear about what he is and is not saying. Against an evolutionary psychology model that posits both a homogenous genome and a single human nature, Buller proposes a polymorphically diverse genome and an array of stable psychological types. The genetic diversity does not map onto racial or ethnic diversity. Instead, the diversity is embedded within population groups. Sexes too: as I read it, there is no reason to assume that the difference between male and female psychology is necessarily greater than the difference found within each sex. An essential feature of this argument, as we saw already in the example of the marine crustacean *Paracerceis sculpta,* is that one should expect to find stable polymorphisms within biological sexes.

A second feature of Buller's critique of evolutionary psychology attacks the notion that the human brain was programmed in response to stable environmental challenges in the deep past. One of the most productive in a long line of arguments seeking to explain the evolution of human intelligence has centered on the complexities associated with negotiating the human social environment. This, the social intelligence hypothesis, assumes that "the majority of adaptive problems that drove human psychological evolution were posed by other humans" and not, say, the needs of the hunt or of toolmaking.[46] But if the adaptive environment consists primarily of other humans, and if their psychologies are evolving so as to maximize their own fitness, then the result is an evolutionary arms race. Typically, biologists invoke the image of an evolutionary arms race when seeking to describe how predator and prey or parasite and host evolve in lockstep, each responding to the other, but there is no reason why the model should not work within a species. So here is the point: if intelligence evolved so as to compete with other evolving intelligences, then it is impossible to speak of stable adaptive problems that generated fixed solutions. The human mind did not just adapt at some fixed moment in the past. It is, instead, continuously adapting.

This position, third and finally, leads Buller to reject one of the most fundamental assumptions of evolutionary psychologists: that the human brain has undergone no significant change for the past 100,000 years or more. Many biologists would naturally find it difficult to swallow this claim. E. O. Wilson has argued that substantial changes can take place in a species over the course of one hundred generations, and two thousand are enough to create a new species if selection pressures are intense enough.[47] According to this argument, "substantial changes" could have taken place in the human genome since the time of the Roman Empire. In support of this argument, there is now considerable hard evidence showing that certain human genes could and did change over the past 10,000 years or so. Many Africans, East Asians, Australians, Pacific Islanders, and Amerindians are allergic to milk because, after weaning, they lose the ability to digest lactose. Some people of Middle Eastern, South Asian, and European descent also become lactose intolerant as adults. In an ancestral environment where humans never drank milk after the age of four or so, it made sense for the body not to waste metabolic energy synthesizing a useless enzyme, lactase. But the first humans to domesticate cattle, sheep, and goats in the Fertile Crescent came under powerful selection pressures to retain, into adulthood, the juvenile ability to synthesize lactase. The ability of most adult Europeans, South Asians, and Middle Easterners nowadays to digest milk products, therefore, is a classic example of microevolution. It is also, not incidentally, a marvelous illustration of what is called gene-culture coevolution, for the new practice of keeping livestock acted as the selection pressure driving this microevolutionary process. Similar arguments hold for patterns of genetic resistance to human diseases, such as sickle-cell anemia, which provides resistance to malaria, or certain blood types, which happen to provide resistance to diseases like smallpox.

But what about the brain? Is it possible to locate powerful selection pressures acting on the genes involved in building the brain? Christopher Boehm has made just such an argument, proposing that an egalitarian ethos and the vast array of behavioral complexes associated with maintaining egalitarianism and reversing the innate primate tendency to form dominance hierarchies first emerged among humans around 100,000 years ago and became at least loosely wired in the human brain.[48] The dispositions of virtually all domesticated animals have undergone remarkable transformations in a much shorter period of time, less than 10,000 years in most cases. One need only compare dogs, cattle, or horses to their wild cousins to see how greatly their basic behavioral complexes have been changed. Even though the human brain is innately more plastic, more educable than that of other mammals, there is no reason to think that the human genome has been immune to recent selection pressures. The high percentage of stable human polymorphisms suggests strongly that the human genome has continuously evolved.

Ultimately, these are issues for biologists and psychologists to settle among themselves without interventions from historians like me. But to reiterate a point I made in the introduction to this book, evolutionary psychology is naturally ahistorical and would resist the best efforts of even a sympathetically minded historian. The field is especially problematic for a deep history of humanity. According to prevailing hypotheses, the mental modules that are the object of the evolutionary psychologist's quest fossilized long ago, in the deep past. They become relevant again only when they resurface as misfits in the modern cultural environment. Nothing that has happened since the moment of fossilization (a million years ago? fifty thousand years ago? who knows—the field has no interest in dates) can have any significance to evolutionary psychology. This kind of attitude makes it impossible to narrate any deep history of change, of migration, of cultural adaptation: one moves straight from the environment of evolutionary adaptation to the present with little need to pause in between. In my reading, moreover, the field's basic suppositions draw a hard line between nature (the modules) and culture (the artificial modern environment). The resulting narrative places the two in a historical sequence, from nature to culture, in a way that is anathema to a seamless deep history. Finally, when evolutionary psychologists stress the idea of Stone Age brains acting clumsily in modern environments, they produce a narrative little different from that of Genesis, where the expulsion from paradise led to pain, misery, and suffering. We can do better than this.

@

Each human brain consists of neural configurations set in place by a combination of genetic, environmental, and random factors. Neural systems are not distributed at random throughout a plastic brain; instead, each part of the brain has a characteristic function. Some, such as those involved in regulating heartbeat, breathing, and body temperature, are put in place by genetic instructions operating through the medium of fetal development.

Other human capacities, such as vision and hearing, are perfected in the developing child. Many such capacities, including behavioral capacities, exist as genetically informed potentials that must be triggered by environmental influence.[49] As such, they are shaped by the development environment in which they are built.

These neural configurations interact, on a daily basis, with the things we see and hear and feel. They are influenced by neurotransmitters released by the brain-body system and by chemicals that we ingest. What results from the subtle play of chemical and electrical signals that take place in our brain-body are a variety of body states that we feel as drives, appetites, motivations, predispositions, emotions, moods, and phobias. According to Damasio and LeDoux, when these body states intersect with consciousness, they produce feelings. Fear, in their model, is automated. You can be frightened of something you are not even aware of, and the feeling of fear arises only when you become aware that you are experiencing the emotion. Some of these body states are accompanied by physiological changes that are invisible or barely visible to another person, such as elevated heart rate or blood pressure and changes in the skin's electroconductivity. Certain other body states, the things we call emotions, are characteristically expressed on the outside of the body in the form of facial expressions, flushing or pallor, swelling, nervous ticks, and so on. Emotions like anger, disgust, and sympathy are publicized on the outside of the body because they are forms of communication. They do useful social and political work.

The will does not necessarily have a great deal of control over the body states that lie behind certain feelings. At the simplest level, most people would find it impossible not to feel hungry once their blood sugar dropped below a certain level. But the same goes for body states that have direct social consequences. Emotional expressions, for example, normally lie outside voluntary control. In this way, the integrity of the emotion is guaranteed by the body. Would a person respond so readily to someone's angry demeanor if anger was easily faked? The response to an angry demeanor, typically, is equally automated for much the same reason.

Necessarily, normally, typically—there are reasons why the preceding paragraph is peppered with such adverbs. People can, after all, learn to fake a reasonably good smile or a sob. Actors do it all the time. By the same token, the fact that body states have a significant chemical component means that they are readily influenced by ingested chemicals of all sorts. Drugs like heroin and cocaine appeal to some of us because they mimic the effects of serotonin and dopamine in the brain and therefore serve to alter body states artificially. Other kinds of behaviors bring internal chemical rewards precisely because the body is designed to respond to stimuli in chemical ways. Recreational sex is the most obvious example of a kind of behavior that allows us the delight of altering our body chemistry.

The body states that lie behind feelings of all kinds help shape both general behavioral patterns and discrete actions. They do not *dictate* behavior. More than a century ago, the anthropologist Edward Westermarck proposed that the origin of the incest taboo, nearly universal in human societies, lies in the fact that incestuous matings are biologically maladaptive. To hinder incest, evolution engineered in people a certain disgust for the idea of copulating with anyone they have grown up with.[50] In the twentieth century, cultural anthropologists unwilling to believe in human biological constants sought cultural explanations for the universality of the incest taboo. But cultural explanations seem increasingly improbable, especially now that we know that many mammals have devices for avoiding kin matings, and Westermarck's proposition again is looking attractive. Research among the Israeli kibbutzim has shown that many will not marry a fellow kibbutznik even though they are unrelated biologically. Simply having shared living quarters as juveniles is enough to persuade the people that the other kibbutzniks are family members. This, incidentally, is an argument made by evolutionary psychologists, and one that I suspect is likely to hold up. But the biological prohibition on incest is *not,* in fact, a prohibition, since incestuous matings can and do happen. In some cases, as in ancient Egypt, cultural evolution led to a preference, albeit short-lived, for brother-sister marriages. The fact of incest in our own culture, especially father-daughter incestuous rape, shows that any distaste generated in the brain can be overruled. The predisposition not to sleep with kin is only that—a predisposition. One of the most important principles of sociobiology is that a general inclination like this can explain behavioral patterns only in the aggregate. It cannot explain individual behaviors, and it runs up against the principle noted earlier: humans are peculiarly predisposed to violate their own predispositions.

The incest taboo is just one example of many kinds of large-scale behavioral patterns that are influenced by body states. It is a situation where a social emotion, in this case disgust, is usually associated with a particular action or stimulus. Yet as I suggested above, disgust, like other social emotions, is otherwise relatively plastic and therefore readily influenced by cultural norms. Thus, one cannot always predict what sorts of body states and behav-

ioral norms will arise from given stimuli, and a good deal of variation can exist from one culture to the next. Men in certain cultures, for example, will explode with rage when faced with challenges to their honor or their masculinity. Victorian women, at
least stereotypically, swooned at the sight of blood. Both kinds of
reactions involve somatic responses—visible swelling; flushing
or the draining of blood from the face; a drop in blood pressure—that are difficult to fake, or at least fake convincingly,
which suggests that they are wired in the brain and brain-body
chemistry. But neither reaction is a human universal. In both
cases, the wiring that typically associates a stimulus with a given
response was put there by culture and upbringing. This is how
gender norms, as cultural constructs, embed themselves in physiology. The existence of such hardwiring has fooled many observers into thinking that gender traits are genetic rather than
cultural.

Whereas the incest taboo makes a good deal of sense, biologically speaking, not all predispositions are so clearly susceptible to
strict adaptationist arguments. This is where we need to bring
exaptations and spandrels back into the picture. Crows, for example, are predisposed to collect bright and shiny objects. I suppose it is possible that crows, like bower birds, use them to attract
mates or for other adaptive purposes. But it seems even more
likely that the corvine desire for flashy things is an exaptation or
a spandrel, one of those features of biological evolution that cannot entirely be explained by adaptive reasoning. Humans are
even more predisposed to possess things than crows and more
subject to the dictates of fashion—if it is flashy and new, it must
be better—than bower birds. One could, if pressed, explain the
human predisposition to collect goods as a genetically induced

adaptation. After all, identity markers and jewelry become commonplace in archeological sites from the time of the creative explosion onward, starting some 50,000 years ago. But the functions served by commodity culture in Postlithic societies go so far beyond the Paleolithic use of objects that it is best to see the desire for goods as primarily exaptive, namely, a trait that may have evolved for one adaptive reason but is now being used for another.

@

By way of conclusion, let me turn to the historical implications of the model I have been proposing in this chapter. Culture, in some fundamental sense, has been revealed as a biological phenomenon. Wired in neurophysiology, taking shape in the form of neural networks and receptors, culture can operate in a relatively mechanistic, quasi-biological fashion. The wiring can be an explicit or intended product of culture patterns, traceable to sets of social practices that shape children in predictable ways during the development process. The wiring can also be accidental, as in cases where pregnant women ingest certain drugs or chemicals that are a natural part of their own culture—alcohol, nicotine, coca—and thereby unwittingly shape fetal development. If historians of eighteenth- and nineteenth-century Europe knew more about the effect of caffeine consumption on fetal development, they might be able to suggest some of the large-scale, albeit wholly unintended, neurophysiological consequences of the rapid growth in consumption of tea and coffee. In either case, there is not much culture without biology. Culture is made possible by the plasticity of human neurophysiology. With this insight, we can finally dispense with the idea, once favored by some historians, that biology gave way to culture with the advent of civilization. This has it all backward. Civilization did not bring an end to biology. Civilization *enabled* important aspects of human biology, and the drama of the past 5,000 years lies in the fact that it did so in ways that were largely unanticipated in the Paleolithic era. What do I mean by this? The expansion in calories available for human consumption, the domestication of animals useful as sources of energy, the practice of sedentism, the growing density of human settlements—such were the changes characteristic of the Neolithic revolution in all parts of the world where agriculture was independently invented: Mesopotamia, Africa, China, Mesoamerica, and other sites. All these changes created, in effect, a new neurophysiological ecosystem, a field of evolutionary adaptation in which the sorts of customs and habits that generate new neural configurations or alter brain-body states could evolve in unpredictable ways. As I shall explore in the final chapter, particularly interesting examples of this are provided by the things I call psychotropic mechanisms: human cultural practices that alter or affect brain-body chemistry.

The neurohistorical approach described in this chapter does not demand a deep historical perspective—a perverse thing to observe, given the preoccupations of this book. Eighteenth-century Europe, with its caffeinated culture, its sentimental novels and pornographic works, and its growing array of consumer goods, provides a gold mine of case studies that could benefit from the adoption of neurohistorical perspectives. I am sure the same holds true for other areas and other histories I do not know so well. And it certainly holds true for the emergence, in the past few decades, of a global youth culture ever more dependent on devices, practices, and commodities that shape or modulate brain-body chemistry, a culture that is fearful of the boredom that ensues when the body is not being continuously stimulated. I would be delighted to see neurohistory used in ways that do not necessarily contribute to a deep history.

Nevertheless, the perspectives of neurohistory matter in the context of this book because they make it possible to see the brain as the narrative focus for a history that begins with early hominins and balances on the Neolithic era. This focus means we can construct a different historical narrative, one that does not have to depend on the framework of political organization, including the rise of the nation-state, that undergirds the grand narratives of general history. A neurohistory is a deep cultural history, offering a way out of the increasingly sterile presentism that constrains the historical imagination and contributes to the growing marginalization of early history in the curriculum. Our feet planted firmly in the deep past, we can look ahead with wonder at the ramifying cultural patterns, the wonderful life, that emerged as human neurophysiology interacted with the rapidly changing ecologies of the Postlithic era.

FIVE

Civilization
and Psychotropy

In everyday life, we do many things that alter our moods and feelings on a regular basis. These alterations are reflected in constantly changing levels of chemical messengers in our tissues and in our brains. In principle, an omniscient observer of human moods should be able to track these changes, like a technician in a recording studio facing an array of dancing meters. Each meter on the board would register a different neurochemical: serotonin, dopamine, all the androgens and estrogens, and dozens of others besides. Most bars, as they rise and fall, would follow a fairly slow rhythm, measured on the order of hours, days, or even weeks. A few, such as those registering epinephrine, norepinephrine, or corticotropin-releasing hormone, would occasionally show rapid spikes and dips, corresponding to the sudden shocks or flashes of rage we experience from time to time. With enough study, patterns would emerge: of the Wall Street trader, say, whose testosterone takes a beating in a bear market and is restored by visits to sex shops. Of the teenager, whose frenetic spikes and dips show as much variation in a week as an older and wiser person would experience in several months. Of whole groups whose levels of dopamine or serotonin, averaged across a month, are distinctly lower and stress hormones, the glucocorticoids, higher than those of other, more-favored groups. Studies like this might show, in fact have shown, how social privilege, a product of cultural patterns and historical trends, correlates strongly with levels of stress hormones.[1]

The array of meters might also reveal how the neurotransmitters and hormones present in our bodies, in theory, could unite to produce an infinite range of different moods and feelings. As a practical matter, however, we soon learn to recognize the familiarity of certain combinations, certain chords, both in ourselves and in others. Our cultures have found it convenient to assign names to these common chords: joy, depression, sadness, anticipation. Your moods and feelings may be tinted with a slightly different range of emotions than mine, and we gossip about the variations so as to calibrate our mood-descriptions more closely to the feelings we actually have. In some cases, we may find that we have nothing to share whatsoever, and that is where we reach the limits of empathy. Our bodies, by virtue of the genomes they carry, are capable of providing us with a whole palette of sounds. But it is our own life histories, the variations between the alleles we carry, and, perhaps above all, the cultures we live in that write the actual music.

This much has become clear from recent work in neuropsychology, though we are a long way from understanding all the details of the neurochemical aspects of moods and feelings and though the omniscience of the sound technician lies far beyond the technological capacity of neuroscience—perhaps to our relief. Yet the mere knowledge that mood and feeling are not impervious to measurement is itself a revelation. It is a revelation for a medical and psychological community trying to find drug therapies for people who suffer from mood swings or personality disorders. But it is also a revelation for students of human society. It is one thing to assert, as I did in the previous chapter, that culture is wired in the brain. It is quite another to measure the physiology of Southern honor by means of cheek swabs. Nothing genetic can explain the results of the experiments undertaken by Richard E. Nisbett and Dov Cohen: that Southern men, when they experience affronts, typically experience rapid increases in levels of testosterone and cortisol, whereas Northerners do not.[2] Culture is indeed coded in human physiology. This fact creates an astonishing new tool for sociologists and anthropologists eager to explore the differences between cultures. It does not necessarily change the nature of the things observed, because observers have long been aware of something called Southern honor. What it changes is the pattern of our explanations and the focus of our attention, which shifts inexorably toward a study of the cultural devices that evolved to instill the feeling of honor in human bodies.

The relevance to history is less obvious, since very few hypotheses deriving from neuropsychology could ever be testable in a historical context. But that is not the point. The point is that historians habitually think with psychology anyway. We are prone to making unguarded assumptions about the psychological states of the people we find in our sources. A historian studying the origins of the state in medieval Europe, writing in 1970, took it for granted that his sources were sufficiently revealing as to allow him to contrast the emotional temperatures of medieval and modern forms of nationalism.[3] Whole works can be shaped by psychological assumptions. Commenting on an important study of memory in post–World War II France, the historian Alon Confino takes note of "the book's main metaphors—syndrome, neurosis, repression, obsession, pathology."[4] Historians have to make psychological assumptions. This chapter suggests how a history might look if written in the light of very recent discoveries in psychology.

Thus, the mere knowledge that the things we do and see and experience have mood-altering effects, that culture impinges on psychology (and vice versa), should encourage us to ask why. The answer to that question takes us into the deep past, for the brain has a history, and that history is a deep history as old as humanity itself—or even older. All animals, after all, engage in mood-altering activities. They consume fermented fruit and nibble catnip. They cuddle and groom and play. Some domestic cats and perhaps most golden retrievers have been bred to enjoy the sensation of being stroked and tickled behind the ears; they are, in a sense, addicted to the wash of oxytocin or dopamine or whatever it is that is generated by patting. Like other primates, humans also enjoy being groomed, though, as with all such things, some like it more than others. Like bonobos, we engage in the pleasures and bonding experience of recreational sex. But to these behaviors Paleolithic human societies added a new range of mood-altering practices, including song, dance, ritual, and a variety of mood-altering substances, often consumed in the context of rituals. The range of mood-altering substances and practices continued to grow in the wake of the agricultural revolution; in the past few centuries, it has expanded at a prodigious pace as the devices became available to an ever-wider spectrum of the population. Thanks to the operations of a consumer economy, we are now surrounded by a dizzying array of practices that stimulate the production and circulation of our own chemical messengers. Think of the instant access to pornography and virtual sex now available on the Internet. Think of the Hollywood thriller that leaves an audience breathless, disoriented, with skin tingling and minds repeatedly shocked by massive doses of epinephrine, nor-epinephrine, and the like. Think of the shopping mall that dis-orients shoppers and induces the production of panic-inducing hormones, a body-state subsequently eased through the act of purchase. Shopping itself has become mildly addictive for the temporary state of euphoria it generates in some. And this is to say nothing about the foods and drugs, both legal and illegal, that de-liver a steady dose of caffeine or opioids or stimulate the human endocrine to produce its own array of neurochemicals. The chords, the melodies, have indeed changed over the course of human history.

The mood-altering practices, behaviors, and institutions gen-erated by human culture are what I refer to, collectively, as *psy-chotropic mechanisms. Psychotropic* is a strong word but not wholly inapt, for these mechanisms have neurochemical effects that are not all that dissimilar from those produced by the drugs normally called psychotropic or psychoactive. It is often pointed out, with reason, that the modern economy is oriented around the delivery of status goods. Yet it is arguable which of the two is more important to the modern economy: status or psychotropy. Movies, gossipy TV shows, novels, music, shopping, sports, cof-fee, alcohol, drugs, sex, pornography—all these institutions, practices, and commodities, and many more besides, have psy-chotropic effects. We can tell because of their mildly addictive properties, because of the mood swings they engender or assuage, because of the confidence or pep they sometimes give us or, especially in the case of the games we lose, the sense of deflation. All of them would cause the display meters in the studio to rise or fall. Our bodies are all different, partly for genetic reasons, partly for reasons rooted in development. But the psychotropic economy caters to everyone. Psychotropy is one of the fundamental conditions of modernity, and explaining its historical trajectory is one of the most valuable results of a deep historical perspective.

So how should we think about history through the lens of psychotropy? For reasons that lie deep in our biological history, the human central nervous system is highly sensitive to the wash of neurotransmitters that comes from everyday experiences and interactions. The advent of civilization and sedentism brought with it an economy and a political system organized increasingly around the delivery of sets of practices, institutions, and goods that alter or subvert human body chemistry. This is what gives civilizations their color and texture. The evolution of a distinctly psychotropic economy, a feature of the past century or two, is one aspect of the story that can be perceived through the lens of neurohistory. This is not necessarily an adaptive story, a story about how human cultural institutions serve biologically adaptive functions. Many psychotropic mechanisms, ranging from psychoactive drugs to pornography and other forms of entertainment, simply cannot be explained by means of adaptive reasoning. The stuff is bad for you. But neither is this a story of intentional change or progress aiming toward a telos. Because no one has ever understood the underlying chemistry, the psychotropic mechanisms that have evolved and disappeared over the past five or ten thousand years necessarily emerged by trial and error and subsequently developed through the small sets of adaptive nudges described in chapter 3. Over the past five thousand years or so there has been an illusion of direction, a sense of progress, if you can call it that, toward an ever-greater concentration of mood-altering mechanisms. But this is the same illusion created by the phylogeny of the panda's thumb, since there is clearly no directing mind, no genetic material, that guides the phylogeny of psychotropy.

This chapter is an essay on the possibilities of psychotropy. In the ensuing pages, I will offer some signposts for how this sort of history might be written. At the very least, we need to acknowledge the crucial role that psychotropic mechanisms play in our story of civilization. For obvious reasons, psychotropy is not necessarily all that friendly to a deep history. If the production, distribution, and use of psychotropic mechanisms could somehow be quantified and graphed, the line would look a lot like the line charting energy expenditure in human societies: rising very slowly across the later Paleolithic, accelerating in the Neolithic, and soaring hyperbolically over the past few centuries. I would suggest, in fact, that the two lines are intimately related: that energy has been captured so as to be expended, at least in part, in pursuit of psychotropy. There is not much here to comfort the paleoanthropologist. Yet the deep history remains essential to the story, since it is the only way to really understand why our brains operate the way they do. Our susceptibility to psychotropic mechanisms ultimately lies in the fact that we are social creatures. Over the course of our evolutionary history, we learned how to assess our status and our standing in the group through chemical clues, and we became dependent on those clues as markers of our self-esteem and our sense of belonging, both of which were vital to survival in the Paleolithic era and remain vital today.

@

Psychotropy comes in different forms: things we do that shape the moods of others; things we do to ourselves; things we ingest. Later in this chapter I shall begin to build some sort of taxonomy. But the taxonomy needs some material to work with, and to that end I would like to begin with a clarifying case study on dominance hierarchies and the stress that can be generated in the context of dominance.

When west Europeans first visited the hunter-gatherer communities of the Pacific Northwest, they remarked on the fact that every person, in villages consisting of hundreds of people, knew with arithmetic precision exactly where he or she ranked in the political hierarchy.[5] But if the precise quality of this ranking system was unusual, modern human societies commonly build and acknowledge dominance hierarchies. Sometimes these are formal and arithmetic, as is the case with the corporate and academic worlds, where hierarchies can be measured in terms of titles, salaries, even the square footage or location of office space. Sometimes they are informal but no less powerful, as in the case of adolescent societies in high schools. The study of dominance hierarchies offers especially fruitful insights for the prospects of a deep history, for two reasons. First, politics remain central to the narrative of general history, which still uses modern nation-states as the natural unit of general historical analysis and, in departments of history at the university level, as the natural unit for categorizing new hires. Second, a good deal of speculative work has been done on the political forms of Paleolithic societies, making it possible to engage in precisely the sorts of cross-time comparisons that justify a deep history using the Neolithic era as the fulcrum of the great transformation.

Dominance hierarchies are deeply rooted in our phylogeny. This much has been suggested by the centrality of precisely ranked dominance hierarchies among our closest relatives, chimpanzees, as reported by Frans de Waal and others.[6] A likely scenario is that our shared common ancestor, a primate who lived some five to seven million years ago, formed a society that was marked by dominance hierarchies. The deep evolutionary history of human dominance hierarchies is also suggested by the way that expressions of dominance and submission have been written into our brains and bodies. All of the social emotions associated with dominance hierarchies, such as anger, fear, contempt, disgust, pity, and embarrassment, are advertised by facial expressions that carry political undertones.[7] Most of this signaling is handled by the autonomic nervous system and takes place outside our conscious control. When facing a superior, one can try hard to prevent one's voice rising into a higher register and, with training, eventually learn how to do it on a consistent basis, but it is not easy.[8] The difficulty reminds us of this very salient point: the brain often likes to do its communicating all by itself, and it only grudgingly allows the mind a say in the process.[9] The fact that human dominance hierarchies are embedded in human neurophysiology suggests that dominance itself is deeply ingrained in several million years of human phylogeny. That dominance hierarchies have deep roots does not necessarily mean that *specific* relations of dominance and submission are hardwired—that women, for example, are naturally subordinate to men because their voices sometimes drift into higher registers while conversing with men. Male household servants can readily be taught to express submission in their faces and postures to their female masters. It is culture, not biology, that wires culturally specific relations of dominance to the neurophysiology by means of which both dominance and submission are felt and acknowledged. Given this lability, we cannot necessarily take current patterns of dominance and submission and project them into the deep past.

Moreover, we cannot assume that the neurophysiological capacity to structure society as a fixed dominance hierarchy is necessarily activated in any given society. In a fascinating argument much discussed in anthropological circles over the past decade or so, Christopher Boehm has argued that human societies in the Paleolithic era were marked by reverse dominance hierarchies—hierarchies in which the weak mastered the powerful by forming coalitions against anyone who threatened to rise to dominance.[10] If Boehm is right, then humans lived for hundreds of thousands of years without the dominance hierarchies that characterize chimpanzee societies. Then, with the agricultural revolution, a long-dormant neurophysiological capacity to recognize and acknowledge dominance hierarchies in human societies was turned back on. In the new environment of the Neolithic and Postlithic eras, devices evolved for accentuating the human neurophysiological capacity of subordinates to "feel" their submission. The actual feeling of submission, as a device for motivating the behavior of subordinates, is far more efficient than the mere knowledge of submission.

Practices that instill a capacity to feel submission can be found in primate societies. Studies of matriarchal baboon societies, for example, show that high-ranking female baboons routinely terrorize subordinate females.[11] As with chimpanzees, a key feature of this terrorism is that it is often random and unpredictable. Since they cannot predict abuse, subordinate females suffer very high levels of stress, which in turn reduces their fertility. This generates a clear biological advantage for the dominant females. Remarkably, subordinate females under stress are much more likely to give birth to males. Baboon groups are matriarchal, and rank is passed down the maternal line. Since baboon males leave their natal group after adolescence and join another group, they are clearly a better bet for subordinate females. The stress hormones that shape baboon society are present in human bodies and have similar though not identical outcomes. Postlithic societies saw an increase in the range or density of devices and mechanisms that generated stress hormones in the bodies of subordinates. Political elites could not have been aware of the precise physiological consequences of their actions and behaviors. Instead, political behaviors converged on these solutions because this is how power was most effectively maintained. One can imagine a given political culture generating a range of behavioral patterns. Those that proved more effective at generating stress hormones, in this ecology, would benefit the adaptive fitness of their practitioners.

This argument has occurred to others with more authority in the field than I can claim. "Agriculture," says the neurophysiologist Robert Sapolsky, "is a fairly recent human invention, and in many ways it was one of the great stupid moves of all time." Agriculture created storable surpluses, and that means a hierarchy based on poverty and wealth. "When humans invented poverty, they came up with a way of subjugating the low-ranking like nothing ever before seen in the primate world."[12] So the invention

of poverty was not, in fact, stupid at all. It was a crucial component in the making of dominance, in neutralizing tens of thousands of years of reverse dominance hierarchies. These are speculative observations, since they are manifestly untestable when
developed as hypotheses in historical contexts. Even so, further
neurophysiological research may well indicate certain areas
where it might be permissible to make certain extrapolations.

Historical sources do sometimes give meaningful clues that
can be read in the new light of neurohistory. When I first began
to read about random abuse in primate societies, for example, I
experienced a shock of recognition, because the authors were describing much the same kind of behavior practiced by castellans
in eleventh- and twelfth-century Europe.[13] Castellans were just
what the name implies: men who built or controlled castles and
surrounded themselves with bands of thugs, the proto-knights of
medieval Europe, for the purpose of terrorizing the peasantry
and extracting tribute from them. Vilified by the contemporary
press, which was largely controlled by monks who did not like
seeing their own serfs oppressed in this way, castellans have
earned a rather sorry though not wholly undeserved reputation.
Some of the stories told about them, such as those regarding the
infamous Thomas de Marle, who used to hang his captives by
their testicles until the weight of the body tore them off, might
even contain a grain of truth.[14] The sources are consistent, however, on the random and unpredictable nature of castellan abuse.

Much the same holds true for the violence committed by
Viking and Norman adventurers wherever they went. A famous
story recounted an incident in which an eleventh-century Norman leader, for no discernible reason, suddenly struck the horse
of a Byzantine Greek diplomat, knocking it senseless with a sin-

gle blow to the neck. With a civil apology, he gave the shaken man a new horse. Robert Bartlett, one of the modern interpreters of this story, describes it as an example of the "controlled use of the uncontrollable."[15] Given the sources at our disposal, we cannot measure the physiological effects of such behaviors today, though the horror attributed to the Byzantine diplomat is easy enough to understand. These kinds of behaviors, however, almost certainly generated powerful, measurable emotional responses. Constant repetition, in turn, could well have induced the formation of specific neural maps or sets of receptors. This much is suggested by modern studies of spousal abuse, which indicate how random abuse creates a psychological dependence on the part of the abused spouse.

The similarity in the patterns of behavior between male castellans, male chimpanzees, and female baboons raises the question of how we explain it. Someone might be tempted to posit a sort of racial memory, as if castellans and spouse abusers were and are controlled by the genes of their distant primate ancestors, genes that had been "turned off" during Boehm's intervening period of reverse dominance hierarchies. But genes do not usually act this way. It is more productive to explain the similarity of these behaviors as the product of convergent evolution. It is similarity of ecology, not relatedness, that often determines similarity of behavior.[16] In societies or relationships where certain conditions are met—where resources are scarce, power is distributed asymmetrically, and the ability to form coalitions is suppressed—alpha individuals manage to reinvent the pattern of random abuse because it is a psychotropic device toward which certain politically adaptive behaviors will converge. In Paleolithic ecologies, as Boehm argues, some of the key ingredients of dominance were missing, notably because power was relatively evenly distributed and because nothing hampered the formation of political coalitions: the Paleolithic counterpart to the public sphere as described by Jürgen Habermas.[17] The Neolithic revolution brought about a return to the ecology of ancestral primate societies, and, as a result, dominance hierarchies were reinvented, though in forms very different from the strictly competitive hierarchies of primate societies. The practice of random abuse, as a useful concomitant of dominance, was, and is, just one of many new psychotropic mechanisms that evolved to reinstill the feeling of dominance and submission among inferiors in Neo- and Postlithic human societies.

@

The case of political dominance hierarchies provides an example of the evolution of psychotropic mechanisms that affect the body states of other people, a key category in the taxonomy of psychotropy. Dominant female baboons and male castellans engage in types of behavior that, arguably, have effects on the moods and feelings of subordinate females and peasants alike. Let us describe these things as "teletropic," a category of psychotropy embracing the various devices used in human societies to create mood changes in other people—across space, as it were (hence "tele"). Teletropy itself is familiar enough in the world of biology. In some sheep pastures, for example, you can find a certain parasite, the lancet liver fluke (*Dicrocoelium dendriticum*), that spends part of its life cycle in ants.[18] Each infected ant harbors roughly fifty parasites, called cercariae, in its stomach. One of the cercariae crawls into the brain of the ant and releases chemicals that have an amazing effect on the ant's behavior. Zombie-like, the infected ant spends an inordinate amount of time on the tips of blades of grass, where it is more likely to be eaten by cattle or sheep, the parasite's definitive host. On some level this behavior is more interesting than that of the ichneumon wasp, which merely paralyzes its host and does not induce any behavioral changes. Both kinds of teletropic mechanisms are common enough in the zoological world. As Richard Dawkins has put it, "any nervous system can be subverted if treated in the right way."[19]

Among humans, this subversion can be done by means of ingested chemicals. In *Brave New World,* Aldous Huxley envisioned a world in which the government distributed soma, a psychotropic drug expressly designed to make people happy and content with their social roles.[20] We do much the same in less sinister ways. A good party host is advised to supply plenty of wine at the dinner table. An irresponsible friend might sneak marijuana into your brownie. A parent takes an ill-attuned child to a doctor and gets a prescription for Prozac; teenagers subsequently sell these pills to their friends taking the SAT exams. The most common teletropic devices, however, do not involve inserting chemical substances into the bodies of others. Instead, the category is largely composed of actions or behaviors that directly influence brain-body chemistry in others by altering the production or reuptake of neurotransmitters in their brains in ways that lie largely outside their voluntary control. These actions can be loosely subdivided into two types of teletropy: symbiotic and exploitative. Both prairie voles and humans practice symbiotic teletropy whenever they do things to their mates that stimulate the production of oxytocin, dopamine, and other chemical messengers and hence render them sexually receptive, a state that does not necessarily run against their own self-interest. Nursing infants stimulate oxytocin production in mothers. In lecturing about medieval European history, I try to amuse, shock, titillate, repulse, or goad my students at fairly regular intervals, since the only mood that is not conducive to remembering is boredom. In the European Middle Ages, teachers routinely beat their students, dimly aware that carefully measured doses of pain can be singularly effective as a memory-retention device. The other category of teletropy consists of mechanisms that appear rather more exploitative, such as those perfected by castellans, dominant female baboons, and advertisers. But although the categories of symbiotic and exploitative seem clear enough, in fact there can be some confusion between them.

Consider the example of liturgy and ritual. Religion has attracted a great deal of attention from cultural evolutionists precisely because religion poses a rather interesting test case. Both functionalist and exaptationist perspectives have been offered in the recent literature.[21] Lately, however, neurophysiologists armed with MRIs have also gotten into the game, using Tibetan monks to demonstrate how meditation produces measurable changes in brain activity. Though it would be difficult, using current technology, to extend this sort of study to church liturgies and other rituals, it is nonetheless easy to imagine that liturgies would tend to have similarly soothing consequences for many people in attendance. The mutual interests between believers and clergy appear to be distinctly symbiotic. Given the psychological benefits of the liturgy, it is easy to understand why many believers would choose to tithe themselves. Yet what appears symbiotic from one perspective will look very different from another. A Marxist, interpreting exactly the same evidence, would draw the conclusion that religious figures are little better than the lancet flukes and ichneumon wasps that hijack the neural pathways of other organisms, the better to exploit them.[22] In this model, the fact that the laity is made to feel good about being duped—we are speaking, after all, of the neurological counterpart to Marxist ideas regarding false consciousness—does not lessen the moral indefensibility of the practice: it might even make it worse. One person's symbiosis, clearly, is another person's exploitation. The psychotropic approach itself is neutral with respect to these sorts of interpretations.

The soothing consequences of religion, in fact, create a problem for the model I outlined earlier that associates stress with political subjugation. The problem is that rulers and their minions sponsor numerous liturgies, ceremonies, and spectacles that arguably *reduce* stress in subordinates. It is possible to be suspicious of the motives, insofar as these and other rituals are supported by the state or the ruler. In his *Discours sur la servitude volontaire,* Etienne de la Boétie (d. 1563) observed that "theatres, games, plays, spectacles, marvellous beasts, medals, *tableaux,* and other such drugs were for the people of Antiquity the allurements of serfdom, the price for their freedom, the tools of tyranny."[23] Numerous studies conducted by psychologists and physiologists in recent years show that La Boétie, in making this pronouncement, was not all that far off the mark. These sorts of spectacles can indeed have mood-altering consequences for those who observe them, and some of these mood-altering consequences, as La Boétie surmised, might well be linked to the exercise of tyranny or other forms of government. By calling them "drugs," La Boétie managed to anticipate the more explicit drug-dependent scenario evoked by Huxley.

Contemplating this system, one cannot help thinking about the behavior of one of the chimpanzees of the Gombe National Forest observed by Jane Goodall. On several occasions, Passion, abetted by her daughter Pom, snatched away and ate the babies of other mothers. The grisly meal complete, Passion then consoled the distressed mothers with hugs and pats.[24] The behavior looks positively pathological. As political behavior, however, it makes a great deal of sense: how better to build or maintain power than to create stress as well as offer the means to alleviate it? The lesson might not apply all that well to Passion, who was not a particularly high-ranking female and was probably just hungry. Even so, it is through behaviors like this that a psychological dependence on hierarchy can be created and enforced.

@

If teletropic mechanisms are those that influence the body chemistry of others, then their counterparts are the mechanisms that influence the body chemistry of the self, which we can call autotropic. One category consists of the chemicals or foods we ingest for their mind-bending effects. Alcohol is the most obvious of these autotropic chemicals and the most culturally widespread; opiates and other chemicals that alter cognitive patterns are not far behind. Many of them, the opiates included, are psychotropic in the usual sense of the word because they mimic or alter the effects of dopamine, serotonin, norepinephrine, and other chemical messengers. Others, like caffeine, sugar, tobacco, and chocolate, do not necessarily include chemical precursors of neurotransmitters but nonetheless influence the body in other ways, typically by causing a cascading set of changes that ultimately generates higher levels of dopamine in synapses, albeit temporarily. Chocolate, for example, is known to stimulate the body to produce its own dopamine, and capsaicin may do the same for serotonin.

A second category of autotropic mechanisms consists of the behaviors we practice that stimulate the production of our own chemical messengers. Long-distance runners can suffer withdrawal symptoms if they stop running, because their bodies are missing their daily dose of endorphins. A vast array of other leisure activities, including sports, music, novel-reading, movies, sex, and pornography, affect the body in similar ways. But rather than go over these obvious cases, let me introduce a subject that is a little less obvious: the practice of gossip. Gossip as a form of communication has been the subject of serious sociological and anthropological analysis since the 1960s. Historians have also gotten into the game, as have psychologists, literary scholars, political scientists, and even a mathematician.[25] But it is from primatology that some of the most interesting work has come lately, for it is through the work of Robin Dunbar that gossip has been unlinked from communication and tied, instead, to grooming.[26] Primate grooming is not simply a hygienic practice. It is also a device for creating, maintaining, and repairing social bonds. Grooming has this effect because it feels not unlike a backrub, stimulating the production of dopamine, oxytocin, and endorphins in the groomee. The key observation in Dunbar's complex and interesting model is that gossip, in human societies, plays exactly the same role that grooming does in primate societies. As early human groups grew larger and larger, the amount of grooming necessary to maintain a full array of social relations grew prohibitively expensive, so early humans switched to gossip, or at least that form of gossip consisting of meaningless social chatter whose only function is the mutual stimulation of peace-and-contentment hormones. Gossip, in this model, remains important as a medium of communication. The difference between Dunbar and others in the field of gossip studies is his assertion that it is not primarily words and their meanings that are communicated. What are communicated, instead, are chemical messengers.

Put this way, gossip looks more teletropic than autotropic. It certainly takes two to gossip, and people do it partly because they hope to build loyalties in other people, loyalties that might be measured in the form of oxytocin production. But the argument also makes it possible to view gossip as mildly addictive to those who practice it. It is the addictive nature of gossip, for example, that presumably explains the need that some people feel these days to talk by cell phone with family and friends at regular intervals, whenever their levels of serotonin or oxytocin have dipped to low levels and need turning up, the way a sound technician might adjust the treble on the sound board. At present, there has been little academic study of whether gossip has any addictive properties, though "gossip addiction" has become a category of folk psychology and seems vivid enough to those who experience it. So let us assume, for the sake of an argument, that gossip turns out to have the same mildly addictive properties as long-distance running. How might we historicize this observation?

We can begin with the general understanding that women gossip more than men—or, to put it more precisely, the kind of talk categorized as "gossip" has been gendered female. There may be deep physiological reasons for this: as Shelley Taylor has argued, women often respond to stress in a different way than do men, and a typical female response includes the production of oxytocin, the peace and bonding hormone. For Taylor, this forms a part of what she calls the "tend and befriend" response, the female counterpart to the stereotypically male "fight or flight" response.[27] We cannot actually know whether this response is rooted in human phylogeny or whether it is a product of the characteristics of gender dynamics in Postlithic societies. Regardless, it is striking how often women's gossip has been subjected to social and moral regulation in Postlithic societies.[28] There are many reasons why this is so, the most interesting of which derives from the very fact that gossip is like grooming: it serves to maintain or solidify social bonds and networks. It is easy to imagine why the powers that be might want to regulate *that*. But the mood-altering properties of gossip add another twist to the story. As I suggested earlier, alpha individuals in human and other primate societies routinely practice a range of behaviors that induce feelings of stress in subordinates. Since gossip, like grooming, is a practice that eases stress, the denigration of female gossip in human societies has the appearance of a cultural device for preventing the alleviation of stress among women, the better to control them in the manner described by Sapolsky. It is no part of this argument that the moral squads who police gossip in some human societies were, or are, aware of what they are doing. Instead, the denigration of gossip should be seen instead as something that has simply evolved through a process of blind variation and selective retention. In this way, gossip, repressed or not, joins a huge range of other mildly addictive practices that are so marked a feature of many Postlithic societies. These are precisely the practices that states, societies, and religious systems spend so much time and energy seeking to regulate. Christianity, for example, is remarkably consistent in its tendency to render as sin a range of autotropic practices—sex for fun, masturbation, gossip, alcohol. These autotropic mechanisms, in some sense, "compete" with the effects of certain Christian teletropic practices, such as liturgies, rituals, prayer, and confession. A dependence on the teletropic mechanisms of religion is fostered whenever people can be persuaded to shun their own autotropic devices for modulating body states.

In recent works of pop sociology, the poisonous consequences of gossip have figured in works that seek to diagnose the pathologies of teenage society.[29] I think gossip probably *is* poisonous in high schools, at least in some contexts, in part because teenagers are notoriously ill-equipped, from the neurobiological point of view, to handle the emotional spikes and dips of the typical teenage body and are, for that reason, much more prone to mood-altering behaviors of all sorts. It would be fanciful, of course, to imagine that the practice of gossip in high schools can be explained only by observing that a high percentage of teenagers are susceptible to its mildly addicting properties. Gossip is doing many other things in high schools. A deep historical perspective on such matters, however, helps in two ways. First, as Dunbar's model so clearly shows, it is impossible to understand the function of gossip in human societies without an appreciation of gossip's deep genealogical roots in human society. Second, the practice of gossip in high schools is an example of what can happen when the institutions generated by Postlithic societies interact with human neurophysiology in unpredictable ways. In the case of schooling, Western societies have been experimenting for nearly two centuries with the biologically unprecedented custom of socializing children in very narrow age-sets rather than the generational layers of a family-based society. We are only just beginning to realize the spectacularly pathological nature of this practice.

⊚

The examples of political dominance hierarchies and gossip are salient ones for this book because they offer suggestive ways for making the long millennia of the Paleolithic relevant to the Postlithic. But, as I argued in the previous chapter, neurohistory has a relevance beyond what it offers to deep history. From my remarks about the eighteenth century, it should already be clear that the progress of European civilization from the Middle Ages to modernity consists of a significant expansion in the range of autotropic mechanisms available on the market. Coffee, sugar, chocolate, and tobacco: all of these products have mildly addictive or mood-altering properties. All are African, Arabic, or New World products that first began circulating broadly in Europe in the seventeenth and eighteenth centuries. To these we can add alcohol, which, though hardly new to the "long eighteenth century" (ca. 1660–1820), nonetheless began to circulate more freely in the form of fortified wines and spirits. Peter Burke cites a famous passage from the German historian August Ludwig Schlözer (d. 1809), who asserted that "the discovery of spirits, the arrival of tobacco, sugar, coffee and tea in Europe have brought about revolutions just as great as, if not greater than, the defeat of the Invincible Armada, the wars of the Spanish Succession, the Paris Peace, etc."[30] Here we find a contemporary aware that his was the great century for the invention of an economy oriented, to a significant degree, around the production and circulation of addictive or alluring substances. To these one can add other characteristic products of the long eighteenth century that have psychotropic consequences, including novels and pornographic literature, as well as a new range of practices, such as consumption patterns, spectacularly gruesome executions, and even the gossip-enabling environment of salons and cafés, that can be seen as mood altering. In the world of neurohistory, the long eighteenth century, the century of the Enlightenment, has a peculiar distinction.[31]

The distribution and consumption of coffee in Europe is emblematic of the emerging psychotropic economy. Coffee, produced almost exclusively in what is now Yemen in the fourteenth through sixteenth centuries, was widely consumed throughout the Islamic world.[32] Among Europeans, the heathen association limited the appeal of coffee early on; it was treated as a curiosity or, at best, a medicine useful for treating gout, scurvy, and ailments of the eye. Only in the decades after 1660 did coffee take off as an item of luxury consumption; coffeehouses and cafés, the very heart of the emerging public sphere, sprouted up in cities and provincial towns throughout Europe.[33] London had thousands of coffeehouses by the early eighteenth century; by 1739, they outnumbered taverns. Valued as a stimulant to mind, body, conversation, and creativity, coffee was associated with the affluent and the leisured class, especially in France.[34] Imports to England and Wales soared after 1790 as "coffee became the alarm clock that marked industrial time."[35]

Seen from a social perspective, the consumption of coffee among the leisure and commercial classes was paralleled by that of gin and other spirits among the lower classes. In medieval Europe, alcohol was consumed across the social spectrum largely in the form of wine or beer. There was a limit to how much the European economy could afford to devote to alcohol, however, since the production of beer and wine necessarily reduced the amount of land available for food. Yet in the early modern era, the production of sugar on the slave plantations of the Caribbean and Brazil allowed for the distillation of rum, imports of which, to England at least, soared between 1720 and 1750. During the so-called gin craze of the mid-eighteenth century, cheap grain was converted into gin, which was consumed in vast quantities by the lower classes. In this way, the two status groups were each tightly associated with a single, mildly psychoactive commodity: the leisure class with caffeine, the lower classes with alcohol. By the very late eighteenth century in England, however, caffeine had made its way into the working-class diet in the form of sweetened tea. Tea imports to the British Isles, which had been steadily increasing over the eighteenth century, soared in the first decade of the nineteenth century as a result.

To these mildly psychoactive goods one can add many others, including tobacco, chocolate, chili pepper, opium, and nitrous oxide. But it is not through food or drugs alone that we engage in autotropy: one of the truly remarkable features of the eighteenth century is the way in which the emergence of autotropic commodities was mirrored by practices such as leisure reading. As Roger Chartier has described it, "travel accounts and descriptions of everyday life stressed the new universality of reading, present in all social circles under a variety of circumstances. A veritable 'reading mania,' also described as a 'reading fever' and a 'reading fury' (German texts refer to *Lesesucht, Lesefieber,* and *Lesewut*) took hold of the population."[36] Observers described this mania as a disease or epidemic, associating it with physical exhaustion, the rejection of reality, and bodily immobility. An imagination excited by reading could be readily drawn to other solitary practices, including masturbation. In England, observers thought that reading matter had a "remarkable power over body and mind alike."[37] Novels, which sprouted up like mushrooms during the eighteenth century, stand out for their druglike qualities. Observers commented on their addictive, page-turning quality and their ability to transform their readers.[38] As William Warner reports, "they were thought especially dangerous for young women, their minds unshielded by a classical education, who would grow addicted to the pleasures induced by novels, turn against serious reading, have their passions awakened, and form false expectations about life."[39] Young female readers were warned not to meddle with romances, novels, and chocolate, all of which were seen as likely to inflame the passions.[40]

Other kinds of literature proved to be equally captivating. Will Slauter has noted how the avid taste for following politics in newspapers was described by observers as a mania, a hot fever, or a malady comparable to tuberculosis.[41] Of particular significance is what Morgan Sonderegger has summarized for me as the "huge profusion of erotic literature in the eighteenth century" in many regions of western Europe:

> Erotic literature's rise was similar to other early modern cultural trends: it took off first in sixteenth-century Italy, then in seventeenth-century France, but largely spread throughout Europe, at first in translation, with the explosion of licit and illicit printing and reading over the eighteenth century. The market for erotic literature was vast, lucrative, and (until the mid-eighteenth century) relatively unregulated. Erotic literature, though potentially very explicit, was in large part textual. Demand was tremendous, both for straightforward erotic novels

and for other genres. Quasi-medical, semi-erotic texts dealt with nymphomania, onanism, the scourge of masturbation generally, homosexuality, and sexual techniques and health; these texts were part of a broader eighteenth-century craze for quasi-medical knowledge. Contemporary fears about reading, and reading erotica in particular, are strikingly similar to today's concerns about television: young and old getting hooked, reading becoming addictive, the first practice of a series of progressively more salacious pastimes. Erotica in particular epitomized the potential of reading to control the mind.[42]

Fears regarding the specter of this sort of mind control crop up frequently in the remarks of alarmed contemporaries. In view of the fact that states and rulers had long had an interest in the things and practices that alter the body chemistry of subjects and citizens, it is no surprise that eighteenth-century states soon got into the business of regulating this emerging market, in much the same way that coffeehouses and cafés came to be licensed by governments during the early eighteenth century.

As all these facts suggest, the long eighteenth century was the century of addiction. The century's psychotropic qualities are suggested by the very fact that the word *addiction* first developed its modern range of meanings in the late seventeenth century.[43] Earlier, the word had implied the state of being bound or indebted to a person—to a lord, for example, or perhaps to the devil. By the seventeenth century, the objects of addiction expanded to include feelings or pursuits. A key shift took place over the course of the seventeenth century as transitive and intransitive usages gave way to reflexive usages in all derivatives: "addiction" went from being an action performed by oneself or by others on oneself to being a self-inflicted action, not necessarily by one's own volition, such as "his genius addicted him to the study of antiquity" (1662). Addiction, which is the state of being (self-) addicted or given *to* a habit or pursuit, emerged as a noun by the third quarter of the seventeenth century; by 1675, for example, it was possible to say that someone had an addiction to books. Alcohol and tobacco were soon added to the list of addictive substances, with others not far behind. As Roy and Dorothy Porter have observed about Britain in the eighteenth century:

> There was, of course, nothing whatsoever new about people neglecting their well-being, drinking or eating themselves to death. What many thought was novel in the Georgian age was the growing tendency of people to *medicate* themselves into a decline or even death; or at least to consume a newly-available cornucopia of *soi-disant* stimulants and pain-killers to relieve their distempers, only to become habituated to their use, with the direst consequences. The century is seminal for both the perception, and the actuality, of addiction.[44]

Nitrous oxide and opium became the new recreational drugs. Like coffee, tea, and tobacco, these had once been used as medicines. But in the new consumer economy, the boundaries between medicinal and recreational uses were breaking down.[45]

All kinds of goods, not just psychotropic ones, were circulating on the markets of eighteenth-century Europe. Perhaps the growing presence of psychotropic commodities was merely a pendant to the expanding economy. But it may be possible to discern a deeper or more meaningful historical pattern. The long eighteenth century, after all, was the century of de-Christianization, of declining attendance at religious services and confession.[46] It is reasonable to suggest that the two go hand in hand: where individuals once relied on religion and ritual as sources of dopamine and other chemical messengers, they turned increasingly to items of consumption, giving up God in favor of mammon. It is possible to push the economic argument even further. Status anxiety of the sort suffered by many people in the twenty-first century induces more or less permanently high levels of stress hormones, as our sound board would reveal. If, as I suspect, the act of buying things helps stimulate the parasympathetic nervous system, cleansing the body of epinephrine and norepinephrine and inducing the production of neurotransmitters, like dopamine, that ease stress, then the demands of autotropy, the desires to alter one's own body chemistry, lie at the very heart of the modern consumer economy. Wherever this argument takes us, I think the point is that an awareness of neurochemistry can help us look at the past three hundred years in a wholly different light. A neurohistorical approach does not change the objects of study. What it offers is a new interpretive framework, where human neurophysiology is one of the environmental factors in macrohistorical change.

These sketchy observations on the situation in modern Europe and the United States are not meant to suggest that other eras did not have their own psychotropic mechanisms. Further study will not fail to illustrate how every Postlithic society has a characteristic psychotropic profile. The whole point about Europe's long eighteenth century is that Europeans picked up psychotropic devices that had circulated in other societies for some time: coffee in the Muslim world; tea and opium in East and South Asia; chili pepper, chocolate, and tobacco in the New World. The pre-Columbian cultures of Mesoamerica, for example, had consumed chocolate for millennia as a stimulant, intoxicant, hallucinogen, and aphrodisiac, often in the form of a paste or a drink.[47] Europe, returning the favor, exported alcohol, Christianity, and other psychotropic goods and practices. Modernity was created when formerly isolated psychotropic mechanisms fell together into a new framework. Much was changed in the process. In modern societies, for example, psychotropic profiles have ceased to be associated with world geographic regions and have become linked instead to class or status identities. This pattern is particularly obvious in the case of the seriously psychoactive drugs like Ecstasy, marijuana, methamphetamine, crack cocaine, and alcohol in its various forms, all of which bespeak powerful class identities, at least in the United States.

By way of offering a grand narrative, it may be possible some day to argue that European societies, between the twelfth and the nineteenth centuries, witnessed a tectonic shift away from teletropic mechanisms manipulated by ruling elites toward a new order in which the teletropies of dominance were replaced by the growing range of autotropic mechanisms available on an increasingly unregulated market. (The rise of the fascist regimes of the twentieth century might well pose a challenge to the simple teleology of this model, reminding us that history is always complex and never linear.) Seen this way, the importance of autotropy to the modern economy and modern society has only been accelerating since the eighteenth century. In this metanarrative, the psychotropic mechanisms that Europeans encountered during Europe's colonial phase acted as the solvent of an old regime. This, as phrased, is unfashionably Eurocentric, but this Eurocentrism reflects my own limitations as a historian and not, I think, the limitations of the model. I welcome every and any effort to translate a neurohistorical paradigm into all corners of world history.

@

From the perspective of neurohistory, the progress of civilization is an illusion of psychotropy. This argument is a deliberate rejoinder to other models of general or universal history that seek to offer explanations for history's apparent direction. Sacred historians saw the unfolding of God's plan. Casual use of the metaphor of the seed in the Western Civ perspective of the twentieth century suggests a similar kind of ontogeny, guided by some internal logic that crystallized in a given epoch and has governed the growth of an institution or a whole society ever since. Still other schemes, too well known to merit much discussion here, offer mechanistic descriptions of progress or change. A neurohistorical model offers an equally grand explanatory paradigm, proposing that some of the direction we detect in recent history has been created by ongoing experiments with new psychotropic mechanisms that themselves evolved against the evolutionary backdrop of human neurophysiology. The Neolithic revolution between 10,000 and 5,000 years ago transformed human ecology and led to fundamental and irreversible changes in demographics, politics, society, and economies. In this changing ecology, new mechanisms for modulating body states emerged through processes of undirected cultural evolution. In recent centuries, the range of psychotropic mechanisms has expanded considerably, giving modernity its characteristically different "feel," and growing sources of energy have been harnessed ever more tightly to an economy that is geared toward psychotropy. Psychotropic mechanisms, once invented, do not necessarily remain fixed in a culture. Some, like gruesome public executions, may have become moribund. Others do manage a certain longevity. It is doubtful that pornography and alcohol will go away in the near future, even if new fashions like virtual sex and Ecstasy might arise and take over some of the market. The one caveat here may lie in our current cultural crisis: the growing homogenization of global society. The universality of basic human physiology may mean that all humans, ultimately, will be tempted by the same package of sensory inputs and body stimulations, and that the capitalistic marketplace, evolving as it does in Darwinian fashion toward optimal solutions, will eventually hit on the perfect package of psychotropic products and mechanisms. This, not freedom, is what Francis Fukuyama should have called "the end of history."[48] For my part, I doubt there is much to worry about. The system is built on an unsustainable demand for energy, meaning that the simple fact of entropy will preserve us from "the end of history." Beyond that, we grow numb to the mechanisms that stimulate our moods and feelings on a daily basis, a neurochemical insensitivity that may help explain why one decade's excitement is another decade's boredom. Psychotropy, I suspect, induces ceaseless change.

To acknowledge the role of psychotropic mechanisms in the development of human societies is to see that what passes for progress in human civilization is often nothing more than new developments in the art of changing body chemistry. The legacy of neo-Lamarckism encourages us to think about and teach history as a progression of increasingly clever ideas that build on one another in a crescendo of civilizational achievement. The clever ideas may lead to good things, like medicine, security, and the emancipation of women. Or they can lead to bad things, like genocide, fascism, and environmental degradation. I do not necessarily want to discard all features of this explanation for historical transformation. But the evolution of psychotropic mechanisms has had a big impact on the shape and nature of human cultural evolution. And because this evolution was and is undirected, many aspects of history itself can be seen as random and undirected. We are being swept along by the things that have arisen as our physiologies have interacted in unpredictable ways with the new ecology forged by our Neolithic ancestors.

Looking Ahead

Around 1.7 million years ago, an early member of our genus, *Homo,* emerged in East Africa in the form of *Homo ergaster.* For all intents and purposes, ergasters were of much the same height and weight as modern humans, and if their braincases were slightly smaller it was not by much, for the upper end of the ergaster range, around 1,100 cubic centimeters, nearly touched the lower end of the modern range, beginning around 1,200 cubic centimeters. The men and women were closer in size, unlike australopiths, among whom males could be as much as half again as large as the females. Other ergaster anatomical features— pelvis, jaw, length of limb—lie close to the modern range. But these are soulless concepts and cannot convey the shock of recognition that many people experience when, for the first time, they come face-to-face with an artist's reconstruction of an ergaster face. Take an ergaster couple, dress them appropriately, and plop them down on a busy Manhattan street: they would earn some stares but many New Yorkers would hurry by without noticing. Lawyers would feel comfortable defending them in a court of law. Judges would not deny them standing. You could not put ergasters in a zoo without cries of outrage, and if they chose to have sex in public you would feel shocked or embarrassed rather than giggly. The same would not be true for an australopith harem. I think it is likely that we would feel more discomfort about caging australopiths than we seem to feel about caging chimpanzees, but, even so, I suspect that australopiths lie on the other side of the frontiers of empathy.

The humanity of ergasters does not lie in their features alone. From subtle morphological clues, paleoanthropologists are able to read off, with some confidence, a number of behavioral insights that indicate a nearly "modern" lifestyle. The arms, legs, and big toe all tell us that they lived on the ground. With the terrestrial lifestyle came a considerably greater risk of predation, and the need for defense against predation may have pushed up ergaster group size, creating even greater pressures to cooperate. The shortened gut, the smaller teeth, and the diminished sagittal crest indicate a rich diet consisting of food that has been predigested through the use of biface choppers and other tools that pound and cut—and possibly even fire, as has been argued lately. The large braincase coupled with the relatively small female pelvis indicate a long period of infant dependency, which in turn required greater maternal and, maybe, paternal investment. The latter possibility is significant: some paleoanthropologists, as they read ergaster morphology, find the first indicators for some degree of pair-bonding. Those who argue in favor of pair-bonding are emboldened by the fact that ergaster women and men were nearly of equal size, within the same range as modern humans. Significant size difference between males and females is characteristic of animal species, including chimpanzees and gorillas, where females copulate with dominant males. In such species, females do all the nurturing anyway; from their point of view, there is no reason not to go for the best. Ergaster women, in contrast, may have needed the extra calories that dedicated mates could provide, and this may have encouraged them to pair off. Features of the bodies of modern women, such as hidden ovulation and menstrual synchrony, have been read for clues that they, too, represent adaptive responses to the need for pair-bonding in early human societies. If so, it is likely that these patterns evolved with ergaster women and not earlier.

The history of the next 1.6 million years is one of a slow elaboration of tool kits, incremental increases in brain size, the continuing flattening of the face and jaw, the gradual descent of the voice box, and other changes besides. But it is, much more vividly, a history of spectacular expansions out of Africa. Somewhat more than a million years ago—the date remains controversial—a few ergasters left Africa and headed east across Asia and north into the unglaciated mountains and steppes of central Asia. Outside of Africa they have become known to paleoanthropologists as *Homo erectus,* though the two species now seem to be one and the same. Erectus survived outside of Africa until 100,000 years ago—and possibly even later than that, if *Homo floresiensis,* the hobbit-people of an isolated Indonesian island, turn out to be descendants of erectus. A second major diaspora may have taken place around 600,000 years ago, resulting in a branch of the hominin bush that died out with the Neanderthals, who went extinct 30,000 to 40,000 years ago. All these dates will become clearer over time. In the meantime, fully modern humans evolved in Africa around 140,000 years ago. It was these people, *Homo sapiens sapiens,* who undertook a third major diaspora, leaving Africa some 85,000 to 50,000 years ago and settling the

Near East, Asia, Australia, Europe, and the Americas in a breathtaking expansion that arguably was not complete until the last of the Pacific islands were settled within the past 1,000 years. All non-African peoples are descended from this diaspora. It remains to be seen whether modern humans will survive out of Africa for as long as erectus. One thing is for sure: *Homo* is a determined colonizer. And it was Africa that was both the cradle of humanity and the source of these waves of colonization. This is worth pondering. Only the final diaspora of *H. sapiens sapiens* resulted in a hominin branch that, for the time being, has managed to survive and flourish in a non-African environment. Until then, Eurasia, for humans, was an evolutionary dead end. It was Africa, not Europe, that generated what nineteenth-century social theorists would have called the "progressive race."

As they slowly filled the world, humans spread apart, like iron filings bearing the same electromagnetic charge. As a result of this disinclination to live cheek by jowl with other groups, we infiltrated every habitable ecosystem. The history of the settlement of the non-African world is a history wherein all available niches were gradually filled up. I think about this historical legacy as I contemplate the internal colonization of medieval Europe, a process that came to an end by A.D. 1300. The settlements made in the marshes of Poland and up the hillsides of the Alps were the last fingers of a rising tide that swept out of Africa, then more slowly inundated the nooks and crannies of the world. Local cultures throughout the world underwent constant cultural microevolution, fine-tuning themselves for local environments. Jared Diamond describes how the original settlers of the Chatham islands, a lonely group of limestone atolls far east of New Zealand, lost both agriculture and their tool kit because the environment of the Chathams could sustain neither agriculture nor stone tools.[1] This is but one example suggesting that, however durable and autonomous culture may be, the environment nonetheless shapes cultural drift, at least when it is given enough time to do so. Culture also allowed humans to adapt to the widely different environments our ancestors faced in new ecosystems. Yet it is important not to underestimate the morphological changes that took place as human populations adapted to different cultural niches. The most notable of these is the loss of dark skin among peoples who moved to the far north, where lighter skin may have evolved because of the need to metabolize vitamin D more efficiently from a sun that shone less often on the skin. The limits of culture can be read off the morphological features that distinguish one human subpopulation from another. Inuits are masters in the art of turning furs and skins into warm clothes, but that cultural skill did not prevent Inuit populations, over the millennia, from developing a smaller and more robust stature that minimized the surface area susceptible to cooling.

In the midst of the drama of the past 50,000 years, our ancestors witnessed an array of environmental spectacles and transformations, not the least of which was a volatile climate that has become so vivid a part of everyday news in the early twenty-first century. According to one recently proposed theory, our ancestors suffered greatly in the aftermath of the eruption of Mt. Toba around 70,000 years ago, a cataclysmic event causing abrupt climatic cooling that killed off all but a few thousand people, resulting in a population bottleneck still visible in the written record of DNA.[2] One can only imagine the mile-high wall of ice at the glacial edge—ever expanding, ever shrinking—that the earliest

Europeans saw on the horizon at the moment of first contact, a wall that has now disappeared, though it will surely come again. The end of the most recent phase of glaciation, starting some 18,000 years ago, caused flooding in low-lying coastal areas, some of it gradual and perhaps unnoticeable, but some of it surely spectacular, such as the flooding of the Black Sea around 6,000 years ago, well into the Neolithic era, well within the limits of human memory. Other events of similar magnitude, the natural counterparts to the wars and epidemics that historians like to relate in introductory surveys, will come to light as the archeological, geological, and genetic evidence accumulates. All of these events provide historians with some of the signposts around which historical narratives can coalesce, though they are not, of course, everything we need to write and teach a deep history.

In the same way that we can read behavioral clues off ergaster morphology, it is possible to propose hypotheses about patterns of human behavior and human culture during the age of the great African diaspora. The reconstructions require careful triangulations between all the available and relevant evidence: morphological, archeological, ethological, molecular, and linguistic. A great deal of evidence, ranging from artistic patterns to the shape of the palate and the position of the voice box, now points to the idea of a creative explosion around the same time as the final African diaspora. Since both African and non-African populations share the capacity for symbolic thought, it seems likely that the creative explosion took place before the final diaspora and in some sense propelled it. Through similar acts of creative reconstruction, students of the Paleolithic have been able to make proposals about topics discussed in the last chapter and a great many others besides.

These reconstructions sometimes depend on the assumption that the behavior of modern hunter-gatherers can provide clues about ancestral behaviors. By observing the behavior of African foragers, for example, it has been possible to estimate that women carry their children, on average, for about 4,000 miles from birth to weaning. This figure has been proposed as a ballpark estimate for the distance a woman would have carried her child, say, 100,000 years ago. The estimate is important because it suggests something about the caloric expenditure of ancestral women, which in turn fits into a pattern of birth-spacing intervals and provisioning that are, in their own right, important features of ancestral societies and economies. These kinds of comparisons can seem both offensive and blind to the reality that there is no foraging population that is untouched, in some way, by the events of the past 5,000 years. There is a something to be said for this resistance, and, if nothing else, it invites a certain caution. Ultimately, however, I do not have a problem with cautious comparisons. Those who reject the possibility out of hand maintain a rigid boundary between the Paleolithic and the Postlithic, denying thereby the validity of any cross-time comparison and abetting the idea of the special creation of man.

These reconstructions cannot be used to create a verbal diorama of an ur-society from which everything subsequently diverges, for it is now quite clear that there never was, and never could be, an ur-society. Even among baboons there is not a "normal" social pattern; we now know that baboon societies vary subtly from location to location: here a kind of matriarchalism created by female coalitions, there patterns of male dominance and abuse. Among humans, every society is likewise molded both by environmental circumstances and by particular cultural patterns.

We can, at best, speak of patterns or tendencies, such as a tendency toward pair-bonding mitigated, to greater or lesser degrees, by patterns of systematic infidelity. It is just like the history, say, of the medieval peasantry, or patterns of lordship, or any other topic that has been framed by historians in recent decades. Collectively, what these reconstructions can be made to reveal is a Paleolithic society with an economy based largely on a single commodity—the calorie—and a system of credit and debt built around memory and enforced by a range of social emotions, including anger and shame. They reveal a society with a political order, patterns of law, family structures, religion, coercive force, and, yes, culture and art. These are the convenient analytic divisions of academic discourse. They are no more real or valid when applied to Paleolithic societies than they are when applied to Postlithic society. Comparison cannot take place without broad categories, so to deny the utility of such categories is to deny that there is much point to writing a deep history. For any deep history to succeed, the use of such categories is a necessary evil.

At one point it was said that humans invented agriculture—that humans became aware of the misery of their uncertain, nomadic existence and came to realize the benefits of a stable food source. Nowadays, some paleoanthropologists are more inclined to say that humans were pushed into agriculture, kicking and screaming, as declining populations of large animals created starvation conditions that could be alleviated only by the growing of food. For who, as Marshall Sahlins once asked, would give up the rich and varied diet and the twenty-hour workweek of the average hunter-gatherer and voluntarily yoke himself or herself to the backbreaking workload and the increasingly impoverished diet of the average agriculturalist?[3] Who would voluntarily consume bread made from grain ground in a stone mortar, producing flour laced with hard particles that erode the dentine, causing painful tooth decay? Who would willingly yoke themselves to a food source so fickle, so dependent on climate, so prone to failure? The misery of agricultural society is hidden in conventional historical sources, which were created by, and typically portray, the easy lifestyle enjoyed by a tiny percentage of the population of agricultural communities and kingdoms. Joan Kelly once asked whether women ever had a Renaissance.[4] In much the same vein, we can ask whether the vast majority of people in ancient and middle societies ever had a civilization.

The shift to agriculture and sedentism had enormous if entirely unplanned implications for human societies. Of these, some of the most significant involve patterns of reproduction. Clay and, later, metal pots suitable for cooking gruel allowed women to wean their babies at a younger age. Sedentism limited women's exercise. Both factors conspired to increase fertility, creating the conditions for rapid population growth. Shorter birth-spacing intervals contributed to the creation or intensification of sibling rivalry. Shifting patterns in the sexual division of labor meant that women, major producers of calories in the Paleolithic economy, lost much of their productive capacity and invested increasing amounts of their own energy instead in reproduction. The reemergence of political dominance hierarchies meant that, in early Postlithic societies, marriage patterns could shift away from partial Paleolithic monogamy to Postlithic polygyny and hypergamy. Women came to serve as markers of men's status, and—depending on the society we are speaking of—their clothing, jewelry, and education served to reflect male status. Even their bodies were marked and bound and sometimes even burned as a reflection of the role that women came to play in the making of male dominance hierarchies.

Some of the eeriest features of Postlithic human society are the products of convergent evolution. Within biology, convergent evolution is a process whereby wholly distinct species independently arrive at the same morphological or physiological solution to a problem or an opportunity presented by their environment. The process can also operate in human culture. Agriculture was independently invented on different continents, as were writing, pottery, royal cults, priestly castes, embalming, astronomy, earrings, coinage, and holy virginity. This list could go on for pages. Diffusion cannot explain these convergences. Watching pyramids sprout up in Egypt and Mesoamerica is like contemplating the emergence of a saber-toothed cat in both marsupial and placental lineages, separated though they were by large oceans and hundreds of millions of years of biological evolution. We celebrate the diversity of human civilizations, but it is the similarities that are the most startling, the thing that continually reminds us of our common humanity.

The emerging societies around the globe were like nothing seen in the Paleolithic era. Although early villages and towns were no bigger or more complex than some late Paleolithic settlements, the cities and empires were unprecedented. And with them came a whole new set of living conditions and a society and economy organized in a fundamental way, as I have argued, around the production, use, and delivery of psychotropic mechanisms. On the one hand, the Postlithic era sustained a sociopolitical order that swayed, cowed, awed, and soothed through political and religious liturgies, spectacles of joy and of suffering, patterns of abuse, monumental architecture, and other devices that played off the subvertibility of the human nervous system. Such systems were essential for the creation of imagined communities. On the other hand, the Postlithic economy also began to deliver goods and devices used by individuals to influence their own body states. Some of these practices and mechanisms constitute highly exaggerated forms of mechanisms that existed in Paleolithic societies. These same mechanisms exist in our own societies: facial expressions, somatic reactions, body postures and gestures, tones of voice, grooming, sex—the list goes on. All of these forms of expression make known such things as patterns of dominance and control, feelings of sympathy and altruism, states of insecurity and confidence. They are felt in the body by means of chemical messengers. Civilizations did not, could not, invent new forms of body chemistry. Instead, civilizations found new devices for exaggerating existing neurochemical states. Persisting patterns could even embed themselves in our synapses, where they underlay relatively durable behavioral forms that have the look and feel of being "biological" without being genetic. None of these patterns was permanent; all were susceptible to the winds of fashion and other unpredictable transformations. We know far too little about how the mind works to understand, yet, how this history might be told. But we know enough to appreciate how each society might be seen as having its own psychotropic profile.

Which brings us, finally, to the prospects for a deep history. From the expansion of the chronology in the 1860s, the time appropriate to history, among Western historians, has been gradually shrinking. It can be a struggle to convince students and readers of the relevance of the premodern. We can strive to rebuild the relevance and interest of the middle and deep pasts in numerous ways. I have mentioned the study of human diseases and human interactions with the environment as compelling devices for building a long historical narrative. The lessons of human population genetics have an intrinsic fascination. To these I have suggested, in this book, that we add a neurohistorical perspective, with sets of tools and concepts that allow us to think about the historical implications of recent developments in neuroscience and human biology. This history is necessarily a deep one, since the genes responsible for building the autonomic nervous system are themselves of considerable antiquity. This history is also a world history, since the equipment is shared by all humans, though it is built, manipulated, and tweaked in different ways by different cultures. Finally, it is a history to which many of us can connect. We will always want to know where our nations and economies and religions came from. We want to know the origins of both human rights and intolerance. We want to follow the histories of women and men and their patterns of sexuality. But we also want to understand why our brains and bodies work the way they do. *That* understanding is impossible without history. Imagine writing a sociology of race relations in a modern city without having some sense of historical patterns. That is more or less what we do when we think about brain, body, and behavior without any sense of historical perspective, without any sense that the workings of the brain are partly dependent on what culture, a product of historical trends, has put there. Without history, we are tempted to overemphasize genes at the expense of gene-culture coevolution, inclined to overlook cultural variations in genetic expression. By bringing the neurophysiology into history, we also bring history to neurophysiology. Although this book has urged historians to think with deep time, it has also urged scientists to think with history. The new science of the brain cannot make sense without history.

Like everything associated with Darwin's dangerous idea, the history that might ultimately emerge from the things I have proposed in this book is unsettling. Yet I think there is grandeur in this view of history. It is the grandeur that the deep time of human history shares with the walls of the Grand Canyon, where the sheer immensity of time is laid out for the wonder of all. We need not dig only in the dusty topsoil of the strata that form the history of humanity. The deep past is also our present and future.

NOTES

INTRODUCTION: TOWARD REUNION IN HISTORY

1. Stephen Jay Gould, *Time's Arrow, Time's Cycle: Myth and Metaphor in the Discovery of Geological Time* (Cambridge, Mass., 1987), 1. See also Stephen Toulmin and June Goodfield, *The Discovery of Time* (New York, 1965).

2. The first edition of William H. McNeill's *The Rise of the West: A History of the Human Community* (Chicago, 1963) devoted eight pages to the Paleolithic. William J. Duiker and Jackson J. Spielvogel cover prehistory in two pages of their *World History: Comprehensive Volume,* 3rd ed. (Belmont, Calif., 2001). A more trade-oriented title, J. R. McNeill and William McNeill's *The Human Web: A Bird's-Eye View of World History* (New York, 2003), covers the Paleolithic in sixteen pages, though their "web" model offers an intriguing device for joining the Paleolithic to the later periods. Michael Cook's general history, *A Brief History of the Human Race* (New York, 2003), suggests that the Paleolithic does not count as history in part because there are no documents from the period that allow us to "study past humans on the basis of what they had to *say* for themselves" (5). The major exception to this general oversight of early human history can be found in David Christian, *Maps of Time: An Introduction to Big History* (Berkeley, 2004).

3. Mott T. Greene, *Natural Knowledge in Preclassical Antiquity* (Baltimore, 1992), 3.

4. I am indebted to Bruce Holsinger for this observation.

5. Ernst Breisach, *Historiography: Ancient, Medieval and Modern,* 2nd ed. (Chicago, 1994), 3.

6. William H. McNeill, *The Human Condition: An Ecological and Historical View* (Princeton, 1980), 5–6; Jared Diamond, *Guns, Germs, and Steel: The Fates of Human Societies* (New York, 1997).

7. James Harvey Robinson, *The New History: Essays Illustrating the Modern Historical Outlook* (New York, 1912), 97, 106.

8. Michael L. Fitzhugh and William H. Leckie, Jr., "Agency, Postmodernism and the Causes of Change," *History and Theory* 40 (2001): 58–81.

9. Clifford Geertz, *The Interpretation of Cultures: Selected Essays* (New York, 1973), 68.

10. Martin Bernal, *Black Athena: The Afroasiatic Roots of Classical Civilization* (New Brunswick, N.J., 1987).

11. Glyn E. Daniel, *The Idea of Prehistory* (London, 1962), 134.

ONE. THE GRIP OF SACRED HISTORY

1. Herbert Butterfield, *Man on His Past: The Study of the History of Historical Scholarship* (Cambridge, Engl., 1955), 103.

2. John A. Garraty and Peter Gay, eds., *The Columbia History of the World* (New York, 1972), 49.

3. John L. Stipp et al., *The Rise and Development of Western Civilization,* vol. 1 (New York, 1967), 41.

4. Samuel Noah Kramer, *History Begins at Sumer* (Garden City, N.Y., 1959).

5. Sir Walter Ralegh, *The History of the World in Five Books* (London, 1687); Jacques Bénigne Bossuet, *An Universal History: From the Beginning of the World to the Empire of Charlemagne,* 13th ed., trans. James Elphinston ([1681] Dublin, 1785).

6. Jean Bodin, *Method for the Easy Comprehension of History,* trans. Beatrice Reynolds (New York, 1966), 298. See also Robert Nisbet, *History of the Idea of Progress* (New York, 1980).

7. In general, see Margaret T. Hodgen, *Early Anthropology in the Sixteenth and Seventeenth Centuries* (Philadelphia, 1964).

8. Peter J. Bowler, *The Invention of Progress: The Victorians and the Past* (Oxford, 1989), 76.

9. Jean-Antoine-Nicolas de Caritat, marquis de Condorcet, *Sketch for a Historical Picture of the Progress of the Human Mind*, trans. June Barraclough (New York, 1955); Anne-Robert-Jacques, baron de Turgot, *Turgot on Progress, Sociology and Economics,* trans. and ed. Ronald Meek (Cambridge, Engl., 1973), 42, 65.

10. Adam Ferguson, *An Essay on the History of Civil Society,* ed. Fania Oz-Salzberger (Cambridge, Engl., 1995), 74.

11. Turgot, *Turgot on Progress,* 42.

12. See, most recently, Norman Cohn, *Noah's Flood: The Genesis Story in Western Thought* (New Haven, Conn., 1996).

13. Cited in Donald K. Grayson, *The Establishment of Human Antiquity* (New York, 1983), 12–13.

14. Ferguson, *Essay,* 74.

15. Bossuet, *Universal History,* 8–10.

16. See, e.g., Sharon Turner, *The History of the Anglo-Saxons from the Earliest Period to the Norman Conquest,* vol. 1 ([1799–1805] Philadelphia, 1841), 27–28, and David Ramsay, *Universal History Americanised; or, an Historical View of the World, from the Earliest Records to the Year 1808* (Philadelphia, 1819), 9–22. See also Charles Coulston Gillispie, *Genesis and Geology: A Study in the Relations of Scientific Thought, Natural Theology and Social Opinion in Great Britain, 1790–1850* (New York, 1951), and George W. Stocking, Jr., *Victorian Anthropology* (New York, 1987), 33–34, 43.

17. Giambattista Vico, *New Science,* 3rd ed., trans. David Marsh (London, 1999).

18. This particular trend had been under way since the fifteenth or sixteenth century; see Ernst Breisach, *Historiography: Ancient, Medieval and Modern,* 2nd ed. (Chicago, 1994), 171–85.

19. For the single bland reference to the flood in the pages where Bodin dismantles the myth of a Golden Age, see *Method,* 298.

20. Vico, *New Science,* 33, 143. The historical neglect of the significance of the Deluge in eighteenth-century society is reflected in the index to the Penguin edition, which contains no entry for the Deluge or the Universal Flood, though see the discussion of the Deluge in Anthony Grafton's introduction, xviii–xix.

21. What follows relies on Paolo Rossi, *The Dark Abyss of Time: The History of the Earth and the History of Nations from Hooke to Vico,* trans. Lydia G. Cochrane (Chicago, 1984).

22. Rossi, *Dark Abyss,* 144.

23. Breisach, *Historiography,* 10, 69–70, 81–82.

24. Rossi, *Dark Abyss,* 136, 140.

25. Bodin, *Method,* 303–33.

26. The leading figure here was Nicholas Steno, most recently discussed in Alan Cutler, *The Seashell on the Mountaintop: A Story of Science, Sainthood, and the Humble Genius Who Discovered a New History of the Earth* (New York, 2003).

27. Rossi, *Dark Abyss,* 109.

28. Claude Albritton, *The Abyss of Time: Changing Conceptions of the Earth's Antiquity after the Sixteenth Century* (San Francisco, 1980), 85; Grayson, *Establishment,* 31–35.

29. Albritton, *Abyss,* 73.

30. Hutton's argument that granite was volcanic in origin and hence massive evidence for the earth's ability to remake itself was challenged by the most prominent geologist of his day, Abraham Werner, who claimed a sedimentary origin that happened to be consistent with the Deluge. Those who resisted the idea of deep time, like Werner, were motivated by prudent empirical caution, not blind Christian dogmatism. Hutton himself was profoundly religious; the only difference was that he believed in a Cartesian God who created the earth and, in His wisdom, endowed it with a set of mechanical laws that ensured its continual re-creation, thus negating any need for future intervention. See Mott T. Greene, *Geology in the Nineteenth Century: Changing Views of a Changing World* (Ithaca, N.Y., 1982), 19–45, and Rossi, *Dark Abyss,* 113–18.

31. Charles Lyell, *Principles of Geology*, 3 vols. (London, 1830–33; reprint Chicago, 1990–91); Joe D. Burchfield, *Lord Kelvin and the Age of the Earth* (London, 1975).

32. Among the many studies of the history of paleoanthropology, see Grayson, *Establishment*, and A. Bowdoin van Riper, *Men among the Mammoths: Victorian Science and the Discovery of Human Prehistory* (Chicago, 1993).

33. Thomas R. Trautmann, *Lewis Henry Morgan and the Invention of Kinship* (Berkeley, 1987), esp. 32–35, 205–30.

34. Ibid., 213.

35. Charles Darwin, *On the Origin of Species* (London, 1859; reprint Cambridge, Mass., 1964); Charles Lyell, *The Geological Evidences of the Antiquity of Man, with Remarks on Theories of the Origin of Species by Variation* (London, 1863); John Lubbock, *Pre-Historic Times, as Illustrated by Ancient Remains, and the Manners and Customs of Modern Savages*, 2nd ed. (New York, 1872).

36. James Harvey Robinson, *The New History: Essays Illustrating the Modern Historical Outlook* (New York, 1912), 26. Later in the same work, he continued: "Fifty years ago it was generally believed that we knew something about man from the very beginning. Of his abrupt appearance on the freshly created earth and his early conduct, there appeared to be a brief but exceptionally authoritative account. To-day we are beginning to recognize the immense antiquity of man" (55). On Robinson, see Daniel A. Segal, "'Western Civ' and the Staging of History in American Higher Education," *American Historical Review* 105 (2000): 771–79.

37. For a useful survey of the important general histories of this period, see Charles Kendall Adams, *A Manual of Historical Literature* (New York, 1882), 31–41.

38. Royal Robbins, *Outlines of Ancient and Modern History on a New Plan* (Hartford, Conn., 1875).

39. Reuben Parsons, *Universal History: An Explanatory Narrative,* vol. 1, *Ancient History from the Creation of Man until the Fall of the Roman Empire* (Yonkers, N.Y., 1902). Resistance persisted in Christian educa-

tional circles for several decades to come; see, e.g., Albert Hyma, *World History: A Christian Interpretation,* rev. ed. (Grand Rapids, Mich., 1947).

40. See Doris Goldstein, "Confronting Time: The Oxford School of History and the Non-Darwinian Revolution," *Storia della Storiografia* 45 (2004): 3–27.

41. Amos Dean, *The History of Civilization,* 7 vols. (Albany, N.Y., 1868), 1: 47, 51.

42. Segal, "Western Civ," 774–75.

43. For a very early example of a general history that notes the possibility of deep time in a footnote, see Richard Green Parker, *Outlines of General History* (New York, 1848), 9.

44. George Park Fisher, *Outlines of Universal History, Designed as a Text-Book and for Private Reading* (New York, 1885), 13–14.

45. Victor Duruy, *General History of the World*, rev. ed. (New York, 1925). Duruy's *Histoire Générale* was first published in France in 1883. It was translated for the U.S. market in 1898 and went through several editions until 1929.

46. Cesare Cantù, *Storia Universale,* 10th ed. (Turin, 1884).

47. Ferguson, *Essay,* 75.

48. Edward Gibbon, *The Decline and Fall of the Roman Empire,* abridged by D. M. Low (New York, 1960), 524–25.

49. Goldstein, "Confronting Time," 25.

50. In general, see Gabrielle M. Spiegel, "L'histoire scientifique et les utilisations antimodernistes du passé dans le médiévisme américain," *Cahiers du Centre de Recherches Historiques, Réflexions Historiographiques* 22 (1999): 87–108.

51. Arthur Richmond Marsh, "Special Introduction," in Henry Hallam, *History of Europe during the Middle Ages,* rev. ed., vol. 1 (New York, 1899), iv–v.

52. Sir Arthur Keith, *New Discoveries Relating to the Antiquity of Man* ([1915] New York, 1931).

53. Cited in Goldstein, "Confronting Time," 21–24.

54. Frederick J. Teggart, *Prolegomena to History: The Relation of History to Literature, Philosophy, and Science* (Berkeley, 1916), 276.

55. Robinson, *New History,* 56.

56. The phrase is from Trautmann, *Lewis Henry Morgan,* 221, cited in Segal, "Western Civ," 772.

57. Ibid., 775, 779.

58. In general, see ibid. Robinson himself cited favorably the 250 pages devoted to anthropology in Eduard Meyer's *History of Antiquity;* see Segal, "Western Civ," 89. Michael Ivanovitch Rostovtzeff, *History of the Ancient World,* vol. 1, *The Orient and Greece,* trans. J. D. Duff (Oxford, 1926), covers all of prehistory up to the Neolithic between pages 13 and 16. Charles Alexander Robinson, Jr., *Ancient History from Prehistoric Times to the Death of Justinian,* 2nd ed., prepared by Alan L. Boegehold (New York, 1967), covers prehistory in twelve pages and the Neolithic in a further five.

59. I consulted the revised and enlarged edition of James Harvey Robinson, *An Introduction to the History of Western Europe* (Boston, 1924), 6.

60. Ibid., 8–9. On Robinson's fusion of medieval with primitive, see also the brief remarks of Gilbert Allardyce, "The Rise and Fall of the Western Civilization Course," *American Historical Review* 87 (1982): 704–5.

61. James Harvey Robinson, *The Ordeal of Civilization* (New York, 1926), 7.

62. Ibid., 35; see also 47, 90.

63. The most noteworthy exception among Western Civ textbooks is Harry Elmer Barnes, *The History of Western Civilization,* 2 vols. (New York, 1935), which was quite serious in its incorporation of the Paleolithic.

64. Breisach, *Historiography,* 398.

65. Ross J. S. Hoffman, ed., *Man and His History: World History and Western Civilization* (Garden City, N.Y., 1958), 28.

66. Mott T. Greene, *Natural Knowledge in Preclassical Antiquity* (Baltimore, 1992), 3.

67. John S. Hoyland, *A Brief History of Civilization* (London, 1925), 24, 48, 49.

68. Hermann Schneider, *The History of World Civilization from Prehistoric Times to the Middle Ages,* vol. 1, trans. Margaret M. Green (New York, 1931), 7.

69. Henry Thomas Buckle, *A History of Civilization in England,* vol. 1 (New York, 1860), 214–18.

70. Geoffrey Parsons, *The Stream of History* (New York, 1928), 142.

71. Schneider, *History of World Civilization,* 37–38.

72. See, e.g., Crane Brinton et al., *A History of Civilization,* vol. 1, *Prehistory to 1715* (New York, 1955), 18, and Shepard Bancroft Clough et al., eds., *A History of the Western World* (Boston, 1964), 14: "The crucial event by which scholars have traditionally divided history from the period known as prehistory or protohistory is the appearance of written records."

73. George Smith, *The Patriarchal Age: or, The History and Religion of Mankind, from the Creation to the Death of Isaac* (London, 1847), 165–67.

74. See ibid., 384–415, esp. the discussion of Sir William Jones from 401 onward.

75. Among the many exemplars of textbooks or pedagogies that begin the course of study with Egypt, see W. C. Taylor, *A Manual of Ancient and Modern History* (New York, 1852); John MacCarthy, *History of the World from the Earliest Period to the Present Time* (New York, 1882); Philip Van Ness Myers, *Ancient History* (Boston, 1904); Robert H. Labberton, *Labberton's Universal History, from the Earliest Times to the Present* (New York, 1902); and Herbert Darling Foster et al., eds., *A History Syllabus for Secondary Schools* (Boston, 1904). Lynn Thorndike includes two chapters on the prehistoric era in his *A Short History of Civilization* (New York, 1930) but then proceeds to Egypt. Some early texts, including Fisher, *Outlines of Universal History*, begin with China and India, then move to Egypt.

76. Among the many examples, see Clough et al., *History of the Western World*, and Garraty and Gay, *Columbia History*. The fourth and most recent edition of William H. McNeill, *A World History* (Oxford, 1999), begins with Mesopotamia, in the valley of the Tigris and Eu-

phrates (13), as does William J. Duiker and Jackson J. Spielvogel, *World History: Comprehensive Volume,* 3rd ed. (Belmont, Calif., 2001), 2–3.

77. H. G. Wells, *The Outline of History; Being a Plain History of Life and Mankind*, 3rd rev. ed. (New York, 1920).

78. Harold Peake and Herbert John Fleure, *The Corridors of Time*, 10 vols. (New Haven, Conn., 1927).

79. Parsons, *Stream of History*; see also G. Elliot Smith, *Human History* (New York, 1929).

80. Jared M. Diamond, *Guns, Germs, and Steel: The Fates of Human Societies* (New York, 1997); see also John Reader, *Africa: A Biography of the Continent* (New York, 1998), and Tim Flannery, *The Eternal Frontier: An Ecological History of North America and Its Peoples* (New York, 2001).

81. William T. Ross, *H. G. Wells's World Reborn: "The Outline of History" and Its Companions* (Selinsgrove, Pa., 2002), 16.

82. Ibid., 20.

83. For a few examples, see Harry Elmer Barnes, *An Intellectual and Cultural History of the Western World,* 3rd rev. ed., vol. 1, *From Earliest Times through the Middle Ages* (New York, 1965), 39, and C. Harold King, *A History of Civilization: Earliest Times to the Mid-seventeenth Century. The Story of Our Heritage* (New York, 1956), 4–5.

TWO. RESISTANCE

1. John Davis, *People of the Mediterranean: An Essay in Comparative Social Anthropology* (London, 1977), 242–45.

2. J. Kelley Sowards, *Western Civilization to 1660* (New York, 1964), 1.

3. Chester G. Starr, *A History of the Ancient World* (New York, 1965), 27.

4. Thomas Walter Wallbank et al., *Civilization: Past and Present,* 5th ed., vol. 1 (Chicago, 1965), 34.

5. John B. Harrison and Richard E. Sullivan, *A Short History of Western Civilization,* 2nd ed. (New York, 1966), 5.

6. John L. Stipp et al., *The Rise and Development of Western Civilization,* vol. 1 (New York, 1967), 12.

7. However, see Michael Cook, *A Brief History of the Human Race* (New York, 2003), 7: "History . . . fits snugly into the warm and stable climatic niche of the Holocene. . . . Human history is founded on farming. . . . The Holocene, then, was the window of opportunity for the making of history. If this is right, there is no reason to ask why humans should have waited so long before making history. . . . [I]t seems that they jumped through the window just about as soon as it opened for them."

8. Quoted in Paolo Rossi, *The Dark Abyss of Time: The History of the Earth and the History of Nations from Hooke to Vico,* trans. Lydia G. Cochrane (Chicago, 1984), 159.

9. John Lubbock, *Pre-Historic Times, as Illustrated by Ancient Remains, and the Manners and Customs of Modern Savages,* 2nd ed. ([1865] New York, 1872), 1.

10. George Park Fisher, *Outlines of Universal History, Designed as a Text-Book and for Private Reading* (New York, 1885), 3.

11. Dorothy Ross, *The Origins of American Social Science* (Cambridge, Engl., 1991).

12. See Leonard Krieger, *Ranke: The Meaning of History* (Chicago, 1977).

13. Leopold von Ranke, *Universal History: The Oldest Historical Group of Nations and the Greeks,* ed. G. W. Prothero, trans. D. C. Tovey and G. W. Prothero (New York, 1885), ix.

14. Frederick J. Teggart, *Theory of History* (New Haven, Conn., 1925), 23 n. 1.

15. Charles V. Langlois and Charles Seignobos, *Introduction to the Study of History,* trans. G. G. Berry (New York, 1898), 17.

16. V. A. Renouf, *Outlines of General History,* 2nd ed., ed. William Starr Myers (New York, 1909), 2.

17. Herbert Butterfield, *Man on His Past: The Study of the History of Historical Scholarship* (Cambridge, Engl., 1955), 103–4.

18. Peter Novick, *That Noble Dream: The "Objectivity Question" and the American Historical Profession* (Cambridge, Engl., 1988), 27. See also Ernst Breisach, *Historiography: Ancient, Medieval and Modern,* 2nd ed. (Chicago, 1994), 233.

19. Quoted in Rossi, *Dark Abyss,* 108.

20. Charles Darwin, *On the Origin of Species* (London, 1859; reprint Cambridge, Mass., 1964), 310–11.

21. Daniel Wilson, *The Archaeology and Prehistoric Annals of Scotland* (Edinburgh, 1851); Lubbock, *Pre-Historic Times,* 1; Harold Peake and Herbert John Fleure, *The Corridors of Time,* vol. 1, *Apes and Men* (New Haven, Conn., 1927), 11.

22. For an example of this metaphor's use, see Brian Sykes, *The Seven Daughters of Eve: The Science that Reveals Our Genetic Ancestry* (New York, 2001), 1: "Our DNA does not fade like an ancient parchment."

23. This is a plausible reading of a fairly obscure passage in Langlois and Seignobos, *Introduction,* 64–65. A generous understanding of *trace* as comprising both written and unwritten sources is more explicit in Henry Johnson, *Teaching of History in Elementary and Secondary Schools* (New York, 1926), 1: "The past cannot be observed directly. What is known about it must be learned from such traces of former conditions and events as time and chance and the foresight of man may have preserved. . . . Traces of past facts of any kind may be regarded as possible material. We speak of a history of plants, of animals, and even of inanimate nature."

24. Paul Connerton, *How Societies Remember* (Cambridge, Engl., 1989), 13.

25. Robert H. Labberton, *Labberton's Universal History, from the Earliest Times to the Present* (New York, 1902), xxi.

26. François Pierre Guillaume Guizot, *A Popular History of France, from the Earliest Times,* vol. 1, trans. Robert Black (Boston, 1869), 15. It is revealing that Guizot's imaginative reconstruction of life in Gaul as it was some two to three thousand years ago bears a resemblance to Vico's depiction of the postdiluvial condition of man.

27. Oswald Spengler, *Aphorisms,* trans. Gisela Koch-Weser O'Brien (Chicago, 1967), 46.

28. Karl Ploetz, *Auszug aus der Geschichte,* 24th ed. (Bielefeld, 1951), 5.

29. John A. Garraty and Peter Gay, eds., *The Columbia History of the World* (New York, 1972), 49.

30. Friedrich Wilhelm Nietzsche, *The Use and Abuse of History,* 2nd rev. ed., trans. Adrian Collins (Indianapolis, 1957), 1. Or, as one historian puts it, "we all know that dogs and cats do not have histories." See J. M. Roberts, *The New History of the World,* 4th rev. ed. (Oxford, 2003), 1.

31. See Connerton, *How Societies Remember,* 102–3.

32. John Hammerton and Harry Elmer Barnes, eds., *The Illustrated World History: A Record of World Events from Earliest Historical Times to the Present Day* (New York, 1935), 7.

33. Langlois and Seignobos, *Introduction,* 145.

34. Eric R. Wolf, *Europe and the People without History* (Berkeley, 1982).

35. John Pfeiffer, *The Creative Explosion: An Inquiry into the Origins of Art and Religion* (New York, 1982), 19–39; Grahame Clark, *World Prehistory in New Perspective* (Cambridge, Engl., 1977), 3–4.

36. James Fentress and Chris Wickham, *Social Memory* (Oxford, 1992); Michael T. Clanchy, *From Memory to Written Record: England 1066–1307,* 2nd ed. (Oxford, 1993); Mary Carruthers, *The Book of Memory: A Study of Memory in Medieval Culture* (Cambridge, Engl., 1990).

37. A model developed by Robert Trivers, "The Evolution of Reciprocal Altruism," *The Quarterly Review of Biology* 46 (1971): 52. See also Elliot Sober and David Sloan Wilson, *Unto Others: The Evolution and Psychology of Unselfish Behavior* (Cambridge, Mass., 1998).

38. In general, see Robin Dunbar, *Grooming, Gossip, and the Evolution of Language* (Cambridge, Mass., 1996).

39. This was the logic that led Steven Mithen to claim that "[h]uman history began in 50,000 BC" in *After the Ice: A Global Human History, 20,000–5000 BC* (Cambridge, Mass., 2004), 3. See also his *The Prehistory of the Mind: The Cognitive Origins of Art, Religion and Science* (London, 1996).

40. See Connerton, *How Societies Remember,* 13.

41. For an extended analysis of the problems of interpretation, see Langlois and Seignobos, *Introduction,* 155–90.

42. Teggart, *Theory of History,* 24.

43. Quoted in Novick, *That Noble Dream,* 89–90.

44. This position is argued aggressively, for example, in Christopher J. Arnold, *Roman Britain to Saxon England: An Archaeological Study* (London, 1984); see also his *An Archaeology of the Early Anglo-Saxon Kingdoms* (London, 1988), xiii.

45. Luigi Luca Cavalli-Sforza, *Genes, Peoples and Languages,* trans. Mark Seielstad (New York, 2000), 151.

46. As reported in Jeffrey L. Sheler, "Rethinking Jamestown," *Smithsonian* 35 (2005): 48–55.

47. As Breisach notes in *Historiography,* 347, commenting on the field of psychohistory.

48. Johnson, *Teaching of History,* 2.

49. Michel Foucault, *The Archaeology of Knowledge,* trans. A. M. Sheridan Smith (New York, 1976); Franco Moretti, "Graphs, Maps, Trees: Abstract Models for Literary History," published in three parts in *New Left Review* 24 (2003): 67–93; 26 (2004): 79–103; and 28 (2004): 43–63.

50. Michael McCormick, *The Origins of the European Economy: Communications and Commerce, A.D. 300–900* (Cambridge, Engl., 2001).

51. Fisher, *Outlines,* 1.

52. John Bagnell Bury, "Darwinism and History," in *Selected Essays of J. B. Bury,* ed. Harold W. V. Temperley (Cambridge, Engl., 1930), 32 n. 1. Similar ideas can be found in Max Savelle, ed., *A History of World Civilization,* vol. 1 (New York, 1957), 28.

53. Tim Flannery, *The Eternal Frontier: An Ecological History of North America and Its Peoples* (New York, 2001), 239–40; Stuart J. Fiedel, *Prehistory of the Americas,* 2nd ed. (Cambridge, Engl., 1992).

54. Hermann Schneider, *The History of World Civilization from Prehistoric Times to the Middle Ages,* vol. 1, trans. Margaret M. Green (New York, 1931), 3.

55. Arnold J. Toynbee, *Mankind and Mother Earth: A Narrative History of the World* (New York, 1976), 15.

56. Roberts, *New History of the World,* 2. This argument, common

to many general histories, may have been influenced by Julian Jaynes, *The Origin of Consciousness in the Breakdown of the Bicameral Mind* (Boston, 1976).

57. William H. McNeill, *A World History* (New York, 1967), 6.

58. Edward Hallett Carr, *What Is History?* (New York, 1961), 55, 60.

59. Ibid., 64.

THREE. BETWEEN DARWIN AND LAMARCK

1. In general, see Herbert Butterfield, *The Whig Interpretation of History* (London, 1931).

2. Daniel C. Dennett, *Darwin's Dangerous Idea: Evolution and the Meanings of Life* (New York, 1995), 26–28, also the index, *s.v.* "Mind-first."

3. George Park Fisher, *Outlines of Universal History, Designed as a Text-Book and for Private Reading* (New York, 1885), 3–4.

4. George Lakoff and Mark Johnson, *Metaphors We Live By* (Chicago, 1980).

5. For an example of the use of this metaphor, see Tyler Volk, *Metapatterns: Across Space, Time, and Mind* (New York, 1995), 114.

6. See, most recently, Francis Fukuyama, who borrows from Kant, Hegel, and others the idea that history, having a beginning, can also have an end: *The End of History and the Last Man* (New York, 1992), 57–70.

7. Robert Bannister, *Sociology and Scientism: The American Quest for Objectivity, 1880–1940* (Chapel Hill, N.C., 1987), 22.

8. Carl Degler, *In Search of Human Nature: The Decline and Revival of Darwinism in American Social Thought* (New York, 1991), 24. See also George W. Stocking, Jr., "Lamarckianism in American Social Science: 1890–1915," *Journal of the History of Ideas* 23 (1962): 239–56.

9. Degler, *In Search of Human Nature,* 344.

10. Cited in ibid., 94.

11. Geoffrey M. Hodgson, "Is Social Evolution Lamarckian or Darwinian?" in *Darwinism and Evolutionary Economics,* ed. John Laurent and John Nightingale, 87–118 (Cheltenham, 2001).

12. However, see the observation in Ernest Gellner, *Plough, Sword, and Book: The Structure of Human History* (London, 1988), 14: "Historical transformations are transmitted by culture, which is a form of transmission which, unlike genetic transmission, *does* perpetuate acquired characteristics. In fact, culture *consists* of sets of acquired characteristics."

13. Edward Hallett Carr, *What Is History?* (New York, 1961), 155.

14. J. M. Roberts, *The New History of the World*, 4th rev. ed. (Oxford, 2003), 2.

15. Stephen Jay Gould, *The Panda's Thumb: More Reflections in Natural History* (New York, 1982), 83–84.

16. Gould's use of *unleashing*, perhaps not coincidentally, is a rejection of an idea expressed by E. O. Wilson four years earlier: "The genes hold culture on a leash." Edward O. Wilson, *On Human Nature* (Cambridge, Mass., 1978), 167, cited in William H. Durham, *Coevolution: Genes, Culture, and Human Diversity* (Stanford, 1991), 34.

17. In general, see Degler, *In Search of Human Nature*, 344–46. See also the more muted remarks in Peter J. Richerson and Robert Boyd, *Not by Genes Alone: How Culture Transformed Human Evolution* (Chicago, 2005), 103–6.

18. Michael Krützen et al., "Cultural Transmission of Tool Use in Bottlenose Dolphins," *Proceedings of the National Academy of Sciences* 102 (2005): 8939–43.

19. Gavin R. Hunt and Russell D. Gray, "Species-wide Manufacture of Stick-type Tools by New Caledonian Crows," *Emu* 102 (2002): 349–53; see also their "Crafting of Hook Tools by Wild New Caledonian Crows," *Proceedings of the Royal Society of London* 271, Biology Letters Supplement (2004): S88–S90.

20. Leslie White, *The Evolution of Culture: The Development of Civilization to the Fall of Rome* (New York, 1959), ix. See also Alexander Alland, Jr., *Evolution and Human Behavior* (Garden City, N.Y., 1967).

21. For some important early works, see Donald T. Campbell, "Variation and Selective Retention in Sociocultural Evolution," in *Social Changes in Developing Areas: A Reinterpretation of Evolutionary The-*

ory, ed. H. R. Baringer, G. I. Blanksten, and R. W. Mack (Cambridge, Mass., 1965), 19–49; Richard D. Alexander, *Darwinism and Human Affairs* (Seattle, 1979), esp. 66–139; Luigi Luca Cavalli-Sforza and M. W. Feldman, *Cultural Transmission and Evolution: A Quantitative Approach* (Princeton, 1981); and Robert Boyd and Peter J. Richerson, *Culture and the Evolutionary Process* (Chicago, 1985). Boyd and Richerson survey some of the historiographical trends in *The Origin and Evolution of Cultures* (Oxford, 2005), 288–90.

22. Boyd and Richerson, *Origin and Evolution of Cultures,* 4.

23. Cavalli-Sforza and Feldman, *Cultural Transmission and Evolution,* 66.

24. Personal communication, September 2005.

25. See Jack Goody, Joan Thirsk, and E. P. Thompson, eds., *Family and Inheritance: Rural Society in Western Europe, 1200–1800* (Cambridge, Engl., 1976), and Richard Wall, ed., *Family Forms in Historic Europe* (Cambridge, Engl., 1983).

26. Charles L. Redman, *Human Impact on Ancient Environments* (Tucson, 1999); Brian M. Fagan, *Floods, Famines, and Emperors: El Niño and the Fate of Civilizations* (New York, 1999); Jared M. Diamond, *Collapse: How Societies Choose to Fail or Succeed* (New York: 2005).

27. Richerson and Boyd, *Not by Genes Alone,* 27.

28. Clifford Geertz, *The Interpretation of Cultures: Selected Essays* (New York, 1973), 44.

29. E.g., ibid., 92. See also Durham, *Coevolution,* 10.

30. Elliot Sober and David Sloan Wilson, *Unto Others: The Evolution and Psychology of Unselfish Behavior* (Cambridge, Mass., 1998); Boyd and Richerson, *Origin and Evolution of Cultures.* See also Christopher Boehm, "Impact of the Human Egalitarian Syndrome on Darwinian Selection Mechanisms," *The American Naturalist* 150, Supplement (1997): S100–S121, and Samuel Bowles and Herbert Gintis, "The Evolution of Strong Reciprocity: Cooperation in Heterogeneous Populations," *Theoretical Population Biology* 65 (2004): 17–28.

31. Richard Dawkins, *The Selfish Gene* (Oxford, 1976); Susan Blackmore, *The Meme Machine* (Oxford, 1999). For criticism, see

Henry Plotkin, *The Imagined World Made Real: Towards a Natural Science of Culture* (London, 2002), 140–60.

32. Dawkins, *Selfish Gene,* 214.

33. Dennett, *Darwin's Dangerous Idea,* 344.

34. Ibid., 367.

35. Richard Dawkins, *The Extended Phenotype: The Long Reach of the Gene,* rev. ed. (Oxford, 1999), 55–80.

36. C. Warren Hollister, *Roots of the Western Tradition: A Short History of the Ancient World* (New York, 1966), 8.

37. Roberts, *New History of the World,* 37.

38. Crane Brinton, John B. Christopher, and Robert Lee Wolff, *A History of Civilization: Prehistory to 1715,* 5th ed. (Englewood Cliffs, N.J., 1976), 8.

39. This image was suggested to me by Patrick Geary.

40. Donald Kagan, Steven Ozment, and Frank M. Turner, *The Western Heritage* (New York, 1979), 3.

41. Gould, *Panda's Thumb,* 95–107.

42. Richerson and Boyd, *Not by Genes Alone,* 131.

43. Ibid., 131–36.

44. Cavalli-Sforza and Feldman, *Cultural Transmission and Evolution,* 53–62.

45. Durham, *Coevolution,* 168.

46. On horses, see Stephen Budiansky, *The Nature of Horses: Exploring Equine Evolution, Intelligence, and Behavior* (New York, 1997).

47. Arjun Appadurai, ed., *The Social Life of Things: Commodities in Cultural Perspective* (Cambridge, Engl., 1986).

48. Benedict Anderson, *Imagined Communities: Reflections on the Origin and Spread of Nationalism* (London, 1983).

49. Benedict Anderson, "Census, Map, Museum," in *Becoming National: A Reader,* ed. Geoff Eley and Ronald Grigor Suny (New York, 1996), 243–48.

50. James C. Scott, *Seeing Like a State: How Certain Schemes to Improve the Human Condition Have Failed* (New Haven, Conn., 1998), 9.

51. Ian Hacking, "Making Up People," in *Reconstructing Individu-*

alism: Autonomy, Individuality, and the Self in Western Thought, ed. Thomas C. Heller, Morton Sosna, and David W. Wellbery (Stanford, 1986), 222–36.

52. Bernard S. Cohn and Nicholas B. Dirks, "Beyond the Fringe: The Nation State, Colonialism, and the Technologies of Power," *The Journal of Historical Sociology* 1 (1988): 225.

53. Scott, *Seeing Like a State*, 2.

54. However, see Mary Douglas, *How Institutions Think* (Syracuse, N.Y., 1986).

55. Daniel Lord Smail, *Imaginary Cartographies: Possession and Identity in Late Medieval Marseille* (Ithaca, N.Y., 1999).

56. This argument was also made in Harvey Sacks, *Lectures on Conversation,* 2 vols., ed. Gail Jefferson (Oxford, 1992), 1: 40–48; see also the index, *s.v.* "categories and classes."

FOUR. THE NEW NEUROHISTORY

1. Michael L. Fitzhugh and William H. Leckie, Jr., "Agency, Postmodernism and the Causes of Change," *History and Theory* 40 (2001): 58–81.

2. See William Ian Miller, *The Anatomy of Disgust* (Cambridge, Mass., 1997).

3. On this, see Sarah Blaffer Hrdy, *Mother Nature: A History of Mothers, Infants, and Natural Selection* (New York, 1999), 130–40.

4. It is interesting to note, however, that electrical stimulation of certain regions of the brain can cause sadness or laughter regardless of the subject's feelings prior to the experiment. For details, see Antonio Damasio, *Looking for Spinoza: Joy, Sorrow, and the Feeling Brain* (Orlando, Fla., 2003), 65–79.

5. Clifford Geertz, *The Interpretation of Cultures: Selected Essays* (New York, 1973), 45.

6. Joseph LeDoux, *The Emotional Brain: The Mysterious Underpinnings of Emotional Life* (New York, 1996), 19.

7. Konrad Lorenz, "Über den Begriff der Instinkthandlung," *Folia Biotheoretica* 2 (1937): 17–50.

8. Richard Dawkins, *The Extended Phenotype: The Long Reach of the Gene,* rev. ed. (Oxford, 1999), 23–24.

9. Paul Ehrlich, *Human Natures: Genes, Cultures, and the Human Prospect* (Washington, D.C., 2000), 34–38.

10. Carl Degler, *In Search of Human Nature: The Decline and Revival of Darwinism in American Social Thought* (New York, 1991), 218.

11. Ibid., 220.

12. Edward O. Wilson, *Sociobiology: The New Synthesis* (Cambridge, Mass., 1975).

13. Degler, *In Search of Human Nature,* 319.

14. Daniel C. Dennett, *Darwin's Dangerous Idea: Evolution and the Meanings of Life* (New York, 1995), 264.

15. Works critical of the political appropriation of biology are numerous. See, among others, Ann Arbor Science for the People Editorial Collective, ed., *Biology as a Social Weapon* (Minneapolis, 1977), and Stephan L. Chorover, *From Genesis to Genocide: The Meaning of Human Nature and the Power of Behavior Control* (Cambridge, Mass., 1979). The geneticist Richard Lewontin is closely associated with this vein of criticism; see, most recently, his *It Ain't Necessarily So: The Dream of the Human Genome and Other Illusions* (New York, 2000).

16. Gabrielle M. Spiegel, "Chance and Necessity: Foucault and the Cultural Inscription of Genetics in Genealogy," unpublished manuscript.

17. David J. Buller, *Adapting Minds: Evolutionary Psychology and the Persistent Quest for Human Nature* (Cambridge, Mass., 2005), 42–43.

18. Stephen Jay Gould and Richard C. Lewontin, "The Spandrels of San Marcos and the Panglossian Paradigm: A Critique of the Adaptationist Programme," *Proceedings of the Royal Society of London* B 205 (1979): 581–98.

19. Stephen Jay Gould and Elizabeth Vrba, "Exaptation: A Missing Term in the Science of Form," *Paleobiology* 8 (1981): 4–15.

20. Donald Symons, *The Evolution of Human Sexuality* (New York,

1979), 90; Stephen Jay Gould, "Male Nipples and Clitoral Ripples," in *Bully for Brontosaurus: Reflections in Natural History* (New York, 1991), 124–38.

21. R. Robin Baker and Mark A. Bellis, *Human Sperm Competition: Copulation, Masturbation, and Infidelity* (London, 1995), 234–38. See also Ehrlich, *Human Natures,* 191–92.

22. For a useful survey, see Robert J. Richards, *Darwin and the Emergence of Evolutionary Theories of Mind and Behavior* (Chicago, 1987), 543–48.

23. The positions are surveyed in Dennett, *Darwin's Dangerous Idea,* 262–312.

24. Niles Eldredge, *Reinventing Darwin: The Great Debate at the High Table of Evolutionary Theory* (New York, 1995).

25. Henry Plotkin, *The Imagined World Made Real: Towards a Natural Science of Culture* (London, 2002), 92–93.

26. Ehrlich, *Human Natures,* 124.

27. See, e.g., Avshalom Caspi et al., "Role of Genotype in the Cycle of Violence in Maltreated Children," *Science* 297, no. 5582 (2002): 851.

28. For what follows I have relied on David S. Moore, *The Dependent Gene: The Fallacy of "Nature vs. Nurture"* (New York, 2001).

29. See Richard Lewontin, *The Triple Helix: Gene, Organism, and Environment* (Cambridge, Mass., 2000), 33–38.

30. For a recent survey, see Daniel M. T. Fessler, "Reproductive Immunosuppression and Diet: An Evolutionary Perspective on Pregnancy Sickness and Meat Consumption," *Current Anthropology* 43 (2003): 19–61.

31. Moore, *Dependent Gene,* 117.

32. Hrdy, *Mother Nature,* 333–34.

33. Gerald M. Edelman, *Neural Darwinism: The Theory of Neuronal Group Selection* (New York, 1987). See also Ehrlich, *Human Natures,* 127, and Lewontin, *Triple Helix,* 38.

34. Alan Leslie, "Pretense, Autism and the Theory-of-Mind Module," *Current Directions in Psychological Science* 1 (1992): 18–21; Simon

Baron-Cohen, *Mindblindness: An Essay on Autism and Theory of Mind* (Cambridge, Mass., 1995).

35. Nobuo Masataka, "Effects of Experience with Live Insects on the Development of Fear of Snakes in Squirrel Monkeys, *Saimiri sciureus,*" *Animal Behaviour* 46 (1993): 741–46.

36. See also Buller, *Adapting Minds,* 122–23.

37. For general introductions, see Steven Pinker, *How the Mind Works* (New York, 1997); Henry Plotkin, *Evolution in Mind: An Introduction to Evolutionary Psychology* (London, 1997); and David M. Buss, *Evolutionary Psychology: The New Science of the Mind* (Boston, 1999). For criticisms, see Jerry A. Fodor, *In Critical Condition: Polemical Essays on Cognitive Science and the Philosophy of Mind* (Cambridge, Mass., 1998), 203–14, and David Sloan Wilson, "Tasty Slice—But Where Is the Rest of the Pie? Review of *Evolutionary Psychology,* by David Buss," *Evolution and Human Behavior* 20 (1999): 279–87.

38. "Hominins" is the term now preferred by many paleoanthropologists to "hominids."

39. Hrdy, *Mother Nature,* 288–97.

40. Jerry A. Fodor, *The Mind Doesn't Work That Way: The Scope and Limits of Computational Psychology* (Cambridge, Mass., 2000).

41. David M. Buss, *The Evolution of Desire: Strategies of Human Mating* (New York, 1994).

42. Kristen Hawkes, "Showing Off: Tests of Another Hypothesis about Men's Foraging Goals," *Ethology and Sociobiology* 11 (1991): 29–54. However, see Frank W. Marlowe, "A Critical Period for Provisioning by Hadza Men: Implications for Pair Bonding," *Evolution and Human Behavior* 24 (2003): 217–29.

43. Hrdy, *Mother Nature,* 266–87.

44. Antonio Damasio, *Descartes' Error: Emotion, Reason, and the Human Brain* (New York, 1994).

45. Buller, *Adapting Minds,* 121.

46. Ibid., 99.

47. Wilson, *Sociobiology,* 569.

48. Christopher Boehm, *Hierarchy in the Forest: The Evolution of Egalitarian Behavior* (Cambridge, Mass., 1999).

49. John Morgan Allman, *Evolving Brains* (New York, 1999); Ehrlich, *Human Natures,* 126–27.

50. See Degler, *In Search of Human Nature,* 245–69, and Donald E. Brown, *Human Universals* (Boston, 1991), 118–29.

FIVE. CIVILIZATION AND PSYCHOTROPY

1. Robert M. Sapolsky, *Why Zebras Don't Get Ulcers,* 3rd ed. (New York, 2004), 364–83.

2. Richard E. Nisbett and Dov Cohen, *The Culture of Honor: The Psychology of Violence in the South* (Boulder, Colo., 1996).

3. Joseph R. Strayer, *On the Medieval Origins of the Modern State* (Princeton, 1970), 10–11.

4. Alon Confino, "Collective Memory and Cultural History: Problems of Method," *American Historical Review* 102 (1997): 1396.

5. Tim Flannery, *The Eternal Frontier: An Ecological History of North America and Its Peoples* (New York, 2001), 242.

6. See, e.g., Frans de Waal, *Chimpanzee Politics: Power and Sex among Apes* (New York, 1982).

7. Good introductions include John Tooby and Leda Cosmides, "The Psychological Foundations of Culture," in *The Adapted Mind: Evolutionary Psychology and the Generation of Culture,* 19–136, ed. Jerome H. Barkow, Leda Cosmides, and John Tooby (New York, 1992).

8. Steven Pinker, *How the Mind Works* (New York, 1997); Henry Plotkin, *Evolution in Mind* (London, 1997).

9. See Tim Wilson, *Strangers to Ourselves: Discovering the Adaptive Unconsciousness* (Cambridge, Mass., 2002).

10. Christopher Boehm, *Hierarchy in the Forest: The Evolution of Egalitarian Behavior* (Cambridge, Mass., 1999). See also David Erdal and Andrew Whiten, "On Human Egalitarianism: An Evolutionary Product of Machiavellian Status Escalation?" *Current Anthropology* 35 (1994): 175–83.

11. Sarah Blaffer Hrdy, *Mother Nature: A History of Mothers, Infants, and Natural Selection* (New York, 1999), 333–34.

12. Sapolsky, *Why Zebras Don't Get Ulcers,* 383.

13. See, e.g., Thomas Bisson, "The 'Feudal Revolution,'" *Past and Present* 142 (1994): 6–42.

14. Guibert of Nogent, *Self and Society in Medieval France: The Memoirs of Abbot Guibert of Nogent,* ed. John F. Benton (1970; reprint, Toronto, 1984), 185.

15. Robert Bartlett, *The Making of Europe: Conquest, Colonization, and Cultural Change, 950–1350* (Princeton, 1993), 86–87. On Norman unpredictability, see ibid., 89.

16. David J. Buller, *Adapting Minds: Evolutionary Psychology and the Persistent Quest for Human Nature* (Cambridge, Mass., 2005), 96.

17. Jürgen Habermas, *The Structural Transformation of the Public Sphere: An Inquiry into a Category of Bourgeois Society*, trans. Thomas Burger with the assistance of Frederick Lawrence (Cambridge, Mass., 1989).

18. Elliot Sober and David Sloan Wilson, *Unto Others: The Evolution and Psychology of Unselfish Behavior* (Cambridge, Mass., 1998), 18.

19. Richard Dawkins, *The Extended Phenotype: The Long Reach of the Gene,* rev. ed. (Oxford, 1999), 69.

20. Aldous Huxley, *Brave New World and Brave New World Revisited* (New York, 2004).

21. David Sloan Wilson, *Darwin's Cathedral: Evolution, Religion, and the Nature of Society* (Chicago, 2002); Scott Atran, *In Gods We Trust: The Evolutionary Landscape of Religion* (Oxford, 2002).

22. See Daniel C. Dennett, *Breaking the Spell: Religion as a Natural Phenomenon* (New York, 2006), 3–5.

23. Etienne de la Boétie, "Discours sur la servitude volontaire," in *Oeuvres politiques*, ed. François Hincker (Paris, 1971), 65, cited in Philippe Buc, *The Dangers of Ritual: Between Early Medieval Texts and Social Scientific Theory* (Princeton, 2001), 189.

24. Jane Goodall, *The Chimpanzees of Gombe: Patterns of Behavior* (Cambridge, Mass., 1986), 283–84.

25. For a survey of some of the literature, see Thelma Fenster and Daniel Lord Smail, eds., *Fama: The Politics of Talk and Reputation in Medieval Europe* (Ithaca, N.Y., 2003).

26. Robin Dunbar, *Grooming, Gossip, and the Evolution of Language* (Cambridge, Mass., 1996).

27. Shelley Taylor et al., "Biobehavioral Response to Stress in Females: Tend-and-Befriend, Not Fight-or-Flight," *Psychological Review* 107 (2000): 411–29.

28. Melanie Tebbutt, *Women's Talk? A Social History of "Gossip" in Working-Class Neighbourhoods, 1880–1960* (Aldershot, Engl., 1995); Jane Kamensky, *Governing the Tongue: The Politics of Speech in Early New England* (New York, 1997).

29. See, e.g., Rachel Simmons, *Odd Girl Out: The Hidden Culture of Aggression in Girls* (New York, 2002).

30. Peter Burke, "Ranke the Reactionary," in *Leopold von Ranke and the Shaping of the Historical Discipline,* ed. George G. Iggers and James M. Powell, 36–44 (Syracuse, N.Y., 1990).

31. I am grateful to my research assistant, Morgan Sonderegger, for his work in putting together much of what follows in this section.

32. Kenneth Pomeranz and Steven Topik, *The World That Trade Created: Society, Culture, and the World Economy, 1400–the Present* (Armonk, N.Y., 1999), 87.

33. Thomas Brennan, "Coffeehouses and Cafes," in *Encyclopedia of the Enlightenment,* 4 vols., ed. Alan Charles Kors (New York, 2003), 1: 267.

34. Daniel Roche, *A History of Everyday Things: The Birth of Consumption in France, 1600–1800,* trans. Brian Pierce (Cambridge, Engl., 2000), 246.

35. Pomeranz and Topik, *World That Trade Created,* 91; the passage refers to the United States but also represents well the situation in England.

36. Roger Chartier, "Reading and Reading Practices," in Kors, *Encyclopedia of the Enlightenment,* 3: 399.

37. Adrian Johns, "The Physiology of Reading in Restoration En-

gland," in *The Practice and Representation of Reading in England,* ed. James Raven, Helen Small, and Naomi Tadmor (Cambridge, Engl., 1996), 140.

38. William Warner, *Licensing Entertainment: The Elevation of Novel Reading in Britain, 1684–1750* (Berkeley, 1998), 105, 137.

39. Ibid., 5.

40. Ibid., 136.

41. Personal communication, November 2006.

42. Personal communication, April 2006.

43. *Oxford English Dictionary, s.v.* "addict" and "addiction."

44. Roy Porter and Dorothy Porter, *In Sickness and in Health: The British Experience, 1650–1850* (London, 1988), 217.

45. Ibid., 220.

46. Michel Vovelle, *Piété baroque et déchristianisation en Provence au XVIIIe siècle: Les attitudes devant la mort d'après les clauses des testaments* (Paris, 1973).

47. Pomeranz and Topik, *World That Trade Created,* 82.

48. Francis Fukuyama, *The End of History and the Last Man* (New York, 1992).

EPILOGUE: LOOKING AHEAD

1. Jared M. Diamond, *Guns, Germs, and Steel: The Fates of Human Societies* (New York, 1997), 54–57.

2. Stanley H. Ambrose, "Late Pleistocene Human Population Bottlenecks, Volcanic Winter, and Differentiation of Modern Humans," *Journal of Human Evolution* 34 (1998): 623–51.

3. Marshall David Sahlins, *Stone Age Economics* (Chicago, 1972).

4. Joan Kelly-Gadol, "Did Women Have a Renaissance?," in *Becoming Visible: Women in European History,* 137–64, ed. Renate Bridenthal and Claudia Koonz (Boston, 1977).

BIBLIOGRAPHY OF
WORKS CITED

Adams, Charles Kendall. *A Manual of Historical Literature*. New York: Harper, 1882.

Albritton, Claude. *The Abyss of Time: Changing Conceptions of the Earth's Antiquity after the Sixteenth Century*. San Francisco: Freeman, Cooper, 1980.

Alexander, Richard D. *Darwinism and Human Affairs*. Seattle: University of Washington Press, 1979.

Alland, Alexander, Jr. *Evolution and Human Behavior*. Garden City, N.Y.: Natural History Press, 1967.

Allardyce, Gilbert. "The Rise and Fall of the Western Civilization Course." *American Historical Review* 87 (1982): 695–725.

Allman, John Morgan. *Evolving Brains*. New York: Scientific American Library, 1999.

Ambrose, Stanley H. "Late Pleistocene Human Population Bottlenecks, Volcanic Winter, and Differentiation of Modern Humans." *Journal of Human Evolution* 34 (1998): 623–51.

Anderson, Benedict. "Census, Map, Museum." In *Becoming National: A Reader*. Edited by Geoff Eley and Ronald Grigor Suny, 243–48. New York: Oxford University Press, 1996.

————. *Imagined Communities: Reflections on the Origin and Spread of Nationalism*. London: Verso, 1983.

Ann Arbor Science for the People Editorial Collective, ed. *Biology as a Social Weapon.* Minneapolis: Burgess, 1977.

Appadurai, Arjun, ed. *The Social Life of Things: Commodities in Cultural Perspective.* Cambridge: Cambridge University Press, 1986.

Arnold, Christopher J. *An Archaeology of the Early Anglo-Saxon Kingdoms.* London: Routledge, 1988.

———. *Roman Britain to Saxon England: An Archaeological Study.* London: Croom Helm, 1984.

Atran, Scott. *In Gods We Trust: The Evolutionary Landscape of Religion.* Oxford: Oxford University Press, 2002.

Baker, R. Robin, and Mark A. Bellis. *Human Sperm Competition: Copulation, Masturbation, and Infidelity.* London: Chapman and Hall, 1995.

Bannister, Robert. *Sociology and Scientism: The American Quest for Objectivity, 1880–1940.* Chapel Hill: University of North Carolina Press, 1987.

Barnes, Harry Elmer. *The History of Western Civilization,* 2 vols. New York: Harcourt, Brace, 1935.

———. *An Intellectual and Cultural History of the Western World,* 3rd rev. ed., vol. 1, *From Earliest Times through the Middle Ages.* New York: Dover Publications, 1965.

Baron-Cohen, Simon. *Mindblindness: An Essay on Autism and Theory of Mind.* Cambridge, Mass.: MIT Press, 1995.

Bartlett, Robert. *The Making of Europe: Conquest, Colonization, and Cultural Change, 950–1350.* Princeton: Princeton University Press, 1993.

Bernal, Martin. *Black Athena: The Afroasiatic Roots of Classical Civilization.* New Brunswick, N.J.: Rutgers University Press, 1987.

Bisson, Thomas. "The 'Feudal Revolution.'" *Past and Present* 142 (1994): 6–42.

Blackmore, Susan. *The Meme Machine.* Oxford: Oxford University Press, 1999.

Bodin, Jean. *Method for the Easy Comprehension of History.* Translated by Beatrice Reynolds. New York: Octagon Books, 1966.

Boehm, Christopher. *Hierarchy in the Forest: The Evolution of Egalitarian Behavior.* Cambridge, Mass.: Harvard University Press, 1999.

———. "Impact of the Human Egalitarian Syndrome on Darwinian Selection Mechanisms." *The American Naturalist* 150, Supplement (1997): S100–S121.

Bossuet, Jacques Bénigne. *An Universal History: From the Beginning of the World to the Empire of Charlemagne,* 13th ed. Translated by James Elphinston. Dublin, 1785. Originally published 1681.

Bowdoin van Riper, A. *Men among the Mammoths: Victorian Science and the Discovery of Human Prehistory.* Chicago: University of Chicago Press, 1993.

Bowler, Peter J. *The Invention of Progress: The Victorians and the Past.* Oxford: Blackwell, 1989.

Bowles, Samuel, and Herbert Gintis. "The Evolution of Strong Reciprocity: Cooperation in Heterogeneous Populations." *Theoretical Population Biology* 65 (2004): 17–28.

Boyd, Robert, and Peter J. Richerson. *Culture and the Evolutionary Process.* Chicago: University of Chicago Press, 1985.

———. *The Origin and Evolution of Cultures.* Oxford: Oxford University Press, 2005.

Breisach, Ernst. *Historiography: Ancient, Medieval and Modern,* 2nd ed. Chicago: University of Chicago Press, 1994.

Brennan, Thomas. "Coffeehouses and Cafes." In *Encyclopedia of the Enlightenment,* 4 vols. Edited by Alan Charles Kors, vol. 1, 267–69. New York: Oxford University Press, 2003.

Brinton, Crane, John B. Christopher, and Robert Lee Wolff. *A History of Civilization,* vol. 1, *Prehistory to 1715.* New York: Prentice-Hall, 1955.

———. *A History of Civilization: Prehistory to 1715,* 5th ed. Englewood Cliffs, N.J.: Prentice-Hall, 1976.

Brown, Donald E. *Human Universals.* Boston: McGraw Hill, 1991.

Buc, Philippe. *The Dangers of Ritual: Between Early Medieval Texts and Social Scientific Theory.* Princeton: Princeton University Press, 2001.

Buckle, Henry Thomas. *A History of Civilization in England,* vol. 1. New York, 1860.

Budiansky, Stephen. *The Nature of Horses: Exploring Equine Evolution, Intelligence, and Behavior.* New York: Free Press, 1997.

Buller, David J. *Adapting Minds: Evolutionary Psychology and the Persistent Quest for Human Nature.* Cambridge, Mass.: MIT Press, 2005.

Burchfield, Joe D. *Lord Kelvin and the Age of the Earth.* London: Science History Publications, 1975.

Burke, Peter. "Ranke the Reactionary." In *Leopold von Ranke and the Shaping of the Historical Discipline.* Edited by George G. Iggers and James M. Powell, 36–44. Syracuse, N.Y.: Syracuse University Press, 1990.

Bury, John Bagnell. "Darwinism and History." In *Selected Essays of J. B. Bury.* Edited by Harold W. V. Temperley, 23–42. Cambridge: Cambridge University Press, 1930.

Buss, David M. *Evolutionary Psychology: The New Science of the Mind.* Boston: Allyn and Bacon, 1999.

———. *The Evolution of Desire: Strategies of Human Mating.* New York: Basic Books, 1994.

Butterfield, Herbert. *Man on His Past: The Study of the History of Historical Scholarship.* Cambridge: Cambridge University Press, 1955.

———. *The Whig Interpretation of History.* London: G. Bell, 1931.

Campbell, Donald T. "Variation and Selective Retention in Sociocultural Evolution." In *Social Changes in Developing Areas: A Reinterpretation of Evolutionary Theory.* Edited by H. R. Baringer, G. I. Blanksten, and R. W. Mack, 19–49. Cambridge, Mass.: Schenkman, 1965.

Cantù, Cesare. *Storia Universale,* 10th ed. Turin, 1884.

Carr, Edward Hallett. *What Is History?* New York: Vintage, 1961.

Carruthers, Mary. *The Book of Memory: A Study of Memory in Medieval Culture.* Cambridge: Cambridge University Press, 1990.

Caspi, Avshalom, et al. "Role of Genotype in the Cycle of Violence in Maltreated Children." *Science* 297, no. 5582 (2002): 851.

Cavalli-Sforza, Luigi Luca. *Genes, Peoples and Languages.* Translated by Mark Seielstad. New York: North Point Press, 2000.

Cavalli-Sforza, Luigi Luca, and M. W. Feldman. *Cultural Transmission and Evolution: A Quantitative Approach.* Princeton: Princeton University Press, 1981.

Chartier, Roger. "Reading and Reading Practices." In *Encyclopedia of the Enlightenment,* 4 vols. Edited by Alan Charles Kors, vol. 3, 399–404. New York: Oxford University Press, 2003.

Chorover, Stephan L. *From Genesis to Genocide: The Meaning of Human Nature and the Power of Behavior Control.* Cambridge, Mass.: MIT Press, 1979.

Christian, David. *Maps of Time: An Introduction to Big History.* Berkeley: University of California Press, 2004.

Clanchy, Michael T. *From Memory to Written Record: England 1066–1307,* 2nd ed. Oxford: Blackwell, 1993.

Clark, Grahame. *World Prehistory in New Perspective.* Cambridge: Cambridge University Press, 1977.

Clough, Shepard Bancroft, et al., eds. *A History of the Western World.* Boston: Heath, 1964.

Cohn, Bernard S., and Nicholas B. Dirks. "Beyond the Fringe: The Nation State, Colonialism, and the Technologies of Power." *Journal of Historical Sociology* 1 (1988): 224–29.

Cohn, Norman. *Noah's Flood: The Genesis Story in Western Thought.* New Haven, Conn.: Yale University Press, 1996.

Condorcet, Jean-Antoine-Nicolas de Caritat, marquis de. *Sketch for a Historical Picture of the Progress of the Human Mind.* Translated by June Barraclough. New York: Noonday Press, 1955.

Confino, Alon. "Collective Memory and Cultural History: Problems of Method." *American Historical Review* 102 (1997): 1386–1403.

Connerton, Paul. *How Societies Remember.* Cambridge: Cambridge University Press, 1989.

Cook, Michael. *A Brief History of the Human Race.* New York: Norton, 2003.

Cutler, Alan. *The Seashell on the Mountaintop: A Story of Science, Sainthood, and the Humble Genius Who Discovered a New History of the Earth.* New York: Dutton, 2003.

Damasio, Antonio. *Descartes' Error: Emotion, Reason, and the Human Brain.* New York: G. P. Putnam, 1994.

———. *Looking for Spinoza: Joy, Sorrow, and the Feeling Brain.* Orlando, Fla.: Harcourt, 2003.

Daniel, Glyn E. *The Idea of Prehistory.* London: Watts, 1962.

Darwin, Charles. *On the Origin of Species.* London, 1859; reprint Cambridge, Mass.: Harvard University Press, 1964.

Davis, John. *People of the Mediterranean: An Essay in Comparative Social Anthropology.* London: Routledge and Kegan Paul, 1977.

Dawkins, Richard. *The Extended Phenotype: The Long Reach of the Gene,* rev. ed. Oxford: Oxford University Press, 1999.

———. *The Selfish Gene.* Oxford: Oxford University Press, 1976.

Dean, Amos. *The History of Civilization,* 7 vols. Albany, N.Y., 1868.

Degler, Carl. *In Search of Human Nature: The Decline and Revival of Darwinism in American Social Thought.* New York: Oxford University Press, 1991.

Dennett, Daniel C. *Breaking the Spell: Religion as a Natural Phenomenon.* New York: Viking, 2006.

———. *Darwin's Dangerous Idea: Evolution and the Meanings of Life.* New York: Simon and Schuster, 1995.

de Waal, Frans. *Chimpanzee Politics: Power and Sex among Apes.* New York: Harper and Row, 1982.

Diamond, Jared M. *Collapse: How Societies Choose to Fail or Succeed.* New York: Viking, 2005.

———. *Guns, Germs, and Steel: The Fates of Human Societies.* New York: W. W. Norton, 1997.

Douglas, Mary. *How Institutions Think.* Syracuse, N.Y.: Syracuse University Press, 1986.

Duiker, William J., and Jackson J. Spielvogel. *World History: Comprehensive Volume,* 3rd ed. Belmont, Calif.: Wadsworth, 2001.

Dunbar, Robin. *Grooming, Gossip, and the Evolution of Language.* Cambridge, Mass.: Harvard University Press, 1996.

Durham, William H. *Coevolution: Genes, Culture, and Human Diversity.* Stanford, Calif.: Stanford University Press, 1991.

Duruy, Victor. *General History of the World,* rev. ed. New York: Thomas Y. Crowell, 1925. Originally published 1883.

Edelman, Gerald M. *Neural Darwinism: The Theory of Neuronal Group Selection.* New York: Basic Books, 1987.

Ehrlich, Paul. *Human Natures: Genes, Cultures, and the Human Prospect.* Washington, D.C.: Island Press, 2000.

Eldredge, Niles. *Reinventing Darwin: The Great Debate at the High Table of Evolutionary Theory.* New York: Wiley, 1995.

Erdal, David, and Andrew Whiten. "On Human Egalitarianism: An Evolutionary Product of Machiavellian Status Escalation?" *Current Anthropology* 35 (1994): 175–83.

Fagan, Brian M. *Floods, Famines, and Emperors: El Niño and the Fate of Civilizations.* New York: Basic Books, 1999.

Fenster, Thelma, and Daniel Lord Smail, eds. *Fama: The Politics of Talk and Reputation in Medieval Europe.* Ithaca, N.Y.: Cornell University Press, 2003.

Fentress, James, and Chris Wickham. *Social Memory.* Oxford: Blackwell, 1992.

Ferguson, Adam. *An Essay on the History of Civil Society.* Edited by Fania Oz-Salzberger. Cambridge: Cambridge University Press, 1995.

Fessler, Daniel M. T. "Reproductive Immunosuppression and Diet: An Evolutionary Perspective on Pregnancy Sickness and Meat Consumption." *Current Anthropology* 43 (2003): 19–61.

Fiedel, Stuart J. *Prehistory of the Americas,* 2nd ed. Cambridge: Cambridge University Press, 1992.

Fisher, George Park. *Outlines of Universal History, Designed as a Text-Book and for Private Reading.* New York, 1885.

Fitzhugh, Michael L., and William H. Leckie, Jr. "Agency, Postmodernism and the Causes of Change." *History and Theory* 40 (2001): 58–81.

Flannery, Tim. *The Eternal Frontier: An Ecological History of North America and Its Peoples.* New York: Atlantic Monthly Press, 2001.

Fodor, Jerry A. *In Critical Condition: Polemical Essays on Cognitive Science and the Philosophy of Mind.* Cambridge, Mass.: MIT Press, 1998.

————. *The Mind Doesn't Work That Way: The Scope and Limits of Computational Psychology.* Cambridge, Mass.: MIT Press, 2000.

Foster, Herbert Darling, et al., eds. *A History Syllabus for Secondary Schools.* Boston: D. C. Heath, 1904.

Foucault, Michel. *The Archaeology of Knowledge.* Translated by A. M. Sheridan Smith. New York: Harper and Row, 1976.

Fukuyama, Francis. *The End of History and the Last Man.* New York: Free Press, 1992.

Garraty, John A., and Peter Gay, eds. *The Columbia History of the World.* New York: Harper and Row, 1972.

Geertz, Clifford. *The Interpretation of Cultures: Selected Essays.* New York: Basic Books, 1973.

Gellner, Ernest. *Plough, Sword, and Book: The Structure of Human History.* London: Collins Harvill, 1988.

Gibbon, Edward. *The Decline and Fall of the Roman Empire.* Abridged by D. M. Low. New York: Washington Square Press, 1960.

Gillispie, Charles Coulston. *Genesis and Geology: A Study in the Relations of Scientific Thought, Natural Theology and Social Opinion in Great Britain, 1790–1850.* New York: Harper, 1951.

Goldstein, Doris. "Confronting Time: The Oxford School of History and the Non-Darwinian Revolution." *Storia della Storiografia* 45 (2004): 3–27.

Goodall, Jane. *The Chimpanzees of Gombe: Patterns of Behavior.* Cambridge, Mass.: Harvard University Press, 1986.

Goody, Jack, Joan Thirsk, and E. P. Thompson, eds. *Family and Inheritance: Rural Society in Western Europe, 1200–1800.* Cambridge: Cambridge University Press, 1976.

Gould, Stephen Jay. "Male Nipples and Clitoral Ripples." In *Bully for Brontosaurus: Reflections in Natural History,* 124–38. New York: Norton, 1991.

————. *The Panda's Thumb: More Reflections in Natural History.* New York: Norton, 1982.

————. *Time's Arrow, Time's Cycle: Myth and Metaphor in the Discovery of Geological Time.* Cambridge, Mass.: Harvard University Press, 1987.

Gould, Stephen Jay, and Richard C. Lewontin. "The Spandrels of San Marcos and the Panglossian Paradigm: A Critique of the Adaptationist Programme." *Proceedings of the Royal Society of London* B 205 (1979): 581–98.

Gould, Stephen Jay, and Elizabeth Vrba. "Exaptation: A Missing Term in the Science of Form." *Paleobiology* 8 (1981): 4–15.

Grayson, Donald K. *The Establishment of Human Antiquity.* New York: Academic Press, 1983.

Greene, Mott T. *Geology in the Nineteenth Century: Changing Views of a Changing World.* Ithaca, N.Y.: Cornell University Press, 1982.

———. *Natural Knowledge in Preclassical Antiquity.* Baltimore: Johns Hopkins University Press, 1992.

Guibert of Nogent. *Self and Society in Medieval France: The Memoirs of Abbot Guibert of Nogent.* Edited by John F. Benton. 1970; reprint Toronto: University of Toronto Press, 1984.

Guizot, François Pierre Guillaume. *A Popular History of France, from the Earliest Times,* vol. 1. Translated by Robert Black. Boston, 1869.

Habermas, Jürgen. *The Structural Transformation of the Public Sphere: An Inquiry into a Category of Bourgeois Society.* Translated by Thomas Burger with the assistance of Frederick Lawrence. Cambridge, Mass.: MIT Press, 1989.

Hacking, Ian. "Making Up People." In *Reconstructing Individualism: Autonomy, Individuality, and the Self in Western Thought.* Edited by Thomas C. Heller, Morton Sosna, and David W. Wellbery, 222–36. Stanford, Calif.: Stanford University Press, 1986.

Hammerton, John, and Harry Elmer Barnes, eds. *The Illustrated World History: A Record of World Events from Earliest Historical Times to the Present Day.* New York: William H. Wise, 1935.

Harrison, John B., and Richard E. Sullivan. *A Short History of Western Civilization,* 2nd ed. New York: McGraw-Hill, 1966.

Hawkes, Kristen. "Showing Off: Tests of Another Hypothesis about Men's Foraging Goals." *Ethology and Sociobiology* 11 (1991): 29–54.

Hodgen, Margaret T. *Early Anthropology in the Sixteenth and Seventeenth Centuries.* Philadelphia: University of Pennsylvania Press, 1964.

Hodgson, Geoffrey M. "Is Social Evolution Lamarckian or Darwinian?" In *Darwinism and Evolutionary Economics.* Edited by John Laurent and John Nightingale, 87–118. Cheltenham: Edward Elgar, 2001.

Hoffman, Ross J. S., ed. *Man and His History: World History and Western Civilization.* Garden City, N.Y.: Doubleday, 1958.

Hollister, C. Warren. *Roots of the Western Tradition: A Short History of the Ancient World.* New York: Wiley, 1966.

Hoyland, John S. *A Brief History of Civilization.* London: Oxford University Press, 1925.

Hrdy, Sarah Blaffer. *Mother Nature: A History of Mothers, Infants, and Natural Selection.* New York: Pantheon Books, 1999.

Hunt, Gavin R., and Russell D. Gray. "Crafting of Hook Tools by Wild New Caledonian Crows." *Proceedings of the Royal Society of London* 271, Biology Letters Supplement (2004): S88–S90.

———. "Species-wide Manufacture of Stick-type Tools by New Caledonian Crows." *Emu* 102 (2002): 349–53.

Huxley, Aldous. *Brave New World and Brave New World Revisited.* New York: Harper Collins, 2004.

Hyma, Albert. *World History: A Christian Interpretation,* rev. ed. Grand Rapids, Mich.: Eerdmans, 1947.

Jaynes, Julian. *The Origin of Consciousness in the Breakdown of the Bicameral Mind.* Boston: Houghton Mifflin, 1976.

Johns, Adrian. "The Physiology of Reading in Restoration England." In *The Practice and Representation of Reading in England.* Edited by James Raven, Helen Small, and Naomi Tadmor, 138–61. Cambridge: Cambridge University Press, 1996.

Johnson, Henry. *Teaching of History in Elementary and Secondary Schools.* New York: Macmillan, 1926.

Kagan, Donald, Steven Ozment, and Frank M. Turner. *The Western Heritage.* New York: Macmillan, 1979.

Kamensky, Jane. *Governing the Tongue: The Politics of Speech in Early New England.* New York: Oxford University Press, 1997.

Keith, Sir Arthur. *New Discoveries Relating to the Antiquity of Man.* New York: Williams and Norgate, 1931. Originally published 1915.

Kelly-Gadol, Joan. "Did Women Have a Renaissance?" In *Becoming Visible: Women in European History,* 137–64. Edited by Renate Bridenthal and Claudia Koonz. Boston: Houghton Mifflin, 1977.

King, C. Harold. *A History of Civilization: Earliest Times to the Mid-seventeenth Century. The Story of Our Heritage.* New York: Scribner, 1956.

Kors, Alan Charles, ed. *Encyclopedia of the Enlightenment.* 4 vols. New York: Oxford University Press, 2003.

Kramer, Samuel Noah. *History Begins at Sumer.* Garden City, N.Y.: Doubleday, 1959.

Krieger, Leonard. *Ranke: The Meaning of History.* Chicago: University of Chicago Press, 1977.

Krützen, Michael, Janet Mann, Michael R. Heithaus, Richard C. Connor, Lars Bejder, and William B. Sherwin. "Cultural Transmission of Tool Use in Bottlenose Dolphins." *Proceedings of the National Academy of Sciences* 102 (2005): 8939–43.

Labberton, Robert H. *Labberton's Universal History, from the Earliest Times to the Present.* New York, 1902. Originally published 1871.

La Boétie, Etienne de. "Discours sur la servitude volontaire." In *Oeuvres politiques.* Edited by François Hincker. Paris: Éditions Sociales, 1971.

Lakoff, George, and Mark Johnson. *Metaphors We Live By.* Chicago: University of Chicago Press, 1980.

Langlois, Charles V., and Charles Seignobos. *Introduction to the Study of History.* Translated by G. G. Berry. New York: Holt, 1898.

LeDoux, Joseph. *The Emotional Brain: The Mysterious Underpinnings of Emotional Life.* New York: Simon and Schuster, 1996.

Leslie, Alan. "Pretense, Autism and the Theory-of-Mind Module." *Current Directions in Psychological Science* 1 (1992): 18–21.

Lewontin, Richard. *It Ain't Necessarily So: The Dream of the Human Genome and Other Illusions.* New York: New York Review of Books, 2000.

———. *The Triple Helix: Gene, Organism, and Environment.* Cambridge, Mass.: Harvard University Press, 2000.

Lorenz, Konrad. "Über den Begriff der Instinkthandlung." *Folia Biotheoretica* 2 (1937): 17–50.

Lubbock, John. *Pre-Historic Times, as Illustrated by Ancient Remains, and the Manners and Customs of Modern Savages,* 2nd ed. New York, 1872. Originally published 1865.

Lyell, Charles. *The Geological Evidences of the Antiquity of Man, with Remarks on Theories of the Origin of Species by Variation.* London, 1863.

———. *Principles of Geology,* 3 vols. London, 1830–33; reprint Chicago: University of Chicago Press, 1990–91.

MacCarthy, John. *History of the World from the Earliest Period to the Present Time.* New York, 1882.

Marlowe, Frank W. "A Critical Period for Provisioning by Hadza Men: Implications for Pair Bonding." *Evolution and Human Behavior* 24 (2003): 217–29.

Marsh, Arthur Richmond. "Special Introduction." In Henry Hallam, *History of Europe during the Middle Ages,* rev. ed., vol. 1. New York: Colonial Press, 1899.

Masataka, Nobuo. "Effects of Experience with Live Insects on the Development of Fear of Snakes in Squirrel Monkeys, *Saimiri sciureus.*" *Animal Behaviour* 46 (1993): 741–46.

McCormick, Michael. *The Origins of the European Economy: Communications and Commerce, A.D. 300–900.* Cambridge: Cambridge University Press, 2001.

McNeill, J. R., and William McNeill. *The Human Web: A Bird's-Eye View of World History.* New York: Norton, 2003.

McNeill, William H. *The Human Condition: An Ecological and Historical View.* Princeton: Princeton University Press, 1980.

———. *The Rise of the West: A History of the Human Community.* Chicago: University of Chicago Press, 1963.

———. *A World History.* 4th ed. Oxford: Oxford University Press, 1999. Originally published 1967.

Miller, William Ian. *The Anatomy of Disgust.* Cambridge, Mass.: Harvard University Press, 1997.

Mithen, Steven. *After the Ice: A Global Human History, 20,000–5000 BC.* Cambridge, Mass.: Harvard University Press, 2004.

———. *The Prehistory of the Mind: The Cognitive Origins of Art, Religion and Science.* London: Thames and Hudson, 1996.

Moore, David S. *The Dependent Gene: The Fallacy of "Nature vs. Nurture."* New York: Times Books, 2001.

Moretti, Franco. "Graphs, Maps, Trees: Abstract Models for Literary History." *New Left Review* 24 (2003): 67–93; 26 (2004): 79–103; and 28 (2004): 43–63.

Myers, Philip Van Ness. *Ancient History*. Boston: Ginn, 1904.

Nietzsche, Friedrich Wilhelm. *The Use and Abuse of History*. 2nd rev. ed. Translated by Adrian Collins. Indianapolis: Bobbs-Merrill, 1957. Originally published 1874.

Nisbet, Robert. *History of the Idea of Progress*. New York: Basic Books, 1980.

Nisbett, Richard E., and Dov Cohen. *The Culture of Honor: The Psychology of Violence in the South*. Boulder, Colo.: Westview Press, 1996.

Novick, Peter. *That Noble Dream: The "Objectivity Question" and the American Historical Profession*. Cambridge: Cambridge University Press, 1988.

Parker, Richard Green. *Outlines of General History*. New York, 1848.

Parsons, Geoffrey. *The Stream of History*. New York: Scribner's, 1928.

Parsons, Reuben. *Universal History: An Explanatory Narrative*, vol. 1, *Ancient History from the Creation of Man until the Fall of the Roman Empire*. Yonkers, N.Y., 1902.

Peake, Harold, and Herbert John Fleure. *The Corridors of Time*, 10 vols. New Haven, Conn.: Yale University Press, 1927.

Pfeiffer, John. *The Creative Explosion: An Inquiry into the Origins of Art and Religion*. New York: Harper and Row, 1982.

Pinker, Steven. *How the Mind Works*. New York: Norton, 1997.

Ploetz, Karl. *Auszug aus der Geschichte*, 24th ed. Bielefeld: A. G. Ploetz, 1951.

Plotkin, Henry. *Evolution in Mind: An Introduction to Evolutionary Psychology*. London: Allen Lane, 1997.

———. *The Imagined World Made Real: Towards a Natural Science of Culture*. London: Penguin, 2002.

Pomeranz, Kenneth, and Steven Topik. *The World That Trade Created:*

Society, Culture, and the World Economy, 1400–the Present. Armonk, N.Y.: M. E. Sharpe, 1999.

Porter, Roy, and Dorothy Porter. *In Sickness and in Health: The British Experience, 1650–1850.* London: Fourth Estate, 1988.

Ralegh, Sir Walter. *The History of the World in Five Books.* London, 1687.

Ramsay, David. *Universal History Americanised; or, an Historical View of the World, from the Earliest Records to the Year 1808.* Philadelphia, 1819.

Ranke, Leopold von. *Universal History: The Oldest Historical Group of Nations and the Greeks.* Edited by G. W. Prothero. Translated by D. C. Tovey and G. W. Prothero. New York, 1885.

Reader, John. *Africa: A Biography of the Continent.* New York: Knopf, 1998.

Redman, Charles L. *Human Impact on Ancient Environments.* Tucson: University of Arizona Press, 1999.

Renouf, V. A. *Outlines of General History,* 2nd ed. Edited by William Starr Myers. New York: Macmillan, 1909.

Richards, Robert J. *Darwin and the Emergence of Evolutionary Theories of Mind and Behavior.* Chicago: University of Chicago Press, 1987.

Richerson, Peter J., and Robert Boyd. *Not by Genes Alone: How Culture Transformed Human Evolution.* Chicago: University of Chicago Press, 2005.

Robbins, Royal. *Outlines of Ancient and Modern History on a New Plan.* Hartford, Conn., 1875. Originally published 1830.

Roberts, J. M. *The New History of the World,* 4th rev. ed. Oxford: Oxford University Press, 2003.

Robinson, Charles Alexander, Jr. *Ancient History from Prehistoric Times to the Death of Justinian,* 2nd ed. Prepared by Alan L. Boegehold. New York: Macmillan, 1967. Originally published 1951.

Robinson, James Harvey. *An Introduction to the History of Western Europe*, rev. ed. Boston: Ginn, 1924. Originally published 1903.

———. *The New History: Essays Illustrating the Modern Historical Outlook.* New York: Macmillan, 1912.

———. *The Ordeal of Civilization.* New York: Harper, 1926.

Roche, Daniel. *A History of Everyday Things: The Birth of Consumption in France, 1600–1800.* Translated by Brian Pierce. Cambridge: Cambridge University Press, 2000.

Ross, Dorothy. *The Origins of American Social Science.* Cambridge: Cambridge University Press, 1991.

Ross, William T. *H. G. Wells's World Reborn: "The Outline of History" and Its Companions.* Selinsgrove, Pa.: Susquehanna University Press, 2002.

Rossi, Paolo. *The Dark Abyss of Time: The History of the Earth and the History of Nations from Hooke to Vico.* Translated by Lydia G. Cochrane. Chicago: University of Chicago Press, 1984.

Rostovtzeff, Michael Ivanovitch. *History of the Ancient World,* vol. 1, *The Orient and Greece.* Translated by J. D. Duff. Oxford: Clarendon Press, 1926.

Sacks, Harvey. *Lectures on Conversation,* 2 vols. Edited by Gail Jefferson. Oxford: Blackwell, 1992.

Sahlins, Marshall David. *Stone Age Economics.* Chicago: University of Chicago Press, 1972.

Sapolsky, Robert M. *Why Zebras Don't Get Ulcers,* 3rd ed. New York: Times Books, 2004.

Savelle, Max, ed. *A History of World Civilization,* vol. 1. New York: Holt, 1957.

Schneider, Hermann. *The History of World Civilization from Prehistoric Times to the Middle Ages,* vol. 1. Translated by Margaret M. Green. New York: Harcourt Brace, 1931. Originally published 1927.

Scott, James C. *Seeing Like a State: How Certain Schemes to Improve the Human Condition Have Failed.* New Haven, Conn.: Yale University Press, 1998.

Segal, Daniel A. " 'Western Civ' and the Staging of History in American Higher Education." *American Historical Review* 105 (2000): 770–805.

Sheler, Jeffrey L. "Rethinking Jamestown." *Smithsonian* 35 (2005): 48–55.

Simmons, Rachel. *Odd Girl Out: The Hidden Culture of Aggression in Girls.* New York: Harcourt, 2002.

Smail, Daniel Lord. *Imaginary Cartographies: Possession and Identity in Late Medieval Marseille.* Ithaca, N.Y.: Cornell University Press, 1999.

Smith, G. Elliot. *Human History*. New York: Norton, 1929.

Smith, George. *The Patriarchal Age: or, The History and Religion of Mankind, from the Creation to the Death of Isaac*. London, 1847.

Sober, Elliot, and David Sloan Wilson. *Unto Others: The Evolution and Psychology of Unselfish Behavior*. Cambridge, Mass.: Harvard University Press, 1998.

Sowards, J. Kelley. *Western Civilization to 1660*. New York: St. Martin's, 1964.

Spengler, Oswald. *Aphorisms*. Translated by Gisela Koch-Weser O'Brien. Chicago: H. Regnery, 1967.

Spiegel, Gabrielle M. "Chance and Necessity: Foucault and the Cultural Inscription of Genetics in Genealogy." Unpublished manuscript.

———. "L'histoire scientifique et les utilisations antimodernistes du passé dans le médiévisme américain." *Cahiers du Centre de Recherches Historiques, Réflexions Historiographiques* 22 (1999): 87–108.

Starr, Chester G. *A History of the Ancient World*. New York: Oxford University Press, 1965.

Stipp, John L., et al. *The Rise and Development of Western Civilization*, vol. 1. New York: Wiley, 1967.

Stocking, George W., Jr. "Lamarckianism in American Social Science: 1890–1915." *Journal of the History of Ideas* 23 (1962): 239–56.

———. *Victorian Anthropology*. New York: Free Press, 1987.

Strayer, Joseph R. *On the Medieval Origins of the Modern State*. Princeton: Princeton University Press, 1970.

Sykes, Brian. *The Seven Daughters of Eve: The Science That Reveals Our Genetic Ancestry*. New York: Norton, 2001.

Symons, Donald. *The Evolution of Human Sexuality*. New York: Oxford University Press, 1979.

Taylor, Shelley, et al. "Biobehavioral Response to Stress in Females: Tend-and-Befriend, Not Fight-or-Flight." *Psychological Review* 107 (2000): 411–29.

Taylor, W. C. *A Manual of Ancient and Modern History*. New York, 1852.

Tebbutt, Melanie. *Women's Talk? A Social History of "Gossip" in*

Working-Class Neighbourhoods, 1880–1960. Aldershot, Engl.: Scolar Press, 1995.

Teggart, Frederick J. *Prolegomena to History: The Relation of History to Literature, Philosophy, and Science.* Berkeley: University of California Press, 1916.

—————. *Theory of History.* New Haven, Conn.: Yale University Press, 1925.

Thorndike, Lynn. *A Short History of Civilization.* New York: F. S. Crofts, 1930.

Tooby, John, and Leda Cosmides. "The Psychological Foundations of Culture." In *The Adapted Mind: Evolutionary Psychology and the Generation of Culture.* Edited by Jerome H. Barkow, Leda Cosmides, and John Tooby, 19–136. New York: Oxford University Press, 1992.

Toulmin, Stephen, and June Goodfield. *The Discovery of Time.* New York: Harper and Row, 1965.

Toynbee, Arnold J. *Mankind and Mother Earth: A Narrative History of the World.* New York: Oxford University Press, 1976.

Trautmann, Thomas R. *Lewis Henry Morgan and the Invention of Kinship.* Berkeley: University of California Press, 1987.

Trivers, Robert. "The Evolution of Reciprocal Altruism." *The Quarterly Review of Biology* 46 (1971): 35–57.

Turgot, Anne-Robert-Jacques, baron de. *Turgot on Progress, Sociology and Economics.* Translated and edited by Ronald Meek. Cambridge: Cambridge University Press, 1973.

Turner, Sharon. *The History of the Anglo-Saxons from the Earliest Period to the Norman Conquest,* vol. 1. Philadelphia, 1841. Originally published 1799–1805.

Vico, Giambattista. *New Science,* 3rd ed. Translated by David Marsh. London: Penguin, 1999. Originally published 1725.

Volk, Tyler. *Metapatterns: Across Space, Time, and Mind.* New York: Columbia University Press, 1995.

Vovelle, Michel. *Piété baroque et déchristianisation en Provence au XVIIIe siècle: Les attitudes devant la mort d'après les clauses des testaments.* Paris: Plon, 1973.

Wall, Richard, ed. *Family Forms in Historic Europe.* Cambridge: Cambridge University Press, 1983.

Wallbank, Thomas Walter, et al. *Civilization: Past and Present,* 5th ed., vol. 1. Chicago: Scott, Foresman, 1965.

Warner, William. *Licensing Entertainment: The Elevation of Novel Reading in Britain, 1684–1750.* Berkeley: University of California Press, 1998.

Wells, H. G. *The Outline of History; Being a Plain History of Life and Mankind,* 3rd rev. ed. New York: Macmillan, 1920.

White, Leslie. *The Evolution of Culture: The Development of Civilization to the Fall of Rome.* New York: McGraw-Hill, 1959.

Wilson, Daniel. *The Archaeology and Prehistoric Annals of Scotland.* Edinburgh, 1851.

Wilson, David Sloan. *Darwin's Cathedral: Evolution, Religion, and the Nature of Society.* Chicago: University of Chicago Press, 2002.

———. "Tasty Slice—But Where Is the Rest of the Pie? Review of *Evolutionary Psychology,* by David Buss." *Evolution and Human Behavior* 20 (1999): 279–87.

Wilson, Edward O. *On Human Nature.* Cambridge, Mass.: Harvard University Press, 1978.

———. *Sociobiology: The New Synthesis.* Cambridge, Mass.: Harvard University Press, 1975.

Wilson, Tim. *Strangers to Ourselves: Discovering the Adaptive Unconsciousness.* Cambridge, Mass.: Harvard University Press, 2002.

Wolf, Eric R. *Europe and the People without History.* Berkeley: University of California Press, 1982.

INDEX

acceleration: cultural, 69, 72, 81, 84–86, 89, 98–103. *See also* speed
acquired characteristics, 81–87, 101, 217n12. *See also* Lamarckism
Adam, 22
Adams, Henry, 77
Adams, Herbert Baxter, 77
adaptation: behavioral, 119–20, 126–30, 145–46; brain, 112, 126–27, 140–42, 146–47; cultural, 90–97, 102–3, 110; exaptations, 126–30, 153–54, 172; genetic, 130, 153–54; new neurophysiological ecosystem, 155; pregnancy, 134–35; psychotropic economy and, 162; spandrels, 128–29, 130, 153
"adaptive nudges," 102
addiction, to mood-altering activities, 160–62, 176–78, 183–84
Africa, 37, 155; autotropic products, 179; beginning of history, 9–10, 15; brain adapted to, 140; colonization, 193; diasporas out of, 192, 193–94, 195; hunter-gatherers, 112; "progressive

race," 193; red-slip pottery, 64; Zimbabwe unwritten history, 53
Agassiz, Louis, 27
agricultural revolution, 26, 155, 212n7; convergent evolution, 199; dominance hierarchies after, 166, 167–68, 198–99; political forms not requiring, 5, 67; resistance to, 197–98; societal effects, 198–99; in Western Civ, 2, 38. *See also* Neolithic
agriculture: Central America, 90; Chatham islands, 193–94; and family history, 67, 91–92; lactose-intolerance and, 147; male labor, 142. *See also* agricultural revolution
alcohol, 179, 186, 188; addictive, 184; autotropic, 174; fetal development affected by, 154; medieval Europe, 180–81
altruism, 94–95, 131
American Historical Association, 75
The American Historical Review, 61
American Museum of Natural History, 69–70, 99

Text:	11/15 Granjon
Display:	Granjon
Indexer:	Barbara Roos
Compositor:	Binghamton Valley Composition, LLC
Printer and binder:	Maple-Vail Manufacturing Group